Water From The Rock

Lectionary Devotional For Cycle C

Stephen P. McCutchan

CSS Publishing Company, Inc., Lima, Ohio

WATER FROM THE ROCK

Copyright © 2009 by
CSS Publishing Company, Inc.
Lima, Ohio

The original purchaser may photocopy material in this publication for use as it was intended (worship material for worship use; educational material for classroom use; dramatic material for staging or production). No additional permission is required from the publisher for such copying by the original purchaser only. Inquiries should be addressed to: Permissions, CSS Publishing Company, Inc., 517 South Main Street, Lima, Ohio 45804.

Scripture quotations are from the New Revised Standard Version of the Bible, copyright 1989 by the Division of Christian Education of the National Council of the Churches of Christ in the USA. Used by permission.

Library of Congress Cataloging-in-Publication Data
McCutchan, Stephen P.
　Water from the rock : lectionary devotional for cycle C / Stephen P. McCutchan.
　　p. cm.
　Includes index.
　ISBN-13: 978-0-7880-2626-3 (perfect bound : alk. paper)
　ISBN-10: 0-7880-2626-7 (perfect bound : alk. paper)
　1. Church year meditations. 2. Common lectionary (1992) I. Title.
BV30.M3965 2009
242'.3—dc22

2009022102

For more information about CSS Publishing Company resources, visit our website at www.csspub.com or email us at csr@csspub.com or call (800) 241-4056.

Cover design by Barbara Spencer
ISBN-13: 978-0-7880-2626-3
ISBN-10: 0-7880-2626-7　　　　　　　　　　　　　　　　　　　　PRINTED IN USA

*This book
is dedicated to
three Presbyterian churches
who, over 38 years of allowing me
to be their pastor,
taught me much about my faith.*

*Bradley Hills Presbyterian Church
Bethesda, Maryland
1968-1975*

*First Presbyterian Church
Wellsboro, Pennsylvania
1975-1983*

*Highland Presbyterian Church
Winston-Salem, North Carolina
1983-2006*

May God continue to bless your ministry.

Table Of Contents

Spiritual Nurture For Pastors	15
Spiritual Nurture For Mainline Christians	19

Five Formats For Your Time Of Prayer

Praising God	25
Confession And Forgiveness	26
Offering Thanksgiving	27
Prayers Of Intercession	28
Benediction	29

Lectionary Meditations For Cycle C

Advent 1   33
  Jeremiah 33:14-16
  Psalm 25:1-10
  1 Thessalonians 3:9-13
  Luke 21:25-36

Advent 2   37
  Malachi 3:1-4
  Luke 1:68-79
  Philippians 1:3-11
  Luke 3:1-6

Advent 3   41
  Zephaniah 3:14-20
  Isaiah 12:2-6
  Philippians 4:4-7
  Luke 3:7-18

Advent 4   46
  Micah 5:2-5a
  Psalm 80:1-7
  Hebrews 10:5-10
  Luke 1:39-45 (46-55)

Christmas Eve/Christmas Day   50
Isaiah 52:7-10
Psalm 98
Hebrews 1:1-4 (5-12)
John 1:1-14

Christmas 1   55
1 Samuel 2:18-20, 26
Psalm 148
Colossians 3:12-17
Luke 2:41-52

Christmas 2   59
Jeremiah 31:7-14
Psalm 147:12-20
Ephesians 1:3-14
John 1:(1-9) 10-18

The Epiphany Of Our Lord   64
Isaiah 60:1-6
Psalm 72:1-7, 10-14
Ephesians 3:1-12
Matthew 2:1-12

The Baptism Of Our Lord/Epiphany 1/Ordinary Time 1   68
Isaiah 43:1-7
Psalm 29
Acts 8:14-17
Luke 3:15-17, 21-22

Epiphany 2/Ordinary Time 2   72
Isaiah 62:1-5
Psalm 36:5-10
1 Corinthians 12:1-11
John 2:1-11

Epiphany 3/Ordinary Time 3   76
Nehemiah 8:1-3, 5-6, 8-10
Psalm 19
1 Corinthians 12:12-31a
Luke 4:14-21

Epiphany 4/Ordinary Time 4   80
Jeremiah 1:4-10
Psalm 71:1-6
1 Corinthians 13:1-13
Luke 4:21-30

Epiphany 5/Ordinary Time 5   85
Isaiah 6:1-8 (9-13)
Psalm 138
1 Corinthians 15:1-11
Luke 5:1-11

Epiphany 6/Ordinary Time 6   90
Jeremiah 17:5-10
Psalm 1
1 Corinthians 15:12-20
Luke 6:17-26

Epiphany 7/Ordinary Time 7   95
Genesis 45:3-11, 15
Psalm 37:1-11, 39-40
1 Corinthians 15:35-38, 42-50
Luke 6:27-38

Epiphany 8/Ordinary Time 8/Proper 3   100
Isaiah 55:10-13
Psalm 92:1-4, 12-15
1 Corinthians 15:51-58
Luke 6:39-49

Epiphany 9/Ordinary Time 9/Proper 4   104
1 Kings 8:22-23, 41-43
Psalm 96:1-9
Galatians 1:1-12
Luke 7:1-10

The Transfiguration Of Our Lord   109
(Last Sunday After Epiphany)
Exodus 34:29-35
Psalm 99
2 Corinthians 3:12—4:2
Luke 9:28-36 (37-43)

Lent 1   114
    Deuteronomy 26:1-11
    Psalm 91:1-2, 9-16
    Romans 10:8b-13
    Luke 4:1-13

Lent 2   118
    Genesis 15:1-12, 17-18
    Psalm 27
    Philippians 3:17—4:1
    Luke 13:31-35

Lent 3   122
    Isaiah 55:1-9
    Psalm 63:1-8
    1 Corinthians 10:1-13
    Luke 13:1-9

Lent 4   126
    Joshua 5:9-12
    Psalm 32
    2 Corinthians 5:16-21
    Luke 15:1-3, 11b-32

Lent 5   131
    Isaiah 43:16-21
    Psalm 126
    Philippians 3:4b-14
    John 12:1-8

Passion/Palm Sunday   135
    Isaiah 50:4-9a
    Psalm 118:1-2, 19-29
    Philippians 2:5-11
    Luke 19:28-40

Easter Day   140
    Isaiah 65:17-25
    Psalm 118:1-2, 14-24
    1 Corinthians 15:19-26
    John 20:1-18

Easter 2   **145**
   Acts 5:27-32
   Psalm 118:14-29
   Revelation 1:4-8
   John 20:19-31

Easter 3   **150**
   Acts 9:1-6 (7-20)
   Psalm 30
   Revelation 5:11-14
   John 21:1-19

Easter 4   **155**
   Acts 9:36-43
   Psalm 23
   Revelation 7:9-17
   John 10:22-30

Easter 5   **159**
   Acts 11:1-18
   Psalm 148
   Revelation 21:1-6
   John 13:31-35

Easter 6   **164**
   Acts 16:9-15
   Psalm 67
   Revelation 21:10, 22—22:5
   John 14:23-29

The Ascension Of Our Lord   **169**
   Acts 1:1-11
   Psalm 47
   Ephesians 1:15-23
   Luke 24:44-53

Easter 7   **174**
   Acts 16:16-34
   Psalm 97
   Revelation 22:12-14, 16-17, 20-21
   John 17:20-26

The Day Of Pentecost 179
Acts 2:1-21
Psalm 104:24-34, 35b
Romans 8:14-17
John 14:8-17 (25-27)

The Holy Trinity 184
Proverbs 8:1-4, 22-31
Psalm 8
Romans 5:1-5
John 16:12-15

Proper 4/Pentecost 2/Ordinary Time 9 189
1 Kings 18:20-21 (22-29) 30-39
Psalm 96
Galatians 1:1-12
Luke 7:1-10

Proper 5/Pentecost 3/Ordinary Time 10 194
1 Kings 17:8-16 (17-24)
Psalm 146
Galatians 1:11-24
Luke 7:11-17

Proper 6/Pentecost 4/Ordinary Time 11 199
1 Kings 21:1-10 (11-14) 15-21a
Psalm 5:1-8
Galatians 2:15-21
Luke 7:36—8:3

Proper 7/Pentecost 5/Ordinary Time 12 204
1 Kings 19:1-4 (5-7) 8-15a
Psalms 42 and 43
Galatians 3:23-29
Luke 8:26-39

Proper 8/Pentecost 6/Ordinary Time 13 208
2 Kings 2:1-2. 6-14
Psalm 77:1-2, 11-20
Galatians 5:1, 13-25
Luke 9:51-62

Proper 9/Pentecost 7/Ordinary Time 14   213
    2 Kings 5:1-14
    Psalm 30
    Galatians 6:(1-6) 7-16
    Luke 10:1-11, 16-20

Proper 10/Pentecost 8/Ordinary Time 15   218
    Amos 7:7-17
    Psalm 82
    Colossians 1:1-14
    Luke 10:25-37

Proper 11/Pentecost 9/Ordinary Time 16   223
    Amos 8:1-12
    Psalm 52
    Colossians 1:15-28
    Luke 10:38-42

Proper 12/Pentecost 10/Ordinary Time 17   228
    Hosea 1:2-10
    Psalm 85
    Colossians 2:6-15 (16-19)
    Luke 11:1-13

Proper 13/Pentecost 11/Ordinary Time 18   233
    Hosea 11:1-11
    Psalm 107:1-9, 43
    Colossians 3:1-11
    Luke 12:13-21

Proper 14/Pentecost 12/Ordinary Time 19   238
    Isaiah 1:1, 10-20
    Psalm 50:1-8, 22-23
    Hebrews 11:1-3, 8-16
    Luke 12:32-40

Proper 15/Pentecost 13/Ordinary Time 20   243
    Isaiah 5:1-7
    Psalm 80:1-2, 8-19
    Hebrews 11:29—12:2
    Luke 12:49-56

Proper 16/Pentecost 14/Ordinary Time 21   **248**
Jeremiah 1:4-10
Psalm 71:1-6
Hebrews 12:18-29
Luke 13:10-17

Proper 17/Pentecost 15/Ordinary Time 22   **253**
Jeremiah 2:4-13
Psalm 81:1, 10-16
Hebrews 13:1-8, 15-16
Luke 14:1, 7-14

Proper 18/Pentecost 16/Ordinary Time 23   **258**
Jeremiah 18:1-11
Psalm 139:1-6, 13-18
Philemon 1-21
Luke 14:25-33

Proper 19/Pentecost 17/Ordinary Time 24   **263**
Jeremiah 4:11-12, 22-28
Psalm 14
1 Timothy 1:12-17
Luke 15:1-10

Proper 20/Pentecost 18/Ordinary Time 25   **268**
Jeremiah 8:18—9:1
Psalm 79:1-9
1 Timothy 2:1-7
Luke 16:1-13

Proper 21/Pentecost 19/Ordinary Time 26   **272**
Jeremiah 32:1-3a, 6-15
Psalm 91:1-6, 14-16
1 Timothy 6:6-19
Luke 16:19-31

Proper 22/Pentecost 20/Ordinary Time 27   **277**
Lamentations 1:1-6
Psalm 137
2 Timothy 1:1-14
Luke 17:5-10

Proper 23/Pentecost 21/Ordinary Time 28   282
Jeremiah 29:1, 4-7
Psalm 66:1-12
2 Timothy 2:8-15
Luke 17:11-19

Proper 24/Pentecost 22/Ordinary Time 29   286
Jeremiah 31:27-34
Psalm 119:97-104
2 Timothy 3:14—4:5
Luke 18:1-8

Proper 25/Pentecost 23/Ordinary Time 30   291
Joel 2:23-32
Psalm 65
2 Timothy 4:6-8, 16-18
Luke 18:9-14

Proper 26/Pentecost 24/Ordinary Time 31   296
Habakkuk 1:1-4; 2:1-4
Psalm 119:137-144
2 Thessalonians 1:1-4, 11-12
Luke 19:1-10

Proper 27/Pentecost 25/Ordinary Time 32   300
Haggai 1:15b—2:9
Psalm 145:1-5, 17-21
2 Thessalonians 2:1-5, 13-17
Luke 20:27-38

Proper 28/Pentecost 26/Ordinary Time 33   304
Isaiah 65:17-25
Isaiah 12
2 Thessalonians 3:6-13
Luke 21:5-19

Christ The King/Proper 29   308
Jeremiah 23:1-6
Luke 1:68-79
Colossians 1:11-20
Luke 23:33-43

Scriptural Index For Cycles A, B, C   313

Spiritual Nurture For Pastors

Water From The Rock is the third volume of the lectionary devotional series and is based on Year C of the Revised Common Lectionary (1992) prepared by the Consultation on Common Texts. The title of this volume is taken from Exodus 17:1-7 where the Israelites were gathered in the wilderness. "They camped at Rephidim, but there was no water for the people to drink." Rather than remember what they had, a God who had liberated them from the tyranny of slavery in Egypt, the Israelites focused on what they lacked in life. Like a congregation that can get testy with a pastor because they are not getting all their needs met, "the people quarreled with Moses, and said, 'Give us water to drink.' " Moses tried to respond from a faith perspective. "Why do you quarrel with me? Why do you test the Lord?" As a pastor, you are fully aware that congregations can become so focused on their perceived needs that they are not interested in listening to you unless you will provide what they demand. As it did for Moses, life in the community of believers can become very frustrating for a pastor. Like Moses, you are invited to cry out to God, "What shall I do with this people?" But when you have cried out, you are also invited to listen to what God will say to you in response. This volume is intended to provide the resources whereby you can listen to God through God's gift of scripture as reflected in the Revised Common Lectionary.

This book is offered in support of your ministry by encouraging you to take time for regular prayer and devotions so that God might continually touch your life and speak to you through scripture. Paul makes an interesting connection to this story of the rock in 1 Corinthians 10:1-4 where he identifies the rock with Christ. Having suggested that Christ transcends the historical moment in which Jesus lived on earth, Paul then speaks to the presence of the living Christ in our experiences. It is not uncommon for pastors to feel overwhelmed by the demands of their profession and feel drained of all spiritual energy. Paul's words seem appropriate to such an occasion. "So if you think you are standing, watch out that you do not fall. No testing has overtaken you that is not common to everyone. God is faithful, and he will not let you be tested beyond your strength, but with the testing he will also provide the way out so that you may be able to endure it" (1 Corinthians 10:12-13). My prayer is that these reflections might be used by God to refresh you with living water from the rock of Christ.

Like the previous volumes, the structure of the book builds on two features of our professional life — the structure of worship and the provision of the Revised Common Lectionary. The basic structure of most experiences of worship include the offering of praise, confession of sins, being nurtured by the word, offering prayers of thanksgiving and intercession, and experiencing the benediction or the blessing of God. The Revised Common Lectionary offers four readings normally drawn from the Hebrew scriptures, the psalms, the gospels, and the epistles.

At the beginning of the book, you are offered five formats for your time of prayer. The first one focuses on the praise of God. The second focuses on the confession of sins and assurance of forgiveness. The third is directed toward a time of thanksgiving. The fourth offers you the opportunity for offering prayers of intercession. Finally there is a time to receive the blessing of God or the benediction. Following these formats for devotions, there is a series of brief meditations on each of the scriptures proposed by the lectionary for the following Sunday.

The intention is that you find at least five times during the week to take time for prayer and meditation for half an hour or more. You would begin the week with a time of praise. Next you would have an opportunity to confess those burdens that are bothering you and experience the grace of a forgiving God. The third day would allow you to spend some time offering your thanksgiving for all that God provides you. On the fourth day you would have an opportunity to focus on the needs of your congregation or the society around you. On the fifth day, you can rest in the blessing of God who has called you to ministry. During this time, you will also be nurtured each day by the scriptures that form the basis of your worship on the following Sunday. I recognize that some may find it more helpful to alter the calendar and use the lectionary readings that will provide the basis of the worship several weeks in advance so that your meditation might also stimulate your thinking with respect to the sermon that you will need to prepare. You may find it helpful to have a pad of paper to capture the thoughts that occur to you.

The appropriate time to use this devotional will vary with the schedule of each individual. Many find that an early morning time can be set aside and is usually not disturbed but for others it is an appropriate way to end the day. I would suggest two other alternatives that have proved helpful to me. Most hospitals have chapels; and if you carry this devotional with you, you could often find a brief time after a hospital visit to nurture yourself in the chapel. Also, I have found a remarkable sanctuary in fast-food restaurants. I order a minimal meal, take it to the most remote corner in the restaurant, and allow the meal to be a spiritual experience that slows down my eating and feeds me with some bread of heaven. No pattern fits all personalities, and I encourage you to explore what time may best fit your pattern and personality. I have deliberately chosen to create just five formats for prayer under the assumption that there will be at least two days each week that do not fit into this rhythm. However, if you are fortunate enough to have a sixth or seventh time, you can simply choose to repeat any of the offered formats.

My hope is that the flexibility of the formats and the opportunity to reflect on the lectionary scriptures will encourage you to be good to yourself and strengthen that connection with God that has drawn you into your calling. God's call in your life was not a mistake, and the church needs your gifts in response to the hunger of God's people. May God strengthen you for the journey that lies ahead.

Spiritual Nurture For Mainline Christians

This is the third volume of the lectionary devotional series. It is based on Year C of the Revised Common Lectionary (1992) prepared by the Consultation on Common Texts. The title of this volume is taken from Exodus 17:1-7 where the Israelites were gathered in the wilderness. "They camped at Rephidim, but there was no water for the people to drink." Rather than remember how they had been blessed by a God who had liberated them from the tyranny of slavery in Egypt, they focused on what they lacked in life. You may be aware of members in your congregation that continually complain that their needs are not getting met. They are like "the people (who) quarreled with Moses, and said, 'Give us water to drink.' " Moses tried to respond from a faith perspective. "Why do you quarrel with me? Why do you test the Lord?" Rarely does a dissatisfied member stop to ask the question, "I wonder what God is trying to say to me through this experience of dissatisfaction?" Throughout scripture there are repeated stories of people crying out to God because life was painful and that was exactly the time when God drew close to them. Like Moses, you may want to cry out to God, "What shall I do with this people?" But when you have cried out, you are also invited to listen to what God will say to you in this situation. This volume is intended to provide you the resources whereby you can listen to God through God's gift of scripture as reflected in the Revised Common Lectionary.

This book is offered in support of your journey of faith within the congregation by encouraging you to take time for regular prayer and devotions so that God might continually touch your life and speak to you through scripture. Paul makes an interesting connection to this story of the rock in 1 Corinthians 10:1-4 where he identifies the rock with Christ. Having suggested that Christ transcends the historical moment in which Jesus lived on earth, he then speaks to the presence of the living Christ in our experiences. It is not uncommon to feel overwhelmed by the demands of your life and feel drained of all spiritual energy. Paul's words seem appropriate to such an occasion. "So if you think you are standing, watch out that you do not fall. No testing has overtaken you that is not common to everyone. God is faithful, and he will not let you be tested beyond your strength, but with the testing he will also provide the way out so that you may be able to endure it" (1 Corinthians 10:12-13). My prayer is that these reflections might be used by God to refresh you with living water from the rock of Christ.

One of the treasures that God has provided to sustain us not only in the mountaintop experiences of faith but also in the valleys of doubt is the discipline of scriptures and prayer. It is the wisdom of the church to have provided us a lectionary to guide us in being immersed in the wisdom of the story of the faith. Here we recall how God has worked in the lives of people in the past so that we can have the courage to await God's presence in our future. Our doubts and even our periods of disbelief are not a barrier to our journey.

For many Christians, those very practices have fallen into disuse or have become a routine that is devoid of power. This book is intended to provide you a means by which to reenergize your prayer life and to hear God speaking to you through scripture. It is intended to support you by encouraging you to take time for regular prayer and devotions so that God might continually touch your life.

The structure of the book builds on two features common to many Christians in mainline churches — the structure of worship and the provision of the Revised Common Lectionary. Whether your church uses the lectionary or not, the format can still be used. You will discover that it will help you feel connected with the wider body of the church that reaches across the world. The basic structure of most experiences of worship include the offering of praise, confessing of our sins, being nurtured by the word, offering prayers of thanksgiving and intercession, and experiencing the benediction or the blessing of God. The common lectionary offers four readings normally drawn from the Hebrew scriptures, the psalms, the gospels, and the epistles.

At the beginning of this book, you are offered five formats for your time of prayer. The first one focuses on the praise of God. The second focuses on the confession of sins and the assurance of forgiveness. The third is directed toward a time of thanksgiving. The fourth offers you the opportunity for offering prayers of intercession. Finally there is a time to receive the blessing of God or the benediction. Following these formats for devotion, there is a series of brief meditations on each of the scriptures proposed by the lectionary for the following Sunday.

The intention is that you will find at least five times during the week to take time for prayer and meditation for one-half hour or more. You will begin the week with a time of praise. Next you will have an opportunity to confess those burdens that are bothering you and experience the grace of a forgiving God. The third day will allow you to spend some time offering your thanksgiving for all that God provides you. On the fourth day you will have an opportunity to focus on the needs of your congregation or the society around you. On the fifth day, you can rest in the blessing of God who has called you to the faith. During this time you will also be nurtured each day by the scriptures that will likely form the basis of your worship on the following Sunday.

The appropriate time to use this devotional will vary with the schedule of each individual. Many find that an early morning time can be set aside and is usually not disturbed, but for others, especially those with children, other times will be more appropriate. It may be an appropriate way to end the day, but there are some who feel so drained by the pressures of life that it is hard to focus when they are so tired. So, before you conclude that your life just does not allow for such a discipline, let me suggest a couple of other opportunities. First, many of you drive to work in your own car and often you can plan to arrive at your parking space in time to have some extra time alone before you enter your place of work. While it may seem shocking at first, let me further suggest that a perfect place to find alone time at many places of work is the stall in the restroom facilities. Also, I have found a remarkable sanctuary in fast-food restaurants. I order a minimal meal, take it to the most remote corner in the restaurant, and allow the meal to be a spiritual experience that slows down my eating and feeds me with some bread of heaven. No pattern fits all personalities, and I encourage you to explore what time may best fit your pattern and personality. I have deliberately chosen to create just five formats for prayer under the assumption that there will be at least two days each week that do not fit into this rhythm. However, if you are fortunate enough to have a sixth or seventh time, you can simply choose to repeat any of the offered formats.

My hope is that the flexibility of the formats and the opportunity to reflect on the lectionary scriptures will encourage you to be good to yourself and strengthen that connection with God that has drawn you into your faith. God's call in your life was not a mistake, and the church needs your gifts in response to the hunger of God's people. May God strengthen you for the journey that lies ahead.

Five Formats For Your Time Of Prayer

Praising God

Invocation
Bless the Lord, O my soul, and all that is within me, bless his holy name. Bless the Lord, O my soul, and do not forget all his benefits. — Psalm 103:1-2

Personal Prayer
Spend ten minutes offering praise to God for the way in which God has called you, nurtured you, strengthened you, and worked miracles in your life.

Nurtured By The Word
Read the Hebrew scripture for the week.

Spend some time asking how God might be speaking to you through this lesson.

Read the meditation on the first lesson for the week.

If thoughts come to your mind as you muse on this passage, jot them down.

Closing Prayer
Either sing or pray the doxology:

Praise God from whom all blessings flow.
Praise God all creatures here below.
Praise God above you heavenly hosts.
Praise Father, Son, and Holy Ghost.

Confession And Forgiveness

Invocation
> *Bless the Lord, O my soul ... who forgives all [my] iniquity, who heals all [my] diseases, who redeems [my] life from the Pit, who crowns [me] with steadfast love and mercy, who satisfies [me] with good as long as [I] live so that [my] youth is renewed like the eagle's.*
> — Psalm 103:2-5 (amended)

Personal Prayer
Take about ten minutes to confess to God those personal and relational sins that burden your soul. Also lay before God the feelings of anger, hurt, and disillusionment that are part of your life.

Assurance Of Forgiveness
Who is in a position to condemn? Only Christ, and Christ died for us, Christ rose for us, Christ reigns in power for us, and Christ prays for us. I claim the good news of the gospel for myself. In Jesus Christ, I am forgiven.

Nurtured By The Word
Read the psalm for the week.
Spend some time asking how God might be speaking to you through this lesson.
Read the meditation on the psalm.
If thoughts come to mind as you muse on this passage, write them down.

Closing Prayer
> *O Lord, I praise you because you do "not deal with us according to our sins, nor repay us according to our iniquities. For as the heavens are high above the earth, so great is [your] steadfast love toward those who fear [you]."*
> — Psalm 103:10-11 (amended)

Offering Thanksgiving

Invocation
I will sing to the Lord as long as I live; I will sing praise to my God while I have being. May my meditation be pleasing to [you], for I rejoice in the Lord.
— Psalm 104:33-34 (amended)

Personal Prayer
Take about ten minutes to thank God for the many blessings in your life. Thank God for the ways God has been present in your life. Thank God for how God has been present to you since birth.

Nurtured By The Word
Read the gospel lesson for the week.

Spend some time asking how God might be speaking to you through this lesson.

Read the meditation on the gospel lesson.

If any thoughts come to you while you are musing on the gospel, write them down.

Closing Prayer
Glory in his holy name; let the hearts of those who seek the Lord rejoice. [I will] seek the Lord and his strength; seek his presence continually. [I will] remember the wonderful works [God] has done.
— Psalm 105:3-5a (amended)

Prayers Of Intercession

Invocation
> Remember me, O Lord, when you show favor to your people; help me when you deliver them; that I may see the prosperity of your chosen ones, that I may rejoice in the gladness of your nation, that I may glory in your heritage. — Psalm 106:4-5

Personal Prayer
Take time to consider and offer in prayer all of the needs of which you are aware within your life. Take note of the spiritual and emotional needs as well as the physical and material needs in your life. Lift up troubled relationships and career challenges as well as family and marital stresses.

Nurtured By The Word
Read the epistle lesson for the week.

Spend some time asking how God might be speaking to you through this lesson.

Read the meditation on this lesson.

If there are thoughts that come to mind as you muse on this scripture, write them down.

Closing Prayer
> Save us, O Lord our God, and gather us from among the nations, that we may give thanks to your holy name and glory in your praise. Blessed be the Lord, the God of Israel, from everlasting to everlasting. And let all the people say, "Amen." Praise the Lord!
> — Psalm 106:47-48

Benediction

Invocation
> My heart is steadfast, O God, my heart is steadfast; I will sing and make melody! Awake, my soul!
>
> — Psalm 108:1

Personal Prayer
Take time to simply rest in the blessings of the Lord in your life. Review times in your life when you have felt the powerful presence of God lifting you up and times when you basked in the sheer joy of the life that God has provided you. Review some high moments in your life and allow them to be signs for you of God's continuing presence calling and guiding you.

Nurtured By The Word
Open the section of meditations at random and choose a particular scripture that is noted. Read it totally free of any agenda for its use.

Spend some time asking how God might be speaking to you through this passage.

Then read the meditation provided.

If there are thoughts that come to you during your musing, write them down.

Closing Prayer
Sing or pray the Gloria Patria:

> *Glory be to the Father, and to the Son*
> *and to the Holy Ghost;*
> *as it was in the beginning,*
> *is now, and ever shall be,*
> *world without end.*
> *Amen, amen.*

Lectionary Meditations For Cycle C

Advent 1

Jeremiah 33:14-16

> *The days are surely coming, says the Lord, when I will fulfill the promise I made to the house of Israel and the house of Judah.* — Jeremiah 33:14

Advent begins not only with promise but also with the very real question, made even more urgent with the passing of time, as to whether God will be faithful to the promises of scripture. Jeremiah stood at the point of destruction of his nation of Judah, long after the destruction of Israel in the north, and was bold enough to proclaim that God was faithful and would fulfill God's promises. What type of faith does it take to "see beyond touch and sight some sign of the kingdom"? This was not some vague promise beyond the reaches of time but a concrete promise that would be fulfilled here on earth. "In those days and at that time I will cause a righteous Branch to spring up for David; and he shall execute justice and righteousness in the land." As Christians we have focused on the "Branch" and applied it to Jesus, but we still await the execution of justice and righteousness in the land.

Jeremiah was quite definite in what he believed the promises of God to be. It would be hard in our own time to say, "In those days Judah will be saved and Jerusalem will live in safety. And this is the name by which it will be called: 'The Lord is our righteousness.'" Our hope rests with our expectation of Christ coming again to complete the reign of God. Therefore, in Advent, we are not just looking back and remembering the birth of a baby 2,000 years ago. Rather, we are looking forward, and, in the face of all the evidence to the contrary, like Jeremiah, we are proclaiming hope for the world. Advent confronts us with the weakness of our trust in God to fulfill the promises of scripture. Far too often we have slipped into cynicism and do not really expect anything new to happen. It takes courage to fully celebrate Advent and to look forward and say, "The days are surely coming...."

Psalm 25:1-10

To you, O Lord, I lift up my soul. — Psalm 25:1

One of the gifts that the psalms offer us is the invitation to be honest with God about the struggles of our lives. In our own lives, and in the life of our congregations, we are always faced with those who oppose us as we attempt to live out the faith. Such opposition goes beyond honest debate and often becomes "wantonly treacherous." It can drive us to such distraction that we begin to doubt our own decisions. It is at such moments that this psalm becomes our prayer. "O my God, in you I trust; do not let me be put to shame; do not let my enemies exult over me." The psalmist avoids euphemisms and names those in opposition to us as "enemies." As we struggle with the challenges of our enemies, those who oppose us, the psalmist invites us to refocus our attention. We are to turn away from the statements of opposition and focus on the true source of our inspiration. "Make me to know your ways, O Lord; teach me your paths. Lead me in your truth and teach me, for you are the God of my salvation; for you I wait all day long."

Because we have been schooled to be cautious of our own self-righteousness, we are often cautious about clearly drawing the lines and naming others as enemies. The psalmist has no such reluctance. The one who is an enemy today may be a loyal companion tomorrow, but, for the moment, we can be honest with God about the one who seems to be our enemy. We can give these feelings over to God rather than try to hide them in ourselves. This invitation is not based on our own goodness but on our trust in the steadfast mercy and love of God. "Do not remember the sins of my youth or my transgressions; according to your steadfast love remember me, for your goodness sake, O Lord!" The next time that you are feeling the pressure of those who oppose you, you are invited to pray this psalm by placing your own name in place of the personal pronouns and allow God's steadfast love and mercy to absorb your hurts and refocus your life. "Good and upright is the Lord; therefore he instructs sinners in the way. He leads the humble in what is right and teaches the humble his way." What more could you ask?

1 Thessalonians 3:9-13

How can we thank God enough for you in return for all the joy that we feel before our God because of you?
— 1 Thessalonians 3:9

In our individualistic society, we often neglect the power of the faith of the larger body to affect our lives. In this letter, Paul was writing to the Thessalonians in a time in which he himself was enduring considerable persecution and suffering (1 Thessalonians 3:4, 7). Timothy had just returned with a report that the Thessalonians had been keeping Paul and his companions in their thoughts and prayers.

For Paul, such awareness gave him strength in his own experience. "For this reason, brothers and sisters, during all our distress and persecution we have been encouraged about you through your faith. For we now live, if you continue to stand firm in the Lord" (1 Thessalonians 3:7-8). It is also important to note that Paul was strengthened by their prayers even though he was fully aware that they were far from perfect in their faith. "Night and day we pray most earnestly that we may see you face to face and restore whatever is lacking in your faith" (v. 10). We are not only strengthened by those who have developed a maturity in the faith but also by those who still have a long way to go.

As we enter this season of Advent and make preparation for celebrating the birth of Christ, it is important that we keep in mind the corporate expression of our faith made manifest in the body of Christ. The community of faith reaches around the world and each part is strengthened by the prayers of the other parts. Some of these communities of Christ are experiencing persecution and are in need of our prayers. Other churches within our community are experiencing stress and conflict and are also in need of our prayers and concern. The great commandment of loving God and loving neighbor finds corporate manifestation as we become aware of and pray for each other. "And may the Lord make you increase and abound in love for one another and for all, just as we abound in love for you" (v. 12). Perhaps praying for other parts of the body of Christ would be an important focus for all of us as we enter Advent.

Luke 21:25-36

> *Truly I tell you, this generation will not pass away until all things have taken place.* — Luke 21:32

These scriptures have been seen as predicting the second coming of Christ, and people have been troubled by Jesus' statement that this generation would not die before it all took place. For some skeptics, this is evidence that Jesus was mistaken. Yet it may be that we confuse a final return of Christ with the second coming of which Jesus was speaking. Is it not true that each Advent is a rehearsal for how to respond to the continuing stresses and challenges of our life and our world? Jesus used cosmic signs to speak of times so distressful that people felt that their world was falling apart. It is precisely when our universe is shaken by the events around us that we should expect the coming of the Son of Man.

Jesus noted, as we are all too aware, that some tried to escape the pressures of such stress through dissipation, drunkenness, or worrying. Each year, in this season before Christmas, we see ample evidence of the vain attempts to escape the pressures of life through forced gaiety or escape into alcohol or drugs. The emphasis on celebration often brings depression to others because they cannot feel what they believe others are feeling. We often view the problems of the church or society as the lack of faith. Yet it is precisely these signs that we should note as the times when Christ will come to us in a new and fresh way. Because Jesus knew that God "hears the cry of God's people" and actively seeks to intervene on their behalf, as God did at the Exodus, so Jesus was confident of the triumphal presence of the Son of Man at the dark times in our lives. The Son of Man comes to us at those moments of direst need if we will raise our heads and be expectant. Each Advent we ask again how to prepare ourselves for Christ's birth afresh in our lives.

Advent 2

Malachi 3:1-4

> *See, I am sending my messenger to prepare the way before me, and the Lord whom you seek will suddenly come to his temple.* — Malachi 3:1

Advent is a season of promise. We read scriptures that reveal the promises of God even as we prepare to recognize their fulfillment in the birth of Christ. Contemporary Christians are often more comfortable thinking of the entire season as a past event. Once upon a time God made a promise to send a messiah and then, over 2,000 years ago, God fulfilled that promise. So today we can feel good that God was faithful, and we can celebrate the results of that faithfulness in the Christmas season. Sometimes it makes us uncomfortable to consider the possibility that we, too, should be anticipating the coming of God. We tend to dismiss such thinking as belonging to a more extreme version of Christianity.

We live as if we were reading a mystery novel but have already peeked at the last chapter and so do not expect any surprises. Yet there is both a past and a future dimension to the Christian faith. It is not only that God came in Jesus but also that God will come again. Our discomfort in such thinking may have a basis in an awareness that the coming of God into our presence would have its negative side as well. "But who can endure the day of his coming, and who can stand when he appears?"

Advent, as a time of preparation, may be an opportunity to reflect on what needs to be purified in each of us and in our church so that we are ready to receive God. Such purification may begin with the pastors and church leaders. "For he is like a refiner's fire and like fullers' soap; he will sit as a refiner and purifier of silver, and he will purify the descendants of Levi and refine them like gold and silver, until they present offerings to the Lord in righteousness." If we were to take the words of the prophet as a word to us during this Advent season, what type of purifying action would we each want to take in our own lives?

Luke 1:68-79

> By the tender mercy of our God, the dawn from on high will break upon us, to give light to those who sit in darkness and in the shadow of death, to guide our feet into the way of peace.   — Luke 1:78-79

This is Zechariah's prophecy once his tongue was loosed upon the naming of John. A major theme of scripture is that the memory of what God has done in the past gives us confidence of what God will do in the future. Zechariah drew on the memory of God's faithfulness to David and the promises that God made through the prophets to build a sense of hope for the future. He saw the history of the people of Israel as fulfillment of the original promise made to Abraham. The vision was of a consistent and faithful God who could be counted upon to raise up prophets who would prepare God's way. In his child, John, Zechariah sees God once again providing hope for God's people. "And you, child, will be called the prophet of the Most High; for you will go before the Lord to prepare his ways, to give knowledge of salvation to his people by the forgiveness of their sins."

All of this would ultimately culminate in the fulfillment of God's intention for the whole world. The vision of Zechariah's prophecy was that God would provide a path "to give light to those who sit in darkness and in the shadow of death, to guide our feet into the way of peace." As we participate in the second Sunday of Advent, we are invited to reflect on the path that leads to light in darkness and peace for the world. For us this path finds its fulfillment in the birth of Christ who becomes our peace. As Paul said in 2 Corinthians 5:19, "... in Christ God was reconciling the world to himself, not counting their trespasses against them, and entrusting the message of reconciliation to us." Are there ways in this Advent season that we, too, might not count people's trespasses against them and take a step toward effecting the reconciliation and peace that we seek in Christ?

Philippians 1:3-11

> *... because of your sharing in the gospel from the first day until now.*   — Philippians 1:5

Paul greeted the Philippians with an affirmation of his relationship with them, a relationship that was sustained by his memory even while he experienced separation from them. "I thank my God every time I remember you...." If the center of the Christian faith is our relationship with God and each other, as Jesus reminds us in the giving of the Great Commandment, then the embodiment of that faith is in the community of faith. We pay too little attention to the role of memory in our faith.

Many people are separated from the faith because of a memory of a painful experience in the church. Others are drawn back to the church after years of separation because of a fond memory of experiences earlier in their life. Paul's memory was one filled with joy "because of your sharing in the gospel from the first day until now." The Greek word translated as sharing is *koinonia* and becomes one of the key words for a description of the church. *Koinonia* occurs again in 2:1 in which Paul spoke of "sharing in the Spirit," and in 3:10 where he spoke of the "sharing of the sufferings" of Christ.

In our passage a version of the word *koinonia* occurs in verse 7 where Paul spoke of his mutual affection for them because they "share in God's grace" with him, both in his imprisonment and in his defense and confirmation of the gospel. During Advent it would be appropriate for a church to reflect on its own history and reflect on the memories of how the members have shared both the good and bad times together. It is through such memories that we gain confidence "that the one who began a good work among (us) will bring it to completion by the day of Jesus Christ."

Luke 3:1-6

> *The voice of one crying out in the wilderness: "Prepare the way of the Lord, make his paths straight."*
> — Luke 3:4

We are living in a wilderness period in which many of the trappings of civilization have proved to be unsatisfying. There are many false starts that reflect a deep spiritual hunger in our society. We use lots of different words, but we seem to be seeking the underlying connection that holds life together and provides us a steadiness and a grasp of the truth. In biblical days when an emperor was going to visit, his entourage went before him to prepare the way of his coming. The path was made smooth and obstacles removed to make his coming as comfortable as possible. The procession route was established so that in his coming the people could see him along the way. Luke used this image to suggest the changes we need to make in preparation for God's coming. He sets us up by naming all of the important people in the power structure of the empire, both political and religious.

However, Luke then suggested that the word of God, the most important message of the universe, comes not to the politically or religiously important people or places but to a man in the wilderness. The wilderness is not a place of importance by our calculations. The wilderness is the opposite of civilization. It is the location where humans are not in control. In Israel's history, the wilderness was also the place where they were clearly dependent on God for survival and salvation. The word of God comes not where we believe we are in charge but in those corners of our life where we lack control. It comes not where we think the important events take place but in the neglected areas of our lives. It comes not where we feel strong and in charge but where we are vulnerable. If we are to make God's path straight, it is in those areas that we need to make preparation.

Advent 3

Zephaniah 3:14-20

... The king of Israel, the Lord, is in your midst....
— Zephaniah 3:15

As we greet the third Sunday of Advent, the excitement of the Christmas holiday increases. The pressure on pastors to skip the Advent hymns and move right to the Christmas carols is strong. The desire of our culture is to now focus on the warm glow of the season and to put aside or cover up any of the negative features of our lives and society. The pressure for joy, cheer, and celebration is so strong that many who are experiencing loneliness or sadness feel as if they are being left behind. The passage from Zephaniah is a sobering message to be read in the midst of this pressure.

First, it reminds us that Christmas is not only about celebrating a historical event that took place 2,000 years ago but also anticipating a future event. The "Day of the Lord" is the culmination of history and is often referred to by Christians as the second coming of Christ. Jesus did not just come once a long time ago but will also return to establish God's kingdom. Christians are to live as if that day is very near. But our very anticipation of the second coming causes us to recognize that all is not well among us. Zephaniah's description of the Day of the Lord is similar to the events preceding Noah and the flood where God said, "I have determined to make an end of all flesh, for the earth is filled with violence because of them; now I am going to destroy them along with the earth" (Genesis 6:13). Perhaps Advent needs to make space for us to pause in our headlong rush to Christmas and to reflect on the hurt and loneliness that exists all around us.

Such an invitation is not meant to kill the joy of the season but to open us to anticipate the only one who can fill our lives with true joy. If we are to sing "Joy To The World," it is helpful to recognize that we do so in light of the thorns that infest the ground, and our real hope is not in ignoring those thorns but in the source of blessing that can flow "far as the curse is found" ("Joy To The World" by Isaac Watts, v. 3).

Isaiah 12:2-6

With joy you will draw water from the wells of salvation.
— Isaiah 12:3

When Moses had led the people across the Red Sea (or Reed Sea), Exodus reported his singing with joy, "The Lord is my strength and my might, and he has become my salvation; this is my God, and I will praise him, my father's God, and I will exalt him" (Exodus 15:2). Now Isaiah uses similar words to report the song that people will sing upon their deliverance. There are moments when, having felt surrounded by enemies, we are suddenly aware of a source of salvation from beyond ourselves, and all we can do is rejoice. Many believers have experienced a moment in the midst of extreme stress or danger when they suddenly felt a deep sense of peace descend upon them, and they knew that they would be all right. As the psalmist records, "You prepare a table before me in the presence of my enemies ..." (Psalm 23:5).

These are the moments of deep joy drawn from the waters of faith that run deep in our lives. It is from the well of those joys, and not the superficial glitter of the season, that our hope truly rests. It is because of the collective memory of such experiences that a congregation can truly "Sing praises to the Lord, for he has done gloriously; let this be known in all the earth." It would be a powerful faith experience for a congregation to invite members to share their stories of the times when they have "drawn water from the wells of salvation" in their own lives and even to recall when, in the history of their congregation, they have experienced God's saving grace. A collection of these stories would make a great devotional for the following year.

Philippians 4:4-7

> *And the peace of God, which surpasses all understanding, will guard your hearts and your minds in Christ Jesus.* — Philippians 4:7

Far too many congregations succumb to the temptation to squabble and fight among themselves and fail to experience the joy that can be theirs in the faith. This is not a recent phenomenon within the church. Paul spent a great deal of energy counseling congregations about their internal fights. As we squabble, however, we seem to reflect more of the world's way of behaving than the gospel that brings us together. Immediately prior to this passage, Paul actually named names in commenting on an apparent quarrel within the church at Philippi. Paul was concerned about two women who were church leaders but who had apparently caused a rift within the church. He acknowledged their prior contributions to the building of the church and urged them to "be of the same mind in the Lord." He then asked others to help them come to an accord. He proceeded to offer his practical advice to the church in such events. "Rejoice in the Lord always; again I will say, Rejoice. Let your gentleness be known to everyone. The Lord is near."

At first that may seem like superficial advice in our problem-solving world. We have been schooled to believe that conflict must be resolved by techniques that force us to face the problem clearly and to seek a workable compromise. Yet Paul was illustrating the practical implications of his earlier admonition to "let the same mind be in you that was in Christ Jesus" (Philippians 2:5). When a church is in conflict, there is a need to shift the focus from the problem that divides it to the Lord who saved the church and to rekindle the joy that the church felt in receiving the gift of faith.

Members of churches have a tendency to allow issues to become so important that they are willing to allow the issues to divide the body of Christ and thus participate in the crucifixion again. It is difficult, but a significant step of faith, to trust that God will help the church to discern the truth in time. "Do not worry about anything, but in everything by prayer and supplication with thanksgiving let your requests be made known to God." When a congregation does not know how to resolve a conflict but is willing to trust God, it begins to experience that "peace of God, [that] passes all understanding...."

Luke 3:7-18

> *He will baptize you with the Holy Spirit and fire.*
> — Luke 3:16

Where is the fire in our faith? Most of us have been baptized with water, but often we wait for the fire. Sometimes we look at the life of our congregation and also want to ask, "Where is the fire?" Too often we rest on the comforts of our faith. The memories of what once was a vital center — Abraham is our ancestor — now becomes a safe, warm memory. John, the prophet, is able to disturb our lives with a demand for repentance, but guilt and admonition only go so far. The fire we are promised is accompanied by the Holy Spirit. If our lives have a sense of being fabricated in response to the expectations of others, then the fire we are promised burns off the false self and releases the true self.

By repentance, we are invited to experience God's burning love that can cleanse us of all the hypocrisies of our lives. The good news of Advent is that the true self, created in the image of God, exists within each of us and that Christ can set us free. We experience a baptism of the Holy Spirit and of fire as we begin to recognize and celebrate the many ways that God touches our lives. How do we prepare others and ourselves for the one who baptizes with the Holy Spirit and fire? "Bear fruit that is worthy of repentance," John said. When we ask what we need to do, he speaks of such practical things as sharing a coat with someone who has none.

We begin the journey back to our true selves through simple acts of compassion for the needy. This is, however, no longer done as a satisfaction of some faith requirement but as a preparation for us to receive the one who comes with fire. The good news is that if we prepare the way, there is one from beyond us who can restore our true selves. Are you feeling rather dull of faith? Search out someone who is in need and respond with compassion. In doing so, you prepare yourself for receiving the one who comes with fire and the Holy Spirit.

Advent 4

Micah 5:2-5a

> *And he shall be the one of peace.* — Micah 5:5a

It is important during the season of Advent that we not treat too casually the hope for peace in our world. The world yearns for a true peace but often seeks it through war and expects that only the weapons of the most powerful can maintain peace. This passage from the prophet Micah speaks of Israel's longing for a leader who would guide them toward peace. According to the gospel of Matthew, this became a central prophecy of the people's hope for a messiah (Matthew 2:6). The gospel declares that this hope was fulfilled in the birth of Jesus. In contrast to worldly wisdom, the passage makes clear that the true source of hope for peace is from God.

Instead of the messiah coming from a powerful nation or even an important family with many resources, this messiah was to come from one of the little clans of Judah. The messiah was to be more than a good man and a good teacher. He was to be, above all, a man of peace, and his coming was to mark the advent of peace in the world. Our faith invites us to look for God's work of peace in areas that are often overlooked by the world and seen as insignificant. As we celebrate the birth of Christ, it behooves the church and its members to reflect on how we act for peace, not only personally but also in the larger world.

It is consistent with the biblical theme that God's peace begins with the birth of a fragile child rather than the development of a new weapon of war. In the same manner, perhaps one congregation seeking to act for peace in the name of that Christ might advance world peace.

Psalm 80:1-7

Restore us, O God; let your face shine, that we may be saved. — Psalm 80:3

Psalm 80 is a community lament. Unlike most individual lament psalms, community laments are prayers that are left unanswered. They are prayers that pour out the communal pain because of trust in God, but they are also prayers that end still waiting for an answer. Psalm 80 is a perfect prayer for a world that seeks the peace of the Christ but has not yet experienced the realization of such a peace. The psalm recalls the intimate relationship of Israel with God by using the image of God as a shepherd of Israel. Later, in verses 7 through 11, it rehearses the history of God having brought the Hebrew slaves out of Egypt and established them as a people.

But the heart of the prayer is the question of why God has not helped them realize the promise contained in their original covenant with God. In many ways it is the Christian question of why the world is not different now that the Christ has come. The psalmist offered this prayer after Jerusalem had fallen (v. 12) and assumed that the reason that Israel was suffering this fate was that God was angry with them. It would be sobering for Christians to reflect on whether the failure of the world to experience the peace of Christ is due to our own disobedience as a church.

The prayers for peace during this season might well include prayers of confession by Christians who have failed to be obedient to the Prince of Peace and are experiencing the consequences of their own disobedience. Yet, along with the psalmist, our hope is not in our own goodness but in our trust that God will not be angry with us forever. If the church has failed to be the obedient people of God, our hope remains in God's goodness. Our prayer, which honestly acknowledges our failures, finally concludes with our plea, "Restore us, O God; let your face shine, that we may be saved." This prayer, like the communal laments of the psalmist, is an open-ended prayer that awaits the response of God.

Hebrews 10:5-10

> *And it is by God's will that we have been sanctified through the offering of the body of Jesus Christ once for all.* — Hebrews 10:10

There has always been a central mystery to our faith. How do we resolve the contradiction between the sinful state of humanity and the holy purpose of God? The prophets agonized over this problem as they recognized that even though God had provided humanity with God's law to direct them in their lives, still they continued to rebel. Jeremiah suggested that God would create a new covenant in which the will of God would be written upon the human heart (Jeremiah 31:31-34). Later, Hebrews suggested that through Christ God inaugurated this new and interior covenant. The law had served a purpose of being a reflection or shadow of the good thing to come, but it was not the real thing itself. The real thing was seen in the perfect obedience of Christ.

In developing this thesis, Hebrews interpreted Psalm 40:6-8. The full psalm was a prayer of thanksgiving for deliverance and a prayer for help. If you substitute Jesus' name for the pronoun and read the psalm in this context, you can imagine it being an important prayer of Jesus in the Garden of Gethsemane or at any of several trials in Jesus' life. Hebrews interpreted the psalm as Jesus' prayer and suggested that the new covenant had been inaugurated through Jesus' full obedience to God's will. In doing so, it had abolished the need for repeated sacrifices because the shadow to which such sacrifices pointed had been replaced by the real thing in Christ's sacrifice.

As we approach Christmas, in the midst of gifts given and received, this passage again confronts us with how we truly receive a gift. What does it really mean to receive this gift of our sanctification from God? When you have received a totally unexpected and wonderful gift from someone, what is the best way to respond?

Luke 1:39-45 (46-55)

> *In those days Mary set out and went with haste to a Judean town in the hill country....* — Luke 1:39

Such a small beginning to such a momentous event. All of the truly great turning points in history begin with small events that are barely noticed. Mary was not a famous or powerful person. We do not even know her, family or much about her. Yet she felt a quickening within her and she responded by taking the first step of a journey that would alter the world. She went to a small village so unimportant that we are not even given its name. There, one small beginning made connection with another small beginning as the unborn child in Elizabeth's womb responded to the embryo in Mary's womb. A synergy began before the actual birth events even took place.

Like the germ of an idea that plants itself in the small corner of a mind, a world-transforming moment began outside the notice of the powerful and the important. One woman responded in faith to that which had not yet taken place, it elicited faith in another woman, and the world began to change.

"When Elizabeth heard Mary's greeting, the child leaped in her womb." The yet-to-be-born John responded to the yet-to-be-born Jesus. John was the one that prepared the way and suggested how we might be prepared to recognize God among us. Before either of these women gave birth, there were signs of what was to come. Even if in the haste of this season we have failed to take the time to prepare to receive Christ in our lives, there are still signs indicating the nearness of Christ to us. Christ may not be fully formed in our lives, and, yet, there is still a quickening within us that hints at what God could make possible in our lives. Now is the time to pause long enough to recognize that our Christmas activities may have neglected the real preparation necessary. We are invited to feel the kick within us and to shift our focus to recognize the Christ among us.

Christmas Eve/Christmas Day

Isaiah 52:7-10

> *How beautiful upon the mountains are the feet of the messenger who announces peace, who brings good news, who announces salvation....* — Isaiah 52:7

One of the shadows that hovers in the background of any Christmas celebration is the haunting fear that after all of the hectic activity leading up to the celebration of Christmas, nothing has really changed when it is over. The world continues as it has with its specters of violence, greed, and lust. This section of Isaiah is often referred to as Second Isaiah and reflects a time when Israel was living in exile. It was in the midst of this time of despair when there was little evidence of any hope that things would actually change in the way that the prophet had spoken. His message was a strong proclamation that despite the apparent reality in which the people lived, God reigns. Christmas in our fractured world is also a good time to proclaim to God's people that God reigns.

In our violence-torn world, what better news could someone bring to the people than the message of peace? Unfortunately, in our cynical world, we are skeptical of such a message. We've heard it before and nothing really has changed. Yet the Christian message to believers living in such a cynical world is the startling news, "Your God reigns!" To counter such cynicism, we are invited to be sentinels who look for signs of God's work in the world. Swimming against the currents of cynicism, worshipers are called to "sing for joy; for in plain sight they see the return of the Lord to Zion." This is not a naive denial of reality. The prophet was fully aware of the contrary signs of the world. "Break forth together into singing, you ruins of Jerusalem...." We are to sing a counter song because we believe a truth that most of the world denies — God reigns! It is because of that truth that, despite the evidence around us, we can look to the future with expectation. It is both a realistic and a much needed message on Christmas Day.

Psalm 98

Make a joyful noise to the Lord, all the earth; break forth into joyous song and sing praises.
— Psalm 98:4

In the formation of the lectionary, the psalm is chosen to respond to the Hebrew selection, in this case Isaiah 52:7-10. There are echoes of that passage in such phrases as "his holy arm" and "in the sight of the nations." The psalmist is inviting the faithful to make a public witness to a revealed reality that seems to run counter to the accepted truths of the larger world. Christmas Day is not just a private celebration of the faithful but a public testimony to the world around us. That public testimony is made in a fashion that can unnerve the cynical power brokers of the world. The whole of the Christmas story undermines the structures of the world that rule through the exercise of power and fear.

God comes into this world not with the loud trumpets of a military charge but the soft cry of an infant. The news is revealed not to the inner circles of the rich who rule in the capital cities but to the poor and almost invisible people who serve the rich by staying up all night to watch the sheep that will later be served to the wealthy. Even the location of this history-changing event is not in an important city or country but in an unimportant village in a small, forgotten corner of the mighty Roman empire. Because, as Christians, we have celebrated this event and sung about Bethlehem and shepherds so frequently, we can easily forget how unimportant these events seemed to the world when they happened. Twelve days from Christmas, we will celebrate the visit of the wise men — pagan astrologers from outside of the faith community. "He has revealed his vindication in the sight of the nations."

Music transcends the rational logic of the world and trumpets a greater truth. The psalmist realizes that such praise cannot be expressed just in words but finds its melody in the lyre (v. 5) and its power in the trumpet and horn (v. 6). Praise recognizes who truly rules in life. When such praise is properly uttered in sounds beyond words, then all creation joins in (v. 7). Both the chaos of the flood and the strength of the hills join in giving joy (v. 8) because it is clear that there is one who judges the world with righteousness and the people with equity (v. 9). Such praise strikes fear in the hearts of those who believe that their power gives them the right to take advantage of the vulnerable. Such praise anticipates, on the basis of signs of one's own saving experience, a time when all peoples will recognize and be obedient to God's purpose. It is a powerful song of hope to be sung on Christmas Day.

Hebrews 1:1-4 (5-12)

> *Long ago God spoke to our ancestors in many and various ways by the prophets, but in these last days he has spoken to us by a Son....* — Hebrews 1:1-2

On Christmas Day we celebrate the in-breaking of God into our time-constrained universe. There is no logical way that one can explain how the eternal can become part of the finite. We can only celebrate this unexplainable mystery in sacramental terms — finite words that point to the eternal truths. In this tightly packed set of verses, the author of Hebrews seeks to pull together a variety of images of the eternal God's past revelations of truth in the finite world. He shows how the images find their fulfillment in the Jesus whose birth we celebrate on Christmas Day.

As a caution to Christians who can be too focused on the birth of a baby, it is perhaps important to hear Hebrews remind us that this Son transcends the historical moment of birth and finds expression in creation itself. In an echo of Proverbs 8:22-31, where the divine wisdom of God is personified as being present at creation, so now the Son is also spoken of as being present at creation.

Speaking to believers all too familiar with the sinful state of humanity that has distorted God's intentions for creation, Hebrews alludes to the assertion in Genesis 1:27 that humanity was created in the image of God and declares that in Christ we can see that image restored. "He is the reflection of God's glory and the exact imprint of God's very being...." At Christmas we are invited to recognize that in Jesus we do have a true revelation of what God expects of us. Recalling the absolute chaos that preceded creation and was only ordered by the expression of God's word, now believers are invited to have renewed hope in Christ's ability to again tame the chaos because "he sustains all things by his powerful word."

Because it is so easy even for believers to become despairing in our turbulent world, Christmas is an excellent time to be reminded that history is not out of God's control. While the intention of God for creation continues to be distorted by the sinful behavior of humanity, God is at work through Christ purifying the sins of the world and redemptively acting through Christ to fulfill God's purposes made evident at the beginning of creation. The birth of Jesus is not the end but the beginning of the story. Still, it is a good time to recommit ourselves to live with Christ through the rest of the story that God is unfolding in the universe.

John 1:1-14

> *The light shines in darkness, and the darkness did not overcome it.* — John 1:5

Like the Hebrew passage in our lectionary selection, this passage, too, draws upon Proverbs 8:22-31 to connect the birth of Jesus with the creation story in Genesis. Both books begin with the phrase "In the beginning...." Since science is restricted to the finite, it has no ability to step beyond the finite and explore eternity. However the Big Bang theory might suggest what happened after the beginning of creation, but from a faith perspective, John invites us to be present in the mind of God before creation began. As Genesis expressed it, before there was order there was only chaos. It was only when God spoke a word that order began to emerge out of that chaos. Now John proclaims that the word of God finds expression in Jesus who was at that beginning with God. "All things came into being through him, and without him not one thing came into being."

When we celebrate Christmas, we are celebrating the beginning of life. When our world seems filled with darkness, we are again hearing our God say, "Let there be light ... and God separated the light from darkness." When everything seems to be going wrong in the world, in our profession, in our lives, we need to hear again that "the light shines in darkness, and the darkness did not overcome it." Sometimes the power of that dark passage is so great in our lives that it is only by faith we cling to the truth that the darkness cannot overcome the light.

The presence of the light is frequently not self-evident in our world. "The true light, which enlightens everyone ... was in the world ... yet the world did not know him." Christmas is not only a celebration of God's gift of a Son but also a powerful reminder of the importance of the community of faith. Like the witness of John the Baptist, sometimes we have to depend on others to testify to the light because we are not able to see it for ourselves. The issue for Christians is not whether our society has taken Christ out of Christmas but whether we will live in a way that puts Christ into Christmas. Will we live in such a manner that others will see Christ present in our lives? "And the word became flesh and lived among us, and we have seen his glory, the glory as of a father's only son, full of grace and truth." Our call is to allow that grace to shine through us.

Christmas 1

1 Samuel 2:18-20, 26

May the Lord repay you with children by this woman for the gift that she made to the Lord.
— 1 Samuel 2:20

Hannah was an example of faith that trusts in God beyond the ordinary circumstances of life. We first hear of Hannah as the barren wife of Elkanah, who also had another wife, Peninnah, mother of several children. A barren woman was considered a failure in life. Peninnah's fertility not only stood as a reproach to Hannah but she also taunted Hannah f or her barrenness. Despite her husband's clear love for her, Hannah felt bereft because of her barrenness.

Then, in response to her repeated prayers, God heard her cry, and she conceived and bore a child that she named Samuel. In response to God's faithfulness to her, she, as a faithful Israelite, offered her first born to the Lord. Instead of child sacrifice, she "lent" her firstborn to serve God for as long as he would live (1 Samuel 1:28). This act of faithfulness in returning to the Lord her most precious gift revealed her absolute trust in God. It echoed the previous story of the offering of Isaac (Genesis 22:1 ff) and foreshadowed God's offer of Jesus. This most powerful symbol of faith comes from "the least of these" — a woman who at first seemed to have failed at her most significant responsibility. Now because of her faithful response to God, God would bless Hannah with three sons and a daughter. A faithful act that risked that which was most precious to her out of trust in God resulted in an abundant return from God. On this first Sunday after Christmas, while we are still celebrating the gift of Christ, we are reminded that the gifts of God should never become idols that we possess. It is often those who have very little that remind us the gifts we receive point to the faithfulness of God whom we must learn to trust.

Psalm 148

> *Let them praise the name of the Lord, for he commanded and they were created.* — Psalm 148:5

Psalm 148 is a psalm of praise that includes every facet of existence. It is a psalm that belongs at the end of the hymn of creation when God "saw everything he had made and behold it was very good" (Genesis 1:31). On that first sabbath day, when God paused, stood back, and rejoiced in this new creation, one could hear the peals of praise echo forth from God's creation. The whole creation was giddy with delight at its newfound existence. Praise came from the heavens, the angels, and the hosts (vv. 1-2). It sprang forth from the sun, moon, and stars (v. 3), and from the waters that were left above the firmament on the second day of creation (v. 4). Even the watery chaos, whose bounds were fixed by God, gave testimony to the sovereignty of God over all the forces of chaos (vv. 5-6).

This same praise echoed from the mystery of the forces within the created world: sea monsters, deeps, fire and hail, snow, frost, and stormy winds all obeyed God's commands (vv. 7-8). From mountains to hills, from fruit trees to cedars, and all forms of animal life reflected God's praises (vv. 9-10). All classes, sexes, ages of people from kings to children should join in such praise (vv. 11-12). Praise is at the center of all creation because every facet of the jewel reflects God's continuing glory (v. 13). It is this same God who has chosen to raise a sign of God's love for a chosen people as a sign of love for all people. God's glory was God's capacity to love a particular people (v. 14). For Christians, as we celebrate the birth of Christ, we see again the glory of God's handiwork and join with the creation to praise the Lord.

Colossians 3:12-17

> *And whatever you do, in word or deed, do everything in the name of the Lord Jesus, giving thanks to God the Father through him.* — Colossians 3:17

In almost all of Paul's letters, he was clear that the evidence of the spiritual life of a congregation must be seen in the fruits of the Spirit. "As God's chosen ones, holy and beloved, clothe yourselves with compassion, kindness, humility, meekness, and patience." The very fact that he had to mention this suggests that such fruits were in tension with a natural inclination of people within a human community. To live in a Christian community does not mean that we are liberated from all of the selfish ego needs of other human groups. Rather, while it is normal for churches to contend with such realities, we also have access to a power from beyond ourselves that can make our less-than-perfect response a redemptive possibility.

When we have a complaint against another member of the church, which we will have, we are to "forgive each other; just as the Lord has forgiven you, so you also must forgive." In most of the world, people's failures to live together in harmony results in the weakening of human community. However, because of the power of Christ working in us, our very failures present us with redemptive possibilities. If a person fails to relate to you properly, it provides you an opportunity to express the same type of love that Christ offers you. "Above all, clothe yourselves with love, which binds everything together in perfect harmony."

The very failure of our relationships presents us the opportunity to "let the peace of Christ rule in our hearts to which we were called in the one body." What enables this to be possible is our continual experience of worship. It is as we worship, singing psalms, hymns, and spiritual songs to God, that we are infused with the word of Christ that dwells within us. Then out of gratitude to Christ, we act to please God in a way that heals the strains between us. We act in this way because we are acting "in the name of the Lord Jesus, giving thanks to God the Father through him." As we celebrate the gift of God to us in Christ, we are enabled to give a gift in return.

Luke 2:41-52

And Jesus increased in wisdom and in years, and in divine and human favor. — Luke 2:52

We can learn much about Jesus from the gospel stories that provide insight for the body of Christ as well as the individual Christian. In Jesus we see the impact of both the human and the divine. Both were a very real part of who Jesus was. He responded to the expectations of two fathers, Joseph and God. On one level, the church must be obedient to God and to God's call. There is a divine expectation that is part of the church as the body of Christ. At the same time, there are appropriate human expectations to which the church must also be obedient. The church is a human institution and subject to the finite realities of all human communities. The individual Christian feels this same tension as well.

The human side of Jesus was seen in his progressive development or increase in wisdom and years. Luke is clear that Jesus progressed or increased in divine as well as human favor. The Christian does not become instantly mature at the moment one first believes. Part of our sanctification is experienced as we are nurtured in the church that is the intersection between the divine and the human. Jesus sat in the temple listening to the teachers and asking them questions. The truth of faith does not come apart from the community of faith.

We, like Jesus, must be in our father's house or seeking specifically to be in the presence of God. Such an effort will often put us in tension with the human expectations within our own lives and with the expectations of those around us. This brief glimpse of Jesus' childhood suggests that it is important that we accept this tension in our lives. For the church or the human to assume that only one part of the equation is necessary or even ideal is to lose the balance that enables us to increase in wisdom. The word of God that is not incarnated in the daily life of humans is an abstraction that denigrates the creation of God.

Christmas 2

Jeremiah 31:7-14

> *Then shall the young women rejoice in the dance, and the young men and the old shall be merry. I will turn their mourning into joy, I will comfort them, and give them gladness for sorrow.* — Jeremiah 31:13

The excitement that Christmas brings to our society is past. Whether we sang carols that celebrated the birth of Christ or songs about Frosty the Snowman and a reindeer with a shiny nose, that music is silent now on our radios and in our stores. Whether it was effective or not, the emphasis on family, gift giving, and holiday parties has now shifted to worries about the weather, the economy, or continued violence in the world.

What are the signs of hope that people of faith now have to offer this weary world? The prophet Jeremiah spoke to a nation on the brink of destruction. In a society whose memory of joy and laughter was replaced with experiences of devastation and despair, Jeremiah spoke of a future that involved music, dance, and ample food. "They shall come and sing aloud on the height of Zion, and they shall be radiant over the goodness of the Lord, over the grain, the wine, and the oil...." Think how important singing, food, and even dance is to building community in the midst of the strains of our society.

In a world torn apart by violence, Jeremiah spoke of gathering people together and erasing the lines that divide. "I am going to bring them from the land of the north, and gather them from the farthest parts of the earth, among them the blind and the lame, those with child and those in labor, together." Here are people divided by distance, physical challenges, or conditions that make them vulnerable. It is in coming together that they find hope and support.

Those who are part of our congregations bear with them a variety of burdens and challenges. The church does not ignore or deny those conditions but provides a community that supports each other and proclaims a God who is not defeated by such realities. Neither in Jeremiah's day nor in ours can we predict with certainty the resolution of all of our problems, but we offer a future free from despair. "I will turn their mourning into joy, I will comfort them, and give them gladness for sorrow."

When we are touched by the fears and despair of the world, it is important that the pastors and church leadership provide their members with experiences of joy that helps them remember the goodness of the Lord. "I will give the priests their fill of fatness, and my people shall be satisfied with my bounty, says the Lord." It is by the gifts of music, dance, food, and drink that we lift people's spirits. The Christmas season may be over but the importance of coming together to praise God is more important than ever.

Psalm 147:12-20

> *He has not dealt thus with any other nation; they do not know his ordinances. Praise the Lord!*
> — Psalm 147:20

Psalm 147 is a prayer of praise that seems to oscillate between the human and the cosmic. Since the birth of Christ moves between the cosmic and the human dimension, this is an appropriate psalm to read on the second Sunday of Christmas. In earlier verses the believer is reminded that the same God who gives order to the cosmos also enters battle between the oppressed and the oppressor (vv. 4-6). It is as if all injustices are a reflection of the chaos that God addressed with a divine word in the creation and still seeks to harness on behalf of creation.

Those whom God has gathered as a witness should praise God (v. 12) because God protects you outside and inside (v. 13) and offers peace and provisions (v. 14). As was true in Genesis 1, God speaks a word to bring order out of chaos in our time as well. It is by God's command that the earth receives its peace and provisions (vv. 15-18).

This cosmic God who cares for the entire universe is the same God who has instructed Israel (and therefore us) as to the will of God. All the nations of the world depend on Israel to declare what God has revealed. Christians are aware that God revealed the divine through the Jewish people and a Jewish person (v. 20). When we pray "Thy will be done on earth as it is in heaven," we accept the same responsibility as Israel in declaring to the nations what makes for peace. We, like the shepherds, hear the angels sing "on earth peace."

Ephesians 1:3-14

> *We, who were first to set our hope on Christ, might live for the praise of his glory.* — Ephesians 1:12

It takes a lot of trust to be a Christian. On this second Sunday after Christmas, consider the audacity of the promise of this season. Over 2,000 years after the birth of Christ, we still sing of peace on earth in a world torn by war. In a world that believes in power, we dare to claim that God came to us in the form of a fragile child. In a world that strives over wealth and fame, we seek the Christ born in a stable to peasant parents in an easily overlooked third-rate colony of the Roman empire. In a church that struggles to stay financially afloat, we claim God was made visible in poverty.

It all seems to challenge the logic of the mind. We are, as the early followers of Christ were called, *people of the way*. It takes a lot of trust to practice the Christian faith. The author of Ephesians said that those who trusted, "heard the word of truth, the gospel of your salvation, and had believed in him, were marked with the seal of the promised Holy Spirit" (v. 13).

Our hope is not in the logic of our minds but in a power from beyond us that interrupts our logic with continued experiences of redemptive hope. These experiences of God's Spirit are like down payments on "our inheritance toward redemption as God's own people, to the praise of his glory."

Look at your church and notice the continual emergence of signs of God's grace. At times you feel almost overwhelmed by the challenges that threaten the church's existence, and then you find community in a world of strangers, forgiveness that interrupts judgment, healing that supports a frightened family, and strength in the midst of weakness. God seems to be especially inclined to be present to those most in need.

"Blessed be the God and Father of our Lord Jesus Christ, who has blessed us in Christ with every spiritual blessing in the heavenly places." There is reason to go forward in hope.

John 1:(1-9) 10-18

> *He was in the world, and the world came into being through him; yet the world did not know him.*
> — John 1:10

After celebrating the greatest gift that God could bestow on humanity, the next few Sundays following Christmas usually have low attendance at worship, which frustrates most pastors. It is almost as if we cannot fully comprehend what we have just celebrated, and it is easier to turn to more mundane areas of life.

Try to comprehend what it means to say that the God of the creation story recorded in Genesis came to this world in the form of a single human being. In Genesis, in the face of absolute chaos, God merely spoke a word and order was formed out of chaos. "Then God said, 'Let there be light'; and there was light ... and God separated the light from the darkness" (Genesis 1:3-4). We are saying this word that God spoke has now found expression in this person we call Jesus. "What has come into being in him was life, and the life was the light of people." This was the light that split the darkness and brought order out of chaos.

In a few brief words, we have moved from the cosmic creation of the entire universe to the life of one person on one planet in one moment of time within that universe. "And the Word became flesh, and lived among us ... full of grace and truth." Is it any wonder that "the world did not know him"? Jesus is only comprehensible if there are those who will bear witness to this truth in a way that we can comprehend. That was John's task before Jesus' birth and is now the task of the church if Jesus is to be present in our own world.

In being able to overcome total chaos by simply speaking a word, God demonstrated absolute power. Now, in Jesus, God is expressed in loving, healing, forgiving, and grace. This is a power that the world has difficulty in trusting. It is as the pastor and church bear fruits of this expression of grace seen in Jesus, people begin to comprehend that something new has been introduced into this world.

As we move beyond the experience of Christmas, which despite skepticism captures the world's imagination, it is the task of the church to so demonstrate the fruits of the Spirit that the world will begin to comprehend this new reality. It may seem incredible to believe what we do in a single church can affect the whole world, but as the angel said to Mary in Luke 1:37, "Nothing will be impossible with God."

The Epiphany Of Our Lord

Isaiah 60:1-6

> *Arise, shine; for your light has come, and the glory of the Lord has risen upon you.* — Isaiah 60:1

As was true on Christmas Day, so the theme of God's light splitting the darkness continues on this Sunday as we celebrate Epiphany. Epiphany is the celebration of the appearance of the Christ to the Gentile world. In a world that is constantly torn by war and conflict, it is easy to be weighed down by the darkness of despair. It would not be hard to organize a good argument that the natural inclination of humanity is toward greed and conflict. The wealth of the world, rather than assisting in the development of people's lives, seems to be a constant source of fear and violence.

Epiphany is a celebration of God's light that splits such darkness. In the time of exile, when all human possibilities of hope for Israel were gone, the prophet spoke of a light that comes from God. It was a light that would reconcile the divisions of the world. "Nations shall come to your light and kings to the brightness of your dawn." The wealth of nations would no longer be a source of continuing conflict but would be brought together in a way that manifested the glory of God. Stop and reflect on the immense wealth of the various nations of the world. Consider all the diverse contributions that they have to make to the richness of humanity. All of this diversity of cultures and nations, the wealth of nations, will come together to praise God.

The praise of God is manifest in this world when the world uses the gifts of God in a manner that fulfills God's purposes. In the later story told in Matthew when the wise men brought their gifts and knelt before the Christ Child, the significance of their act was in the fulfillment of this glorious vision of Isaiah. In contrast to the world's means of accomplishing its purposes, the purpose of God was not accomplished through the use of force. Rather God brought the diversity of creation together through the birth of a small child. This reconciliation began through an expression of God's love that gives light.

Psalm 72:1-7, 10-14

> *For he delivers the needy when they call, the poor and those who have no helper.* — Psalm 72:12

Psalm 72 was originally written as a royal psalm to praise the king of Israel. Each king of Israel was anointed as a sign of God's choice. What we translate in English as anointed, the Hebrew uses the word "messiah" and the Greek uses the word "Christ." Each of Israel's kings was called to be the messiah. For Christians, Jesus fulfilled his call as the Messiah or Christ. Therefore, as we read this royal psalm, we can recognize it as a celebration of Jesus who fulfilled his purpose as determined by God.

Jesus is the king's Son who bears justice and righteousness for the people, especially the poor (vv. 1-2). In the feeding of the 5,000, he became an advocate for the poor and needy (vv. 3-4). By his resurrection, he not only lives for all generations (v. 5) but also refreshes people like rain (v. 6). By his ministry, he is a continual source of righteousness and peace (v. 7). His dominion or power to rule is not limited today by national boundaries (v. 8). As the Roman soldier acknowledged him at the foot of the cross (v. 9), and the wise men brought him gifts from the east (v. 10), so today those who rule find themselves serving him (v. 11).

Not only in his physical life but even today in the body of Christ, he delivers the needy, has pity on the weak, and redeems life from violence and oppression (vv. 12-14). The wise men brought gold, and prayers continue to be invoked for him (v. 15). There is a fruitfulness among his people (v. 16), and his name clearly endures for all time (v. 17). Jesus, as the Christ, is the blessing of God that reflects God's glory throughout the earth (vv. 18-19). In this way, Jesus in his resurrection appearance reveals how he has fulfilled the psalms (Luke 24:44).

Ephesians 3:1-12

> *... enable you to perceive my understanding of the mystery of Christ.* — Ephesians 3:4

As we enter the third millennium, it is important that we explore what Paul calls the mystery of Christ. It is far too small a thing to think of the church as a good religious organization that we casually participate in as one among several good organizations in our lives. The mystery of Christ reveals a plan of God for the reconciling of the whole world, not just those who are believers, be they Jew or Gentile. "In him the whole structure is joined together and grows into a holy temple in the Lord; in whom you also are built together spiritually into a dwelling place for God" (Ephesians 2:21-22). Epiphany has implications not only for the world coming to understand the significance of Christ but also for the church coming to understand the significance of the church for the world. Jesus lives on in the body that we call the church. Each of us, by our baptism, becomes a part of God's story unfolding in history. God's purpose is that "through the church the wisdom of God in its rich variety might now be made known to the rulers and authorities in the heavenly places."

God's reason for our being part of the church is to have us participate in something larger than ourselves. In the same way that we have sacrificed some personal pleasure for the sake of our family, so we are invited to make a commitment as part of God's family. As one part of the body, we are to act in a way that makes visible the whole body. How we treat our neighbor, or honor God's presence, reveals or beclouds God's purpose. The first Epiphany celebrated Christ's appearance to the larger world in the form of the magi who brought their gifts. Today Epiphany is ultimately revealed as the world brings its gifts to bear on behalf of the love of God seen in the birth of Christ. It is also revealed as we demonstrate our willingness to submit our wealth to the way of Christ for the sake of the world.

Matthew 2:1-12

... and they knelt down and paid him homage....
— Matthew 2:11

The intellectual elite knelt before the baby Jesus. They offered him their wealth for his use. Here is where the gospel has its epiphany or is revealed to the human soul. The darkness of the world is maintained in our hearts as long as the arrogance of our own wisdom or the seduction of wealth and power take priority over our obedience to the seemingly fragile presence of God's word. King Herod was correct in seeing that the worship of God in Christ undermined his authority in the world. Herod was a pragmatic man and ran his kingdom on what was effective. Each of us is confronted with the choice of what we allow to take priority in our lives. When our values are challenged by the demands of the gospel, do we insist that our wisdom is superior to the gospel? When God asks that we devote our hard-earned money or precious time to the work of God, do we say that God is asking too much? Can our wisdom be in service to Christ rather than the filter through which we determine whether the mandates of faith are reasonable?

Leadership that is shaped by wisdom and power that are subordinated to Christ approaches the world from a whole different perspective. The wise men still paid attention to the ways of the world. "And having been warned in a dream not to return to Herod, they left for their own country by another road." They neither rejected the benefits of their own wisdom nor dismissed the threats of the world. Yet their world and their decision making were now shaped by a different source. The New Testament or new covenant begins with the Gentile world kneeling before God in Christ Jesus. Much of the Christian church is now made up of Gentiles. The question we have to ask as we begin each year is whether we are still willing to submit all that we have in service to our Lord.

The Baptism Of Our Lord
Epiphany 1
Ordinary Time 1

Isaiah 43:1-7

> ... he who formed you, O Israel: Do not fear, for I have redeemed you; I have called you by name, you are mine.
> — Isaiah 43:1

Israel was in exile. All that confirmed their identity and well-being had been taken away. The land, which had been a confirmation of God's promise to Abraham; the kingdom, which also fulfilled God's promise to David; and the temple, which was the very seat of God's presence with them had been taken away from them. They had been forcibly resettled in a foreign land with other customs and other gods. In the midst of every sign that they were dying as a people, the prophet spoke words of hope and future. He spoke of God having created or formed them. The one who gave them life had the power to redeem them.

This was not a private spiritual promise removed from the historical reality of their life as a nation. The prophet was speaking of corporate redemption. This was not a cost-free redemption caused by some cosmic wave of a magical wand. There was a cost to every change of circumstance in a group's condition. Egypt, Ethiopia, and Seba would pay a price for Israel's redemption. The world would conform to God's purpose.

All this was done for the glory of God. God would not be defeated by history but would shape history to fulfill the divine purpose that was embodied in the physical reality of Israel. Such hope was not based on Israel's actions; certainly not on its faithfulness. It was based on God's decision to love this people. If God is consistent and the scriptures accurately record the nature of God's involvement in this world, what are the implications for Israel and the church today? Is there a cost to the rest of the world for the sake of the future of Israel and the church? There is a mystery in the election of God that defies rational explanation. In light of the event of the cross, we are left with the further question as to our responsibility to the world in light of the price the world is paying for our sake.

Psalm 29

> *... and in his temple, all say glory!* — Psalm 29:9

Psalm 29 can serve as a reflection on the doxology: "For thine is the kingdom, the power, and the glory." The imagery is that of a powerful storm that sweeps over land and water. The thunder (v. 3), lightning (v. 4), and driving winds (v. 5) evoke a response of awe and humility. Witnessing such a storm reminds one of the awesome power of God. Apparently the cedars of Lebanon (v. 6) and the great oaks (v. 9) were seen as symbols of great strength. In the face of God's power, however, they seem like mere playthings. This exhibition of power evokes a response from the heavenly beings (v. 1) and those in the temple (v. 9). Cry "Glory!" To glorify God is to acknowledge the incomparable contrast between our earthly symbols of power and the reality of God.

The storm is but a metaphor that reminds us that we have not begun to probe the dimensions of God's majesty. The flood is a symbol of chaos in Israel's literature, yet God sits enthroned over it (v. 10), even as God effortlessly controlled the chaos of Genesis 1. There are no limits to God's kingdom, power, and glory (v. 10). When we recognize the indescribable dimensions of God's power, all we can do is petition God for strength and peace (v. 11). In worship, when we sing, "For thine is the kingdom, the power, and the glory," we are acknowledging that strength and peace are ultimately a gift from God. This makes our human pretensions to being in charge a rather specious claim. It could also raise questions about how the church relates to the world around it.

Acts 8:14-17

> *... they had only been baptized in the name of the Lord Jesus.* — Acts 8:16

Beginning with chapter 2, Acts began to describe this strange experience of the Holy Spirit among the believers. If the Spirit created life out of the formless void described in Genesis 1 ff, this same Spirit visited them at Pentecost in a way that united them. This Spirit seemed to be creating new life in the church out of the chaotic world around it. This Spirit not only converted people to a new way of life, but that way of life overcame greed (Acts 2:43-47), healed people crippled from birth (Acts 3:1-10), gave frightened fishermen great boldness in front of the religious leaders of the day (Acts 4:1-12), demanded honesty among believers (Acts 5:1-11), set prisoners free from prison (Acts 5:17-21), and inspired recent converts with great wisdom (Acts 6:8-15). The Spirit seemed to break down walls and pull the church along with it. Understanding the word of God was not sufficient.

When the news arrived that some had accepted the word of God in Samaria, according to Acts, what was missing was the power of the Holy Spirit. As the story that will soon follow makes clear, this power was not for sale nor was it open to being controlled or manipulated by others. Even the apostles had to pray that these new believers would receive the Spirit. Only then did they lay their hands on them, and these new believers received the Holy Spirit. It is easy for the church to become so focused on church growth strategies that it forgets that the real power of the church is beyond the church's control. For the church to grow, there must be both proclamation and reception.

The power of God in our midst is a gift that breaks down all barriers but is totally beyond all our clever strategies. At the same time, the story suggests that the gift of the Spirit came as a result of laying their hands on these new believers. It is through the intimate contact with the fellowship of believers that the power of belief is made visible in the life of new believers. The Spirit arrives through the community and not as a result of the special belief or actions of individuals.

Luke 3:15-17, 21-22

> *As the people were filled with expectation, and all were questioning in their hearts concerning John, whether he might be the Messiah.*   — Luke 3:15

What does it take to be the Messiah? Or, to extend the question to our context, what does it take to be the messianic community? Many communities can draw attention to themselves through their powerful actions. The distinction that the gospel makes between a powerful organization dedicated to the improvement of society and the messianic community that reveals the very presence of God is the presence of the Holy Spirit. By John's powerful sermons, many were convicted of the need to change their lives. They were ready to follow John as their new leader. With remarkable insight, John saw that there was something still to come. People needed not only to repent, but they also needed to be purified in a way that human will power cannot bring about. John looked for one who could baptize them with the Holy Spirit and fire.

Pentecostal churches evoke the presence of the Holy Spirit as an authenticating power. This can make participants of many of our mainline religious communities very nervous. The power of the Spirit seems so uncontrollable. It appears to make people do strange things. Yet what both Pentecostal and non-Pentecostal churches need to experience is that purification of one's ego that enables one to submit to the direction of God. The community of faith that is willing to "not count equality with God a thing to be grasped" discovers in the servant nature of Jesus' ministry a model for their own cleansing and renewal. They begin to experience the power of God's Spirit that affirms them as beloved children of God.

Epiphany 2
Ordinary Time 2

Isaiah 62:1-5

> *For Zion's sake I will not keep silent, and for Jerusalem's sake I will not rest....* — Isaiah 62:1

Given the seemingly intractable violence of the Middle East, this prophecy has a hauntingly unfulfilled promise. If Jerusalem is the city of peace, its history seems to belie its name. God promises not to rest until "her vindication shines out like the dawn, and her salvation like a burning torch." Therefore, we know that God is not resting but still is at work in our world seeking to bring about shalom. This is a promise not only for Jerusalem but also for the world as well. "The nations shall see your vindication, and all the kings your glory...." The fulfillment of the promise to Zion will become an emblem of hope for the world. In the interim, however, believers live in a tension between the hope of the promise of shalom and the violent reality that we experience. In troubled Jerusalem, we see the struggle of faith. We want to trust in the promises of God, but the world around us seems to defy God's intent.

The church becomes a provisional Jerusalem. Its chaotic life can cause its members to feel forsaken and the land of their faith to seem desolate. Just as we are ready to give in to despair, we discover again that God's delight is in us, and there is a mystical sense of the unity of God and creation that suggests that God is married to the earth. Jerusalem becomes the window through which we seek to glimpse the marriage of eternity and time. If we restrict our vision to the limits of our time-bound life, we often find ourselves giving in to despair. If through the experience of the church and the promise of scripture we allow ourselves to glimpse eternity, we hear again the hope that sings, "as the bridegroom rejoices over the bride, so shall your God rejoice over you."

Psalm 36:5-10

> *... you save humans and animals alike, O Lord.*
> — Psalm 36:6

This passage is a selection from a larger psalm that contrasts the self-centered nature of evil with the expansive nature of God's love. In contrast to humans that flatter themselves in their own eyes (v. 2), God's love extends to humans and animals alike (v. 6c). The absolute otherness of God is described as a love that is neither confined by time nor space. "Your steadfast love, O Lord, extends to the heavens, your faithfulness to the clouds." The image of a mighty mountain (v. 6a) is offered to describe God's righteousness. It is not going to be moved by the incidentals of life. God's judgments, upon which all human hopes and fears ultimately rest, are described like the great deep (v. 6b). For Israel, a land-based people, there was nothing quite so unfathomable as the depth of the ocean. The expansiveness of God's saving grace extended itself not just to humans but to animals as well (v. 6c).

The thread woven throughout scripture of God's care not only for the chosen people but also for all people is expressed here. The heart of all life is found in God. All people can find their security in God. "All people may take refuge in the shadow of your wings" (v. 7b). It is God's intent that they also find nurture in the abundance of God's creation (v. 8a) and joy in the vitality of life (v. 8b). While this part of the psalm is a magnificent hymn of praise, it also is a strong reminder to the faithful that God's love is not limited to the community of faith. While those who are separated from God may experience life as a parched desert, it is God's intention and therefore, the responsibility of those provided the gift of faith that they also discover the fountain and light of all life (v. 9).

1 Corinthians 12:1-11

> *Now concerning spiritual gifts, brothers and sisters, I do not want you to be uninformed.*
> — 1 Corinthians 12:1

It is curious that in talking about spiritual gifts, the first thing that Paul wanted to speak about was the danger of being "enticed and led astray to idols." Why does the topic of spiritual gifts immediately bring to Paul's mind the issue of idolatry? If idolatry is worshiping, or giving worth to, that which is less than God, then are we in danger of giving too much worth, even worshiping, certain spiritual gifts? Isn't a constant source of tension within a church the overvaluing of some people's gifts and devaluing the gifts of others?

To give too much value to the person who has the gift of wealth, the gift of faith, speaking in tongues, or preaching runs the risk of practicing a form of idolatry. The strength of the Christian community is the recognition that "each is given a manifestation of the Spirit for the common good." The danger for the Christian community is to accept the world's criteria for measuring the value of such gifts. The challenge for the Christian community is not to rest until each person's gift is identified and lifted up for the common good. Even the most celebrated gift is only a part of the larger purpose set by God. Later Paul suggested that God might give the greater gifts to the lesser members and the lesser gifts to the more important members (1 Corinthians 12:23).

It would certainly upset the value system of our world if the church recognized this as a given truth. Suddenly those who lacked what the world celebrates as important gifts would be seen as important in God's eyes, and the whole community of faith would find reason to celebrate the life of each of its members. The appeal of the church to the disenfranchised in our society would be overwhelming. Perhaps this is what Jesus meant when in his inaugural sermon in Nazareth, he quoted Isaiah saying, "He has anointed me to bring good news to the poor" (Luke 4:18b).

John 2:1-11

But you have kept the good wine until now.
— John 2:10

This story begins with a strange interchange between Jesus and his mother. She pointed out that they had run out of wine. He seemed to respond that such an ordinary event was not his concern. Yet his mother's response was to assume that Jesus would indeed respond to this need, so she instructed the stewards. His mother was right, Jesus did respond, and the gospel suggests that this revealed Jesus' glory. Jesus made visible his divine side by responding to a seemingly small human need. Jesus' glory is in demonstrating the grace of God in the most ordinary aspects of life. For believers, it is a caution to not overlook the ordinary when we are seeking to experience the spiritual.

This passage is often read at a wedding service, and it can serve as an effective parable for marriage. In every marriage there is the promise of wine, a heady experience of physical attraction that enriches the relationship. Sex is the wine of marriage. As the steward said to the bridegroom, most people serve the good wine early at the party and the quality declines as the party progresses. When Mary told Jesus, "They have no wine," we hear the common story of a relationship that has lost its zest. It would be easy for people to begin to drift away from the party, but Mary invited Christ to help renew the relationship.

Jesus began to instruct the servants to fill jars of purification with water. Friends, by their support, often help hold marriages together during a dry spell in the relationship. If the couple will permit Christ not only to attend their relationship but also to be involved in its enrichment, Jesus is capable of taking those aspects that appear to be diluted beyond recognition and transform them into new bonds of excitement. It is not just restoring the old attraction but discovering a heady wine that is superior to the first and rewards the faithful with new quality.

Epiphany 3
Ordinary Time 3

Nehemiah 8:1-3, 5-6, 8-10

> *This day is holy to the Lord your God; do not mourn or weep.*
> — Nehemiah 8:9

When our lives are in chaos, one of the first things we need is a very clear discipline and structure to help us stabilize. The story of the people's return from exile is a story of return from chaos. Almost everything that provided them identity — land, temple, government — had been ripped away from them. They were allowed to return to the land.

Metaphorically, it is like people whose faith had been destroyed and who ventured back into the land of faith. One of the first things they did was to hear the law read to them. They heard what the discipline of this new way of life required. They were given a set of practices that would help reorder their lives from that which had been their practices. It is a new orientation.

Their first response was to compare the way of life provided by God through the scriptures with the life they had been living, and they were filled with guilt for time lost. "For all the people wept when they heard the words of the law." But they were counseled to rejoice instead. The law was not meant to condemn them for their failures in the past but to provide them with a structure by which some new order might come to their chaotic lives. The law was like the word of God that split the darkness in Genesis 1. The first day of a new life is when we begin again under God's guidance. It is a holy day: "For the joy of the Lord is your strength."

Psalm 19

> *Let the words of my mouth and the meditation of my heart be acceptable to you, O Lord, my rock and my redeemer.* — Psalm 19:14

Psalm 19 could serve as a foundation for Paul's declaration in Romans 1:20: "Ever since the creation of the world his eternal power and divine nature, invisible though they are, have been understood and seen through the things he has made." The psalmist, too, believes that the heavens and the firmament declare the glory of God to the ends of the earth (vv. 1-4). As an example, he gives the strong and steady course of the sun that evokes awe in the observer (vv. 5-6). In this sense, recalcitrant members are right when they suggest that communing with nature can inspire them. The experience of such awe evoked by nature stimulates in such people the desire to respond. But nature, no matter how inspiring, gives no instruction.

The law of the Lord is God's gift that informs us, in a way that nature cannot, of how we can respond to this mysterious power that orders our universe. The law revives the soul, makes the simple wise, rejoices the heart, and so on (vv. 7-10). It enables life to have direction and purpose in relation to one's creator. Yet, the law also makes us aware of our inadequacies and makes us even more aware of how dependent we are on God to liberate us from sin (vv. 11-13). This, too, was Paul's message in Romans 1.

Only as both rock and redeemer can the words of our mouths and the meditations of our hearts be found acceptable to God (v. 14). The rock alone becomes a harsh judgment. The redeemer alone can easily slip into cheap grace. It is the balance of experiencing God as one who expects something of us and provides us redeeming possibilities when we fail that enables us to be fully open to the goodness of God's gift of life.

1 Corinthians 12:12-31a

If one member suffers, all suffer together with it; if one member is honored, all rejoice together with it.
— 1 Corinthians 12:26

Like Paul, we, too, are confronted by the fractured body of the church. While Paul was particularly speaking of the church in Corinth and while we could find many churches that exhibit the squabbling and infighting that Paul addressed in Corinth, perhaps the greatest scandal of the body of Christ is our calm acceptance of the divisions that separate us denominationally. Paul was not content to dismiss such divisions as characteristic of human nature. At the same time, he was not an advocate that we should all conform to some common formula that was to fit all. In fact, Paul saw great value in the diversity within the body of Christ. The unity of the body was not to be found in uniformity but in recognition that each of our unique qualities was a gift from God "for the common good." This diversity was itself the intention of God and served to foster the health of the church. His familiar analogy of the human body emphasized his appreciation of the strength of the diversity within the common body.

That which unifies the church is its recognition of our formation into one body by one spirit. The practical means by which we unite is the emphasis on mutual care. "If one member suffers, all suffer together with it; if one member is honored, all rejoice together with it." One can imagine the impact of churches applying this admonition in their relationship with other churches. Imagine the powerful impact on a single city if all the churches in that city demonstrated a mutual care for each other and a celebration of the gifts that each contributed to the good of the whole.

How would we implement Paul's suggestion that "the members of the body that seem to be weaker are indispensable, and those members of the body that we think less honorable we clothe with greater honor, and our less respectable members are treated with greater respect"? Perhaps if we could even recognize that our financial resources were part of our spiritual witness, we might begin to wrestle with what Paul will describe in the next chapter as a "more excellent way."

Luke 4:14-21

> *Today this scripture has been fulfilled in your hearing.*
> — Luke 4:21

Have some sympathy for those who found Jesus' words difficult to accept. To accept that Jesus was filled with God's Spirit and charged with the proclamation of good news to the poor, release to the captives, recovery of sight to the blind, and to let the oppressed go free is no easier for us to accept today than it was for people in Jesus' time. No matter how much we try to spiritualize those words, they haunt us with their concrete reality. "The hopes and fears of all the years are met in thee tonight" may be sung on Christmas Eve, but we leave the church and go into a world that gives evidence of many dreams unfulfilled. There is something in us that wants to resist the full acceptance of Jesus as the divine revelation of God.

In this passage Jesus confronted his neighbors with the fact that God contradicted and challenged the narrowness of their ego-centered world. God did not exist to do their bidding or to confirm their status in the world. There is something within us that wants to believe that we are the chosen, and it is up to God to figure out how to respond to our needs.

Show us a sign, Jesus. We've heard you are a healer. I've got this pain. Heal it, and I will believe in you. And Jesus responds, "It is not your pain that is the center of the universe. Rather it is God's purpose around which the universe revolves." If Jesus is the fulfillment of scripture, then obedience even in the face of pain or suffering is more important than our being healed. Jesus is not here to prove himself to us but rather to call us to obedience to God.

Epiphany 4
Ordinary Time 4

Jeremiah 1:4-10

> *Before I formed you in the womb, I knew you....*
> — Jeremiah 1:5

Consider what it means that you were in the mind of God before you were a "glint in your parents' eyes." What does it mean that your life has an intentionality to it that transcends the fact that you were the result of lust or love? The purpose, and therefore the meaning, of your life is lodged not in your circumstances or environment but in the mind of God. There is a mystery to the call of God in our lives. We dare to suggest that there is an intersection between eternity and finite time. In a way that precedes our very existence, "before I formed you in the womb," we are part of a much larger story that takes shape in the mind of God. There is a natural resistance and a sense of inadequacy to such a thought.

Who are we to have a purpose that has eternal dimensions? It almost seems arrogant to contemplate such a possibility. It is captured in Jeremiah's words, "Ah, Lord God! Truly I do not know how to speak for I am only a boy." We also resist because such a thought suggests that we do not belong to ourselves. Yet, at the same time, it gives our life a dignity that is ennobling. Despite all our fears, we are reassured that our existence is a matter of importance to God. "Do not be afraid of them, for I am with you to deliver you."

While most clergy have known the feelings of inadequacy in the face of the task before us, we have also experienced the mystery of having been given words to say that seem to come from beyond ourselves. "Now I have put words in your mouth." Jesus makes the same promise in Matthew 10:19-20. "When they hand you over, do not worry about how you are to speak or what you are to say; for what you are to say will be given to you at that time; for it is not you who speak, but the Spirit of your Father speaking through you." Our calling experiences the brush of eternity but is embedded thoroughly in our own time. We can be dragged before authorities and have our every decision second-guessed, but the ultimate power that shapes our destiny belongs to another. The scary reality is to trust the power that we cannot control.

Psalm 71:1-6

> *In you, O Lord, I take refuge; let me never be put to shame.* — Psalm 71:1

This psalm is often referred to as the prayer of the elderly. Verses 9 and 17-18 make specific reference to the age of the psalmist. If you pray these first six verses from that perspective, you can hear a person who has been feeling the pressures of aging seeking strength from beyond. Another intriguing feature of this psalm is its liberal use of allusions to other psalms. In the verses assigned to this reading, verses 1-3 allude to Psalm 31:1-3, and verses 5-6 seem to reflect the words of Psalm 22:9-10.

In both psalms, the petitioner feels isolated from human community and only feels restored to community through his absolute trust in the faithfulness of God. The psalms in the lectionary are chosen in response to the previous Old Testament lesson; in this case, the reference is the call and commission of the prophet Jeremiah. The psalmist teaches us how to pray when we feel threatened by our environment. There are some parallels between the threat felt by the elderly and the threat of those who seek to respond to God's call vocationally. In both cases, the world around us seeks to diminish our worthiness.

In both cases, the petitioners are invited to find their true worth in the God who has formed them. And that sense of renewal begins in reviving the memory of where God has been before in their lives. "Upon you I have leaned from my birth; it was you who took me from my mother's womb." This sense of renewal does not deny the reality of the threat but seeks help by reminding God of their prior relationship. In the call of Jeremiah, there is the suggestion that their relationship precedes birth. The power of prayer is that it restores our relationship with God and, therefore, reminds us that we are valued in a way that transcends our circumstances.

1 Corinthians 13:1-13

> *... if I hand over my body so that I may boast, but do not have love, I gain nothing.* — 1 Corinthians 13:3

This chapter has been read in weddings so often that it is difficult to extract it from that context and hear it freshly. It is important to recall the context in which Paul placed it in this letter. It was not the romantic love between two individuals of which Paul spoke but the glue that enabled a congregation to transcend petty jealousies and rivalries. Given the tragic factionalism that is affecting the Christian church in our time, and the excessive emphasis on technique as the Savior of the church, it may be important to hear Paul's words addressing our churches.

In the previous chapter, Paul has been speaking about spiritual gifts and the necessity of not seeing one set of gifts as more important than others in the overall functioning of the congregation. He concluded chapter 12 by saying, "And I will show you a still more excellent way." He then made reference to some of the more prominent spiritual gifts that are manifested in congregations such as speaking in tongues, having prophetic powers, showing great wisdom, and the willingness to demonstrate the power of one's faith through making great personal sacrifices. Individuals and religious communities continue to be powerfully impressed by those who can demonstrate some version of such gifts. Yet, repeatedly, we discover that such powerful witnesses can become tragically distorted and destructive unless they are channeled by a transcending love that seeks to serve others rather than self.

If Jesus clarified that God's way is a way of relationships with God and neighbor, then Paul was providing the practical prism through which we should measure our attempt to live in God's way. In the same way that Jesus' love was demonstrated in his willingness to be a servant to others, so the church is invited to trust God enough to risk itself for the sake of others.

Luke 4:21-30

> *All spoke well of him and were amazed at the gracious words that came from his mouth. They said: "Is not this Joseph's son?"* — Luke 4:22

There is something in us that is amazed at the gracious words of Christ in our lives. At the same time, we also want to reduce Christ to the practical knowledge of "what's in it for me?" We want Jesus to demonstrate his usefulness in our lives. We want Jesus to be a service provider rather than a prophet. That same consumer mentality surfaces in our relationship with the body of Christ. It is far more common to complain that the church has failed to meet my needs than it is to complain that I have failed to meet the needs of Christ in his body. As a congregation, it is easy for us to want to think about our survival as an organization rather than about our faithfulness as the body of Christ. How often do we survey our needs as an organization and find them in tension with a faith that calls us to serve those beyond us?

Unlike Jesus, the head of the church, we consider survival to be the first order of business and only then do we turn and consider our mission. Yet God keeps forcing us outside of ourselves. What is hard for us to accept is that we are healed by our becoming a channel through which the word of God is made plain. While there is no evidence that Jesus sought out the opportunity to suffer, he did not make the avoidance of suffering the primary purpose in his life. We are blessed by becoming a blessing. The Christian faith often asks for sacrifice at a time when we are demanding service. Our faith invites us to risk responding to the needs of others precisely at the time when we feel needy. To respond to such an invitation requires an act of faith. It is much easier for us to recall the human origin of the one who brings us the word of invitation: "Is not this Joseph's son?"

We say that the church is a business, and we cannot do any good if we go out of business. But then we pause and consider where we might be if Jesus had responded to the threat to his life in the same way.

Epiphany 5
Ordinary Time 5

Isaiah 6:1-8 (9-13)

In the year that king Uzziah died, I saw the Lord sitting on a throne, high and lofty ... — Isaiah 6:1

Uzziah, also known as Azariah, had such a long and successful reign in Judah that for many it would have been difficult to remember when he was not their king. Imagine having the same president for fifty years. Whether you liked or disliked some of his decisions, you would become accustomed to a society structured and ruled over by him. Then suddenly this figure that had dominated the governing of your society for as long as you could remember dies. Uzziah's death signaled a major change in Judah's society. All the familiar structures that shaped life were suddenly subject to change. At times of major change, people lose their sense of security. With that new vulnerability, there is often an openness to the spiritual dimension of life. For Isaiah, it was an experience of God and a strong sense of call in his life. The framework of this experience has provided an outline for reformed worship. We come into the sanctuary and encounter the holy with a sense of awe and praise. "Holy, holy, holy is the Lord of hosts; the whole earth is full of his glory."

It is natural, when we do have the sense of divine presence, to feel our own sense of inadequacy and the need to confess our sinfulness. "Woe is me! I am lost, for I am a man of unclean lips, and I live among a people of unclean lips." In our liturgy, the confession of sins is immediately followed by an assurance of forgiveness. "Now that this has touched your lips, your guilt has departed and your sin is blotted out." Having been assured of our forgiveness, we are now prepared to hear the word of God proclaimed. In that proclamation, we hear God's call in our lives. "Whom shall I send, and who will go for us?" Having heard that call, we are invited to make an offering or response. "Here am I; send me!" Yet even as we offer ourselves, the resistance of the world to God's word confronts us. "Keep listening, but do not comprehend." The benediction is a prayer for and an assurance of our hope in the midst of a resistant world. "The holy seed is in its stump." Every week we relive in the liturgy the basic outline of the spiritual journey of our lives and in doing so find our place in the larger story of God.

Psalm 138

I give you thanks, O Lord, with my whole heart ...
— Psalm 138:1a

This psalm is listed in our lectionary as a response to the Isaiah 6 passage in which Isaiah, following the death of Uzziah, entered the temple and had the overwhelming experience of the presence of God. It was a time of national trauma following the death of a king who had ruled for fifty years, as long as most people could remember. The psalm is a personal prayer of thanksgiving that may seem unusual at a time of national and, perhaps, personal trauma. Praying this psalm with Isaiah's experience of Uzziah's death in mind can remind us of the power of immersing ourselves in thanksgiving at such times.

Thanking God with our whole hearts in times of trauma reminds us of the power of thanksgiving when we are in deep distress. Our bowing down in thanksgiving causes us to recall that the true source of our blessing is the steadfast love and faithfulness of God (v. 2). In such prayers, we recall how God has been faithful to us in the past and sustained us in times of need (v. 3). Our thanksgiving is in anticipation of the time when all the powers on earth will recognize and praise God as the source of blessing (vv. 4-5). When the rulers of the earth are aware of the character of God, they will humble themselves because they know God responds to the lowly (v. 6). We already know this because as we reflect back over our lives, we know God responded to us when we were lowly and in need (v. 7). Our thanksgiving is completed when having acknowledged how often God has been there for us, it suddenly dawns on us that God has a purpose for us. We are the work of God's hands, and we can pray with confidence, "Do not forsake the work of your hands" (v. 8).

It is a worthy psalm to pray at times of personal or national trauma.

1 Corinthians 15:1-11

Whether then it was I or they, so we proclaim and so you have come to believe. — 1 Corinthians 15:11

It is difficult in our media- and personality-obsessed world to keep in mind what is important is that a person comes to believe and not by whom they have come to believe. It is equally important to keep in mind that how another person comes to believe is beyond our control and often defies our explanation. The core of Paul's understanding of the gospel centered on the death and resurrection of Jesus. He showed very little interest in the life and even the teachings of Jesus. He marveled at the transforming power of God's love. If Jesus was raised and was to appear to only a select few, it would be natural that he would appear to those who had been his companions during his ministry. And while he did do that, "last of all, as to one untimely born, he appeared also to me," Paul declared.

God's choice could hardly be explained either by previous relationship with Jesus, of which he had none, or by his behavior. He had, after all, "persecuted the church of God." The only explanation is this totally unexplainable and utterly mysterious grace of God. When you think of your own journey, can you identify totally unexpected events or people who profoundly affected your personal journey? In some cases the event may have seemed entirely negative at the time or the person may have been some person that you have a great deal of difficulty admiring. Yet, by the grace of God, that experience or encounter has utterly transformed your life.

It is somewhat humbling to consider that someone else may have been utterly transformed by an act or a comment you made that you have long since forgotten. Can it be that one of the manifestations of God's grace is God's ability to work within the church, even when it appears dysfunctional, to transform the lives of others? Perhaps we need to spend at least an equal amount of energy noticing the presence of God's transforming grace within the church as we spend criticizing its failure to live up to our expectations. After all, it is not as important who or what brings a person to belief as it is that they have come to believe.

Luke 5:1-11

> *Go away from me, Lord, for I am a sinful man!*
> — Luke 5:8

What was it in Peter's experience that so convicted him of his sinfulness? Why was his response to Jesus in light of that sinfulness to want to send Jesus away? Is there something in us that is afraid of getting too close to holiness? Notice the contrast between the crowd that "was pressing in on him to hear the word of God" and Peter who wanted to send Jesus away. If Peter is the symbol of the church and the crowd is the world of spiritually hungry people, then this story speaks to the issue of evangelism. It is important to recognize the association between work and evangelism. It was while the four disciples were engaged in their profession of fishing that they experienced the power of Christ in their lives. It was while they were exercising their profession that Jesus addressed the spiritual hunger of the world.

Too often we separate any effort at evangelism from our work as if it were an extracurricular activity. Following the story line, we recognize that Jesus enters our boat and teaches the crowd even while we are just mending our nets. The possibility for spreading the good news of Christ will come when we least expect it while we are engaged in the most ordinary procedures of our lives. When Jesus asked the disciples to let down their nets in deeper water, they reluctantly obeyed while explaining why it would not work. It is not unusual for the most powerful message of good news to come in a way that we think will not work.

When God worked through the disciples to accomplish what they did not believe possible, they were suddenly aware of how they were more willing to trust their judgment of what was possible than to trust God. Our awareness of the weakness of our faith makes us want to send Jesus away because we feel unworthy. But Jesus says to us, as he did to those first disciples, "Don't be afraid," I will use you to save others. It is because Jesus trusts us more than we trust Jesus that we can share good news.

Epiphany 6
Ordinary Time 6

Jeremiah 17:5-10

> *Cursed are those who trust in mere mortals and make mere flesh their strength ...* — Jeremiah 17:5

Jeremiah serves as a prophet during the destruction of Judah as a nation. The heights the Israelites achieved in the reigns of David and Solomon, and even the strength they found after the split into the two nations of Israel in the north and Judah in the south, was rapidly falling apart. While prophets had long warned of the destruction of the nation, now it appeared to be occurring before their eyes. All they had worked for, taken pride in, and saw as a sign of God's favor was rapidly disappearing. It was as if the urbane civilization of human achievement was returning once again to the uncivilized state of the desert. Yet the image of the desert provided for Jeremiah a means by which he also could help them recall their source of hope. It was in the wilderness or desert, where they wandered for forty years, that they were formed into a people of God.

It was during the wilderness experience that they learned the danger of depending on their own ability and the sureness of God to provide for them if they would simply trust in God. "Blessed are those who trust in the Lord, whose trust is the Lord," said Jeremiah. He reminded his people who were currently teetering on the brink of chaos that there was one who has already demonstrated that he was not defeated by chaos. Using the image that is also found in Psalm 1, Jeremiah contrasted trust in God with trust in mortals. It was, suggested Jeremiah, "like a tree planted by water, sending out its roots by the stream."

The danger for the nation was not the external conditions. They had faced such dangers before. The danger was that they had lost the capacity to place their trust in God. The threat to their nation was a test of God. "I the Lord test the mind and search the heart, to give to all according to their ways, according to the fruit of their doings." Given all of the dark predictions about the fate of the church in our time, perhaps it is again time to examine how much we trust God and how much we are placing our hope on the strength of mortals.

Psalm 1

> *They are like trees planted by streams of water, which yield their fruit in its season, and their leaves do not wither.* — Psalm 1:3

By placing this psalm as a response to the Jeremiah 17:5-10 passage, the lectionary has emphasized the issue of choice and the impact on life of one's connection with God. Psalm 1 also recalls the context of Joshua 24:15 in which Joshua has reminded the people of all that God has done for them and challenges them, "... choose this day whom you will serve ... but as for me and my household, we will serve the Lord." The scriptures continually emphasized the amazement that God had not only chosen them but also the necessity of the people responding by making their own choice.

We are both destined and responsible for our own choice in life. Using the hyperbole common to the psalmist, the choice is described as an "either/or" choice. The choice was between the wicked and the righteous. The righteous were those whose "delight is in the law of the Lord, and on his law they meditate day and night" (v. 2). The anchor to such a life was a focus on the way of God as seen in the law or instruction of God. Those who did not have such an anchor "are like chaff that the wind drives away" (v. 4). For the psalmist, God was the author of life, and, therefore, seeking God's purpose meant that you were drawing on the very source of nutrients in life. The image is that such a person was "like trees planted by streams of water" (v. 3).

While the choice is painted in either/or terms, with no room for ambiguity, the invitation is not to a life of narrow rigidity. Life that has direction is freer than life that is aimless. The price of that freedom, however, is a constant alertness to how you might best reflect the purpose that feeds your life with energy. Now you draw energy not from satisfying your own ego but from fulfilling God's purpose. Your life finds its meaning in a much larger story to which you are now contributing. This psalm serves as an introduction to the book of Psalms that will explore these themes in greater detail.

1 Corinthians 15:12-20

> *Now if Christ is proclaimed as raised from the dead, how can some of you say there is no resurrection of the dead?* — 1 Corinthians 15:12

We have tried to shield ourselves from the reality of death. In most attempts by the media to picture anything beyond death, there is the assumption of the immortality of the soul. Some of the movies that attempt to depict this picture as the essence of the person in some ghostlike form leaving the body and floating away. The logical conclusion from such an image is that the body is a mere hindrance and that death sets us free from its restrictions. The result is a denial of the reality of death. If the soul is immortal, then there is no need for the resurrection since you are never really dead. You are simply transitioning to a new stage of life.

To believe in the resurrection is to accept the reality of death. Death is the end of our body and soul. Our hope is not in our immortality but in God who can defeat the very real power of death. It is curious that in this passage Paul reverses our logic with respect to Christ's resurrection. It is normal to think that because Jesus was raised from the dead, therefore, the barrier of death was defeated, and we can have hope that we, too, will be raised with him. Yet in this passage, Paul suggested that the belief in Christ's resurrection depended on the reality of general resurrection. "If there is no resurrection of the dead," Paul stated, "then Christ has not been raised."

In that sense, Christ's resurrection was not an exception to the norm but a revealing of the truth of God's power to defeat death. To place our trust in God's power to defeat death, we have to first acknowledge the reality of death. If death is not real, if somehow we all are immortal, then there is no need for our belief in the resurrection. But if death is real, then our hope is only in God's power to defeat death. The resurrection of Christ revealed the power of God to defeat the power of death. Our source of hope is not in our individual goodness but in the goodness of God who is not defeated by death.

Luke 6:17-26

Blessed are you who are poor, for yours is the kingdom of God. — Luke 6:20

In Matthew this beatitude is phrased a little differently. "Blessed are the poor in spirit," Matthew said. It is easier for us to translate such a beatitude into a need to be humble. Luke did not allow such wiggle room. Luke's version of the beatitudes challenges almost everything for which we strive. While we may have sympathy for the poor, the hungry, and those who weep, at best we want to raise them up to our much more comfortable state. We certainly have no desire to join them. We are forced by Luke to ask why we do not want to be poor, hungry, or to weep, or to be excluded on account of the Son of Man. In any of these conditions, we become needy and most of us would prefer to be independent and secure.

Luke invites us to consider the condition of life that the Hebrews experienced as they journeyed through the wilderness. They were poor, hungry, and wailing because of their condition. Yet, as their faith celebrates, it was in that state that they were drawn closer to God. When they were in a clear state of need, they learned that they could trust God to provide for them each day their daily bread. They did not have to be dependent on any other condition of life.

We have been raised to believe that by being secure in our physical, emotional, and relational situation, we are then free to choose our own direction in life. The problem is that we are still dependent on the sources of those conditions. The kingdom of God, which we say that we would like to enter, is that state in which we can trust God totally. Only then are we free to be the people God created us to be.

Epiphany 7
Ordinary Time 7

Genesis 45:3-11, 15

I am your brother, Joseph, whom you sold into Egypt.
— Genesis 45:4

Many people live with a horrendous sin locked away in their heart. They continue to live their lives and may even have repressed conscious thought of that sin, but it shapes who they are. Joseph's brothers had sold him into slavery and then went on with their lives. Whether their act haunted them or whether they had repressed it, we are not told, but they continued with their lives. Then, when they least expected it, they encountered Joseph, and their past came hurtling back. The reason that we seek to repress the memory of such guilty acts is that we assume that their exposure would be destructive to us. It is no wonder that his brothers were speechless when he first revealed himself to them: "Joseph said to his brothers, 'I am Joseph. Is my father still alive?' But his brothers could not answer him, so dismayed were they at his presence." Not only had their past suddenly been exposed, but also it happened at a time when they were very vulnerable. Then the next shock arrived.

"And now do not be distressed, or angry with yourselves, because you sold me here; for God sent me before you to preserve life." First the sin of their past was exposed, but next they heard that God had worked with their sin in a redemptive way. The question for Joseph's brothers was whether they could accept that God, through Joseph, had moved on beyond the guilt of their sin to a redemptive possibility. What the brothers were confronted with was the power of grace. They had clearly been guilty, but God was not locked into their guilt. God had used their deed to save the Hebrews from starvation. Joseph, the victim of their deed, had arrived at a position to save them from starvation.

As the story progresses, the brothers had a great deal of difficulty accepting that Joseph would not at some time in the future seek revenge for the evil that they had done to him. The power of grace is not seen in God's overlooking your sins but in accepting that God is capable of working through even the worst of your sins for a redemptive possibility. Many years later this same revelation of the transforming power of God's grace would be revealed again as God transformed the violent act of crucifixion into a means of salvation for the whole world.

Psalm 37:1-11, 39-40

> *Refrain from anger, and forsake wrath. Do not fret — it leads only to evil.* — Psalm 37:8

These verses become a beautiful reflection on the story of Joseph, his journey into slavery, and his rise to a position of power in Egypt. It is natural for people to be disturbed by the apparent success of people who do evil deeds. This psalm counsels patience in such circumstances. "Do not fret because of the wicked; do not be envious of wrongdoers." It is important to recognize that the psalmist is not counseling passivity in the face of wrongdoing. Rather the psalmist is warning against becoming consumed by one's reaction to such wrongdoing and, therefore, doing even further harm to oneself.

Consider what would have happened to Joseph if he had been consumed with anger or even self-pity at what his brothers had done to him. "Be still before the Lord, and wait patiently for him; do not fret over those who prosper in their way, over those who carry out evil devices." Joseph became a living example of the psalmist's admonition: "Trust in the Lord, and do good; so you will live in the land, and enjoy security." When one combines the narrative story of Joseph with the psalmist's exhortation, one recognizes the power of the beatitude that Jesus drew from this psalm. "Blessed are the meek, for they will inherit the earth" (Matthew 5:5). See Psalm 37:11 for the foundation for this beatitude. If the meek to which Jesus referred were those depicted in this psalm, then their strength is derived from the power to not allow the actions of wrongdoers to dissuade them from trusting in the transforming power of God.

While we may not all have the almost magical outcome that Joseph did in his life, we can work to prevent ourselves from being consumed by our envy of others by developing a greater trust in God for the unfolding of our life.

1 Corinthians 15:35-38, 42-50

> *... you do not sow the body that is to be, but a bare seed, perhaps of wheat or of some other grain.*
> — 1 Corinthians 15:37

There is always the danger that we will push an analogy too far, but Paul was trying to speak of a mystery beyond our experience. He may well have been contending with Corinthian forbearers of his contemporaries who believed that we are immortal souls captured in a physical body. Paul believed that the resurrection of the body preserved the physicality of our current body in some manner that reflected continuity with who we had been during our life here on earth. While the seed was transformed through its death, we know that there is a direct physical continuity between the seed that was sown and the plant that emerged. A seed does not contain some inner spiritual essence that escapes its outer husk. The body or plant that is produced is directly connected with the actual seed that is planted.

Our current society prefers to believe in an immortal soul encased in a physical body that can be discarded at death. Paul spoke of our body being transformed: "It is sown a physical body, it is raised a spiritual body." Also, it was not something automatic but depended upon God: "Flesh and blood cannot inherit the kingdom of God, nor does the perishable inherit the imperishable." What takes place at our death depends on God and not on some inherent characteristic of our own being. "But God gives it a body as he has chosen, and to each kind of seed its own body." Paul also spoke of our bearing the image of Christ in our resurrection.

The reports of Christ's resurrection suggested both continuity and discontinuity as well. He was able to be touched by his disciples and to digest food that was given to him. At the same time, the gospels suggested that he was not bound by time and space in the same way that he was before his death. He seemed to enter a room with locked doors and to move about without the constrictions that we normally assume. When we seek to understand the resurrection, we are entering into a dimension of eternity but retain our touch with time. Analogies are useful, but in the end we return to our capacity to trust God who is good and is not defeated by death.

Luke 6:27-38

> *Love your enemies, do good to those who hate you, bless those who curse you, pray for those who abuse you.*
> — Luke 6:27-28

These commandments of our Lord appear especially impossible to those who are accustomed to living with some measure of power and possessions in this world. We would be glad to counsel terrorists that their violent behavior is self-defeating, but we resist accepting that these verses could make for good foreign policy. We are quick to suggest all sorts of circumstances in which it is impractical for us to "give to everyone who begs from you; and if anyone takes away your goods, do not ask for them again." Yet consider what it means if we reject such admonitions in light of practical considerations. "If you love those who love you, what credit is that to you? For even sinners love those who love them. If you do good to those who do good to you, what credit is that to you? For even sinners do the same." If we are guided by the pragmatic wisdom of the world, is there any significant difference between those who believe and those who do not? Perhaps we need to focus on exactly what the difference is between those who claim Christ as Lord and those who do not make such an affirmation.

The Christian faith offers us the challenge of an alternate worldview that seems to be contradicted by worldly pragmatism. What would be the impact on church life if we chose to focus our energies on demonstrating the wisdom of the Christian faith within the body of Christ? Would we suffer as Christ suffered, if instead of judging others we lived out the grace that Jesus taught? Could financially strong churches give to financially weaker churches without expecting anything in return? Could a church trust as a practical truth for its life as a community the admonition "for the measure you give will be the measure you get back"? Would the willingness to turn the other cheek and bless those who curse you have a significant impact on the witness of the whole body of Christ? Would we then have a stronger testimony to offer the world as a practical alternative to the violence that threatens to engulf us?

Epiphany 8
Ordinary Time 8
Proper 3

Isaiah 55:10-13

> *... so shall my word be that goes out from my mouth; it shall not return to me empty, but it shall accomplish that which I purpose....*   — Isaiah 55:11

Consider how much effort pastors exert in examining the scriptures and trying to proclaim them in a way that is in accord with the accepted wisdom of the world. Now consider what the prophet Isaiah was saying. In the face of any normal assumption of a realistic view of the world, Isaiah was making an incredible claim. Isaiah lived in a time when the people of God had been defeated by a super power. All the symbols of their existence as a nation had been destroyed from the walls of the palace of their king to the temple of their God. The leading citizens had been carried off and relocated in foreign lands. All practical wisdom would suggest that there was no way that this nation could ever be reconstituted.

Isaiah claimed that the evil that appeared to have defeated the purpose of God through the destruction of God's people was not more powerful than God. We live and practice the faith as if it may fail. We give sin and evil so much credit that we assume that evil may win. Isaiah never suggested that God wanted the people to be defeated and go into exile. Rather he claimed that even in the midst of the people's disobedience, which resulted in their defeat, God would not be defeated. For Isaiah to believe that God was more powerful than the evil that had defeated God's people, he had to believe that God could work even through this experience of exile that appeared by any human standards to be a total defeat.

If we hold to the same faith today, then don't we have to ask what God is doing when the church appears to fail to grow or to have any significant influence on society? Don't we have to ask what God's word is doing when there is a major scandal in the church? If God's word does not fail, then doesn't this change how we evaluate all that is happening in our world? If Isaiah was right that we shall "go out in joy and be led back in peace," then is our attitude of despair and cynicism a reflection of our lack of understanding of what God is doing? Is this similar to what Jesus said, "Peace I leave with you; my peace I give to you. I do not give to you as the world gives. Do not let your hearts be troubled, and do not let them be afraid" (John 14:27)?

Psalm 92:1-4, 12-15

It is good to give thanks to the Lord, to sing praises to your name, O Most High ... — Psalm 92:1

Psalm 92 has the superscription that says it is a song for the sabbath day. On the sabbath the person of faith steps aside from work and productivity to give thanks, sing praise, and to declare God's steadfast love and faithfulness to the music of the lute, harp, and lyre (vv. 1-3). As an echo of God's ceasing to work on the sabbath, so humans are invited to step back from their productivity and rest. "For you, O Lord, have made me glad by your work; at the works of your hands I sing for joy" (v. 4). In worship one steps out of the pressures of time to reflect on life and receives an entirely different perspective even on the occasional success of wickedness in our world (vv. 5-9). In worship one can feel the exuberant joy to which God has anointed you (v. 10), and you recognize that in the eternity of God, evil acts have no lasting influence (v. 11). In worship you can feel the flowering of the self because your life finds its true center in God's presence (vv. 12-13).

When you are centered in God, age is not the determinative factor of your worth (v. 14). It is the fresh creativity of the elderly in worship that demonstrates God's steady righteousness. So Sarah, Abraham, Zechariah, and Elizabeth all gave evidence that in God's presence, life is never over. In worship we touch eternity where both the frustrations of age and the wounds of injustice pale in light of the eternal presence of God who draws us forward.

1 Corinthians 15:51-58

> *Listen, I will tell you a mystery! We will not all die, but we will be changed, in a moment, in the twinkling of an eye, at the last trumpet.* — 1 Corinthians 15:51-52

Paul concluded his remarks on the significance of Christ's resurrection and how we view our present lives with a triumphant song of praise. In contrast to the mystery cults that believed in the immortality of the soul, Paul, as a good Jew, believed in the resurrection of the body. Contemporary Christians have often been more influenced by the pagan beliefs that suggest we have an immortal soul than the Jewish belief that both our body and soul perish apart from the life-giving Spirit of God and our hope is that all of us, body and soul, will be resurrected. At the same time Paul recognized that the resurrected body was not just resuscitated: "For this perishable body must put on imperishability, and this mortal body must put on immortality."

He had undoubtedly heard the reports of the disciples that the resurrected Jesus could eat, drink, and be touched like other humans and that he also could pass through doors and move from place to place. He was physical and yet his body had been transformed. This was the firstfruit of what the rest of us could hope for as well. Resurrection has implications not only for what happens after we die but also for how we live our current life. The ultimate threat of most powers in this world is the power of death. If you do not do what we tell you to do, we will kill you. By the victory of Christ over death, we have been liberated from the power of those who seek to control us. We are free to do what we believe God wants us to do, even when it appears to be ineffective, because we "know that in the Lord [our] labor is not in vain."

Luke 6:39-49

> *Why do you call me "Lord, Lord," and do not do what I tell you?* — Luke 6:46

Given the frequency with which surveys suggest that there is no significant distinction between the behavior of those who attend church and those who do not within our society, this verse stands as a disturbing challenge to the church. It is not a new problem for Christianity. Some have tried to resolve it by suggesting that there is an invisible church within the visible church. That is, the real church is made up of the invisible faithful who exist in the midst of the larger group that makes up the visible church. The problem with such a suggestion is that the line that separates the faithful Christian from the unfaithful one often cuts right down the middle of each of our hearts. The question of how to distinguish the true people of God from those who merely go through the motions is one that has plagued both Judaism and Christianity from the beginning.

Jesus' response to such a question was both simple and profound: "No good tree bears bad fruit, nor again does a bad tree bear good fruit; for each tree is known by its own fruit." Jesus had already warned about the problem of being too quick to judge others while having a blind spot to your own deficiencies. Now he suggested that we discern good from evil in terms of the fruit or results of our lives. The true church does not consist of a few perfect people in the midst of the larger society. Rather the true church, the body of Christ, is made visible at those moments when we do act in response to the word of Christ in our lives.

While each of us will have faithful and unfaithful moments in our lives, rather than spending energy judging others, we are invited to act on Jesus' word as a means of developing a solid foundation for our lives that will help us withstand the storms that are bound to occur.

Epiphany 9
Ordinary Time 9
Proper 4

1 Kings 8:22-23, 41-43

> *Likewise when a foreigner, who is not of your people Israel, comes from a distant land because of your name....* — 1 Kings 8:41

There is a constant theme of universalism throughout scripture. It begins with the assertion at the beginning of the Bible that all humanity is of one stock and was created by the same God. Adam was a Hebrew word that could best be translated as earthling, and Eve was the mother of all the living. When a particular people was selected by God in the call of Abram, the purpose of the call continued to benefit the rest of humanity: "And in you all the families of the earth shall be blessed" (Genesis 12:3b). Here in this triumphal moment of Israel's history, in Solomon's prayer dedicating the temple that he has built for Yahweh, the prayer included the stranger. The purpose of Israel's special relationship with God was never for Israel alone but for the sake of the whole world. "When a foreigner comes and prays toward this house, then hear in heaven your dwelling place, and do according to all that the foreigner calls to you ..." God's desire is that all the world might be reconciled to God's purpose (2 Corinthians 5:19).

This prayer is enacted in Acts 8:26-40 when Philip encountered the Ethiopian eunuch who had come to Jerusalem to worship God. While Solomon in his prayer recognized that no building could contain the universal God (1 Kings 8:27), he acknowledged the importance of a physical place toward which people could look when they wanted to direct their thoughts toward God. While we recognize that God is not in our churches, we also recognize that the very symbol of a church can evoke the sense of awe that prepares a person to turn and seek a relationship with the divine. At the same time, it is a critical part of our faith to remember that the God whose name is evoked by the physical symbol of a church is the God who calls us to be aware of and sensitive to the needs of the stranger that comes to us. It is, after all, in welcoming the stranger that we encounter God in our midst (Genesis 18:1-15; Luke 24:13-35).

Psalm 96:1-9

> *O sing to the Lord a new song; sing to the Lord, all the earth.* — Psalm 96:1

The lectionary deliberately chooses the reading from Psalms as a response to the reading from the Hebrew scripture. In this case, the emphasis is on the impact of faith on the whole world. Psalm 96 is a proleptic celebration of the culmination of God's purpose for the world. It is in anticipation of the time when the whole earth will sing together a new song (v. 1) that will bless God's name and daily tell of God's salvation (v. 2). All the nations will continually tell the stories of how God works to save (v. 3), which will in turn evoke awe among the peoples (v. 4). They will recognize the contrast between what they have been worshiping (giving worth or ultimate value to) (v. 5) and the source of true honor, majesty, strength, and glory (v. 6).

All peoples will be able to recognize what God does in life (v. 7) and want to respond with an appropriate offering (v. 8). It will be a time when the whole earth will be unified in their common worship of God (v. 9). They will recognize God's authority and justice (v. 10), and then the created world that has been suffering as a consequence of human arrogance (Romans 8:18-25) will join in the celebration (vv. 11-12). The center of our ecological imbalance, as well as the violent divisiveness among nations, is our failure to recognize and give worship to God.

It is our arrogance that denies God is the center of truth and justice. God's presence on earth is the fulfillment of righteousness and truth intended from the beginning (v. 13). Before the world can fully recognize this truth, those who have been called to be part of God's people must come to this recognition.

Galatians 1:1-12

> *I am astonished that you are so quickly deserting the one who called you in the grace of Christ and are turning to a different gospel ...* — Galatians 1:6

Unlike all of the other letters of Paul, following his opening greeting (1:1-5), Paul did not offer a thanksgiving for the work of the church in Galatia. Instead, he immediately launched an offensive against those whom he believed were distorting the gospel. In an age when we are so accustomed to a variety of interpretations of the gospel among the churches, it is challenging to hear this direct attack of Paul's against those who suggested another way of understanding the gospel. The issue quickly became one of authority. In fact, most liberal Christians would hear Paul's approach as very authoritarian. Convince us by your arguments, if you can, but by what authority do you claim to have the only perspective on the truth? It is somewhat ironic that this strong approach from Paul was expressed in Galatians, which is normally spoken of as a letter that emphasizes the freedom of Christ.

At the same time, even in our post-modern world that emphasizes truth is in the eye of the beholder, some of the most rapidly growing communities in the name of Christ are those whose leaders speak with full confidence in their authority. Perhaps it is because we live in a very confusing world that people are attracted to people who can speak with authority. For most Christians, the issue is how we can recapture the authority of our proclamation without succumbing to an authoritarian approach. Paul made very clear that what he was proclaiming was more than a philosophy of life taught to him by others. He was absolutely convinced that what he was proclaiming was a revelation of truth received directly from God. At the same time, he made clear that his gospel was not an individualistic understanding but was one that had been tested with the community (Galatians 2:1-2).

As you approach the season of Lent, it is perhaps important that you take time to reflect on the message that you believe you can proclaim with authority and allow it to be tested by the community. What are the basic truths about which you have no doubt? Paul's central understanding of the gospel returned again and again to the crucifixion and resurrection of Christ.

Luke 7:1-10

> ... *the centurion sent friends to say to him, "Lord, do not trouble yourself, for I am not worthy to have you come under my roof... But only speak the word, and let my servant be healed."* — Luke 7:6

There are several aspects to this event that draw our attention. First of all, it is quite clear that the centurion was not a member of the Jewish faith. He had shown respect for the Jewish people, but there was no evidence that he had sought to become a convert. The elders who came to Jesus on his behalf said, "He is worthy of having you do this for him, for he loves our people, and it is he who built our synagogue for us." Second, the centurion was not seeking a favor from Jesus for himself but for a slave "whom he values highly." Even if we understand that slavery had a different connotation in Palestine than it does in America because of our unique history, the slave was still considered to be of lesser value than the free members of the family. Third, the centurion was not acting on behalf of any personal experience with Jesus but simply on what he had heard about him from others.

It is also noteworthy that the centurion felt no need of any personal encounter or relationship with Jesus himself. He made no suggestion that if Jesus would respond to his request that the centurion would become a follower of Jesus. This was a one-time request with no promise of any further response. Finally, he declared an absolute conviction about the authority of Jesus to command that which was causing his slave to be ill. For Jesus' part, there was no request of any further response from the centurion. Nor did Jesus feel any need to meet or have a relationship with him.

As the body of Christ, or even as an individual Christian, what is the implication of your responding to a person's need who neither believes as you do or shows any interest in doing so? Is there a significant gospel message being proclaimed when the church responds to human need without asking anything in return? Are there times when those who come to us astonish us by their belief in our capacity to help them? Does the response of Jesus to this stranger he never met reveal an aspect of the extravagant grace of God that overflows into the world? In what way is the church called upon to enact a similar grace?

The Transfiguration Of Our Lord
(Last Sunday After Epiphany)

Exodus 34:29-35

> ... *Moses did not know that the skin of his face shone because he had been talking with God.*
> — Exodus 34:29

On Transfiguration Sunday we confront the mystery of time touching eternity. It is hard for us to conceive of a reality that has no past, present, or future. We often use a circle that has no beginning or end to symbolize the eternal but even that seems inadequate. It is even harder to imagine the impact of eternity touching time. When we speak of the eternal God entering into a moment in time, our words fail to do other than hint at that reality. In this passage, we hear of Moses' talking with God. A human being who was confined to space and time was able to communicate across the division with eternity. What you bring back from eternity has to be encapsulated in time-shaped words.

Moses reduced the experience to commandments that he gave to the people. This was something that they could hear and comprehend. Moses himself was affected by the experience. The impact on Moses was seen in his shining face. We cannot be touched by eternity without being altered. The people saw a hint of eternity in Moses' face and were fearful. It is like coming to the edge of the world and looking over at the abyss that has no end. Moses put a veil on his face as he moved about among the people in between conversations with God. Paul later suggested that Moses was doing that to keep the people "from gazing at the end of the glory that was being set aside" (2 Corinthians 3:12—4:2). The dizzy vision of the abyss is too much. It is easier to hear about the abyss, or the eternal God, than it is to experience it from your time-based platform.

Later the disciples would be terrified by a similar transfiguration of Jesus. Moses would again be involved along with Elijah. The Bible keeps hinting at this crossover, but only three people were shown to experience it. In each case there were witnesses that could tell of the experience. It is as if God knows that we cannot endure eternity for long, but we must know that we have been touched by it. It is the hint of eternity that enables us to gain perspective on the present in which we live.

Psalm 99

> *The Lord is king; let the peoples tremble!*
> — Psalm 99:1

Psalm 99 is best heard as a psalm to the people of God when they have grown comfortable and indifferent to their relationship with God. "The Lord is king; let the peoples tremble! He sits enthroned upon the cherubim; let the earth quake" (v. 1)! Few people in our church tremble at the thought that God might really be in charge. Even in the church, we are more focused on the moment than we are touched by the eternal. The psalm challenged the people to praise God because God is holy — totally different from and apart from us and yet rules over us: "The Lord is great in Zion; he is exalted over all the peoples" (v. 2).

It is more than just the presence of the eternal God. This God who rules over life is a lover of justice and an establisher of equity as has been demonstrated in the past (v. 4). We are charged to worship or give first priority to this God of justice. "Extol the Lord our God; worship at his footstool. Holy is he" (v. 5)! The psalmist reminds us of Moses, Aaron, and Samuel as people who cried out to God, and God responded to them (v. 6). God told them how they should live. "He spoke to them in the pillar of cloud; they kept his decrees, and statutes that he gave them" (v. 7). This God who answered them was not only a forgiving God but also punished their wrongdoing (v. 8).

Now we know why we should tremble. God is more than a magic amulet that assists us in living. God is someone totally different from us who expects us to reflect God's love for justice and equality. "Extol the Lord our God, and worship at his holy mountain; for the Lord our God is holy" (v. 9). Precisely because God has responded to us, we know that God expects something from our lives. There is reason for us to tremble when we come into God's presence. "Extol the Lord our God; worship at his footstool. Holy is he!"

2 Corinthians 3:12—4:2

> *... where the Spirit of the Lord is, there is freedom.*
> — 2 Corinthians 3:17

Paul responded to the age-old conundrum of law and freedom. God communicated God's expectations through Moses and the Ten Commandments. The very reception of this gift from God, however, created in people more a sense of guilt than freedom. Consider whether in today's church there is more emphasis on guilt or grace as a motivating factor. Paul was convinced that the law, which he agreed was given by God, had failed to save people. He had discovered the power of the Spirit to do what the law could not do: "... a new covenant, not of letter but of spirit; for the letter kills, but the Spirit gives life" (3:6). He drew a sharp contrast between the attempt of Israel to be shaped by the law of God and what he now saw as the freedom of the Spirit of Christ. He used the image of Moses veiling his face in Exodus 34:29-35 as an image of the people's inability to view the truth of God.

The current attempt of the church to legislate a new morality would have astonished Paul. He saw Israel as having been granted the grace of God in the old covenant but having wrapped it in tradition and fear until they missed "the end of the glory that was being set aside" (v. 13). Paul believed that the glory of God's unmerited grace was revealed "when they hear the reading of the old covenant" but "their minds were hardened" (v. 14). The echo of

God's hardening the heart of Pharaoh comes to mind. For Paul "when one turns to the Lord, the veil is removed ..." (v. 16). As we see what God has done in Christ, we "are being transformed into the same image from one degree of glory to another" (v. 18).

The question for the church is whether we have again veiled the new covenant in tradition and fear and pulled back from the freedom of Christ. Is that why we are such a fractured body of Christ that veils the true glory of Christ?

Luke 9:28-36 (37-43)

> *And while he was praying, the appearance of his face changed....* — Luke 9:29

With the Transfiguration, the disciples are confronted with the difference between seeing Jesus as just a special person and suddenly experiencing him as the Christ of God. The theological challenge for the church is whether it is just a special organization or whether it is the body of Christ. Is there just a historic connection between the present church and the traditions and scriptures that precede it or is the church the living story of God's continuing revelation that began with the law and the prophets and found its fulfillment in Jesus? If one looks at this story of the Transfiguration as the story of the church and not just a historic incident in the life of Jesus, then we see our own journey being described. The Transfiguration happened at a time when Jesus was at prayer. It is in prayer that we grow closer to God.

When we experience the closeness of God, something changes. Consider Peter, James, and John as representatives of the active faithful in the church. They experienced the church, the body of Christ, at prayer. They resisted the physical needs of their body (sleep) and focused on the church at prayer. Because of their devotion, they saw not just a group of humans going through a set of rituals but rather the glory of God manifested in the body. The church was transfigured before their eyes, and they saw how the law and the prophets testified to God's presence among his people.

They responded by wanting to build three booths symbolizing the law, the prophets, and the Christ.

Were they trying to enshrine the holy moment or were they demonstrating hospitality for the divine? It is uncertain, but, at that moment, they were overshadowed by God. Their epiphany, when they saw clearly that God confirmed Jesus and his body, was confirmed. Now they knew for certain that the church was the vehicle of their salvation, and they were told to listen to what Christ would tell them. It was not so much a message that they could tell others about as a message that must be experienced. So we should spend less time telling others about the church than we do being the church for others.

Lent 1

Deuteronomy 26:1-11

> *So now I bring the first of the fruit of the ground that you, O Lord, have given me.* — Deuteronomy 26:10

Too often the act of receiving the offering in church is seen as a necessary interruption of worship in order to collect money to pay the bills. Liturgically, the offering is an act of gratitude in response to what God has done for us as a people. Each year the Israelites brought the firstfruits of their harvest and placed them before the priest. As agrarian farmers who depended on their harvest for their survival, they were symbolizing their trust in God for their future and acknowledging that all that they had was a gift from God. Because the growth of their crop was so dependent on elements that were beyond their control, they could experience each season the necessity of help from beyond themselves if they were to be successful. In our urban culture, there is a greater disconnect between our work and the food that is necessary for our survival. It is easier to assume that our possessions are the result of our efforts and forget that everything begins as a gift from God.

The firstfruits were considered the best of the harvest. The Israelites returned the best portion to God. It was also a time to rehearse what God had done for them from the beginning. So as they placed their offering before the priest, they would recite a concise history of their faith. "A wandering Aramean was my ancestor; he went down into Egypt and lived there as an alien ... The Lord brought us out of Egypt with a mighty hand and an outstretched arm...." When we take time to reflect back on our life with all the significant events that shaped who we are, it is easier to see the "outstretched arm" that has guided us. As we begin the season of Lent, it would be a powerful experience for a congregation to reflect on its own history and acknowledge God's hand in its journey as preparation for bringing their offering before God as an act of thanksgiving.

Psalm 91:1-2, 9-16

On their hands they will bear you up, so that you will not dash your foot against a stone. — Psalm 91:12

Psalm 91 is a psalm of trust in the power of God to deliver us from all that threatens us. The reader will recognize that this was the psalm Satan quoted when he was tempting Jesus in the wilderness (Matthew 4:6). It is an appropriate psalm with which to begin the season of Lent.

If the one we affirm as the Christ can be tempted by scripture, we are warned how scripture can be misused even when it reflects a central core of our belief. For Israel and the church, a central belief is our trust in God (vv. 1-8) who has the power to deliver us from both the human and the natural elements. "For he will deliver you from the snare of the fowler and from the deadly pestilence ..." (v. 3). Like a mother bird protects her young (another image that Jesus used later on), God's faithfulness can be counted on (v. 4). God's faithfulness can ease the terror of night or the threat in the day (vv. 5-6). You can trust in God even when the wicked seem to be triumphing (vv. 7-8) because God stands between you and the evil that threatens you (vv. 9-10).

Those who trust in God will be protected in their daily walk (vv. 11-12) and from the threats of both lion and serpent (v. 13). This does not say that no threats will come to the believer but that God will hear the cry of the faithful, be present in times of trouble, and rescue and honor the one who clings to God in love and calls on God's name (v. 14). It is precisely when one is facing overwhelming odds that one is tempted to place self, rather than God, at the center of one's belief. We want to make God an instrument of, rather than the source of, our salvation (v. 16). As we begin Lent and reflect on the temptations of Christ, we are offered the opportunity to reflect again on our own temptation to treat God as an instrument of our desires rather than the source of our salvation.

Romans 10:8b-13

> *... if you confess with your lips that Jesus is Lord and believe in your heart that God raised him from the dead, you will be saved.* — Romans 10:9

Are you saved? It is an ancient question. Today we often associate such a question with the more conservative branches of Christianity. It speaks to an uneasy concern at the center of many people's hearts. We can see it in the thousands who respond each year to the invitations issued at evangelistic crusades.

What does it mean to be saved? For Paul it has to do with living in response to the word of faith that is available to us. The opposite, to be lost, is to live our lives disconnected from the God who gives us life. The life of salvation is to "confess with your lips that Jesus is Lord and believe in your heart that God raised him from the dead." To confess with your lips is to make public your commitment to have Jesus be Lord in your daily living. To live a life that reflects Jesus as Lord will necessarily put you in conflict with some of the values and temptations of our society. Jesus, as the exemplar of faithful living, not only faced resistance but also ultimately was faced with the loss of his life. The courage to overcome that resistance comes from believing that God affirmed Jesus' life of obedience with the resurrection.

By allowing the Christ that God affirmed to guide us in our decisions in life, we are liberated from the fears and shame that often shape people's decision-making. To be free of shame and fear is to be saved because you experience the daily connection with God that infuses you with life. "No one who believes in him will be put to shame." The ultimate shame is that before God. Once we accept that in Christ we are forgiven, we no longer have to live in a manner that earns God's favor. Now we are free to live in a manner that reflects our thanksgiving for what God has already done for us. Now our life is not a life lived in fear that we will not measure up but rather in joyful thanksgiving that we have already been accepted.

Luke 4:1-13

> *Jesus, full of the Holy Spirit, returned from the Jordan and was led by the Spirit in the wilderness, where for forty days he was tempted by the devil.* — Luke 4:1-2

It is interesting to note that it was the Holy Spirit that led Jesus into the wilderness to be tempted. This was immediately after Jesus had been confirmed and affirmed as God's Son (Luke 3:22). The gospel of John declares, "But to all who received him, who believed in his name, he gave power to become children of God" (John 1:12). It is important for Christians to recognize that, like Jesus, it is as we recognize that we are children of God that we face our greatest temptations. To live as a child of God offers as many temptations as it does blessings. The devil tempts us to worship him by worshiping us. He raises the "I" in each of us to become the central place in each of our universes. Our desire for power, to feel the surge of adrenalin caused by our ability to shape and control events, even in the best of causes, makes us dangerously oblivious to the need to have our life centered in God. "One does not live by bread alone."

Deuteronomy says that the trip through the wilderness was meant to teach Israel this truth. We need to be fed in a different way by God if life is to have real meaning. What is the bread of God by which we have life abundant? "You shall worship the Lord your God and serve only him." Our priorities become very confused when we place ourselves at the center of our lives. We become enslaved to impulse, fear, craving, other people's ideas, and luxuries. To keep life in perspective, God must be at the center. "Do not put the Lord to the test." It is so easy to wonder what the benefits of being God-centered are. We want to find out what God will do for us. We quickly shift from our being the servants of God to wanting God to be our servant. It is only worth making sacrifice of our needs and interests if we can trust that God is at the center of all that happens. Lent is a good time for us to reflect on our capacity to center our lives on God.

Lent 2

Genesis 15:1-12, 17-18

> *And he believed the Lord; and the Lord reckoned it to him as righteousness.* — Genesis 15:6

This is the passage Paul used to demonstrate that we are saved by faith and not by law (Romans 4:3). Paul's suggestion was that Abram trusted in God instead of the practical wisdom of the world that would suggest that he and Sarai were too old to have children. " 'Look toward heaven and count the stars, if you are able to count them.' Then he said to him, 'So shall your descendants be.' And he believed the Lord; and the Lord reckoned it to him as righteousness." This happened, suggested Paul, before Abram was circumcised and long before the people had received the commandments. Therefore, we can say that in a sense Abram was still a Gentile and it was before God had given the law.

In this sense, God is inviting the entire world to respond in faith. The image of covenant-making is also important because of what it says about the permanency of the covenant. God instructs Abram to slaughter certain animals and lay their halves on opposite sides of a path. This was an ancient covenant-making ritual. The parties to the agreement were to pass between the animal pieces as if to say that if either of the parties broke the agreement, they should be cut in two as were the animals. However, in this case, it was only the smoking fire pot and the flaming torch, both symbols of God, that passed through the cut up animals. The fulfillment of the promise that was made depended on God and not on Abram or his descendents. Abram's part was to believe that God could accomplish what God had promised. It was up to God to actually fulfill the promise. The Hebrews, and later the Christians, believed that salvation belonged to God. Paul said that we are saved by faith and not by works.

Psalm 27

> *Do not give me up to the will of my adversaries, for false witnesses have risen against me, and they are breathing out violence.* — Psalm 27:12

Dietrich Bonhoeffer once suggested that all of the psalms could be grouped according to the categories of the Lord's Prayer. Psalm 27 could serve as a reflection on the petition, "Lead us not into temptation but deliver us from evil." The psalm begins with an affirmation in the midst of reasons for fear that could tempt us (v. 1). But then it describes the reasons that people do fear the evildoers and adversaries who assail, slander, and rise against them (vv. 2-3). In such a world, we are tempted to abandon God. Deliverance is seen as being in the presence of God (v. 4) who will hide and conceal us from trouble (v. 5). We are invited to discover such deliverance in the practice of worship (v. 6) when we cannot only sing but also cry out to God and seek God's face (vv. 7-9a).

We pray to be delivered from the absence of God because we know that the worst evil that pursues us is the anger that causes those we count on to forsake us (vv. 9-10). It is that very fear of the destruction of relationships created by false witness that causes us to plead to know more of the way of the Lord (vv. 11-12). In the face of a deceitful world where we are tempted to abandon all hope, we are admonished to wait, be strong, and take courage but, above all, to wait for the Lord (vv. 13-14). Part of our deliverance from evil is our confidence that in time we shall see the goodness of the Lord in the land of the living (v. 13).

Philippians 3:17—4:1

He will transform the body of our humiliation that it may be conformed to the body of his glory ...
— Philippians 3:21

The focus of Paul's ministry was more on the corporate community of the church than it was on the individual. In Philippians, Paul saw a tension within the church that was caused by members whose vision was too limited. It is easy for a community to be focused on survival, community admiration, success, or even comfort. The god of such a church, suggested Paul, was their belly and "their glory is in their shame; their minds are set on earthly things." For Paul this limited vision was a denial of the cross of Christ. The church, as the body of Christ, can expect suffering and humiliation in the same manner that Jesus experienced it. The reason Jesus was able to endure this was that his perspective was from eternity. "But our citizenship is in heaven."

In the same way that God responded to Jesus' faithful obedience by transforming his humiliation on the cross into the resurrected body of glory, so the church can expect God to respond to their faithfulness. As Jesus could take Peter who denied him and make him the leader of the church, so he can take the denials of the church and transform them into signs of glory. The key symbol of this transforming power is the cross. To be an enemy of the cross is to deny this transforming power and rely on our own wisdom and insight. The challenge for the church is to not be overwhelmed by the immediate threats and seductions and to trust in God's transforming power.

Luke 13:31-35

Jerusalem, Jerusalem, the city that kills the prophets and stones those who are sent to it! — Luke 13:34

If Jesus is the head of the church and the church is his body, then what do we do when the church fails us? The church becomes the mobile Jerusalem for Christians. Jerusalem exists wherever two or three are gathered in Christ's name. This mobile Jerusalem often can be mean-spirited and judgmental or so caught up in its organizational concerns that it squeezes the Spirit right out of it. If the church is the mobile Jerusalem destined to be the center of holiness, then we have to hear that it has by its behavior often scattered its own children. We have watched the church kill the very prophets through which God seeks to speak to it, and we have seen the church stone the victims of our society's prejudice whom God sends to the church for healing.

Many people have tried to accept Jesus as their Lord and Savior but reject Christ's body. The result has been that they keep trying to carry a head around that is severed from its body. Jesus' understanding of the necessity of going to Jerusalem and his compassion for Jerusalem challenges any temptation to dismiss institutions in favor of an individualistic approach to the faith. There are certainly miraculous things that Christ can do in the world outside the church. Christ's Spirit does cast out demons and performs cures. But the goal of Christ's work still finds its center in Jerusalem, that killer of the prophets. Christ, like a mother hen, desires to gather her brood together in the one body, but the church keeps alienating itself into factions and scattering Christ's brood. Jerusalem, the center of Christ's work, needs a conversion that shifts its focus so that it can say, "Blessed is the one who comes in the name of the Lord."

Lent 3

Isaiah 55:1-9

> *Why do you spend your money for that which is not bread, and your labor for that which does not satisfy?*
> — Isaiah 55:2

This passage begins with an invitation that seems to be straight from the mouth of a con artist. You can almost hear the voice of a telemarketer who has just called you on the phone: "Have I got a deal for you! If my boss knew that I was making this offer, I'd really be in trouble." "Ho everyone who thirsts, come to the waters; and you that have no money come, buy, and eat! Come, buy wine and milk without money and without price." It is this offer that is too good to be true that the prophet dares to suggest is the offer God is making to this people.

There is a scandal to the grace of God that seems hard for contemporary people to fully grasp. We are more comfortable with the proverbial wisdom that "you get what you pay for." In the face of our skepticism, the prophet challenges us to consider what it is we are paying for. "Why do you spend your money for that which is not bread, and your labor for that which does not satisfy?" We are seduced by our consumer society, abetted by the skilled art of advertising into seeking, through our labors and wealth, products that cannot fulfill their promise. Continuing with Isaiah's image of food and drink, consider all of the food and drink we consume that is actually contributing to the deterioration of our health. Isaiah declared that God is offering an alternative way to live, which is in response to an unmerited grace of God.

Instead of killing ourselves with empty calories, God offers "rich food" that can fill our lives with meaning. "Seek the Lord while he may be found, call upon him while he is near." He then offers David as a paradigm of the relationship that God offers us. David had broken all of the Ten Commandments but discovered again and again the healing grace of God. David did not earn God's love by his behavior. He could only receive it. This unmerited love of God is the wine and milk that you can buy without money and without price. It seems to contradict all we assume about the nature of reality. Lent is not only a time to acknowledge our sins before God, but also it is a preparation to receive the grace of God. "Let them return to the Lord that he may have mercy on them, and to our God, for he will abundantly pardon." Lent is a time to learn again that God's "thoughts are not your thoughts, nor are your ways [God's] ways...."

Psalm 63:1-8

Because your steadfast love is better than life, my lips will praise you. — Psalm 63:3

The lectionary places this psalm in response to the passage from Isaiah about the incredible grace of God. It is a reminder that we discover that longed-for relationship through worship. Psalm 63 was given the context of David when he was in the wilderness of Judah by its superscription. That wilderness had been his sanctuary when Saul sought to kill him and later when his son, Absalom, tried to overthrow him. We pray this psalm as one who has been stripped of power, so our soul thirsts for God like we were in the desert (v. 1).

That was possible for David because this sanctuary in the desert was in the context of a life of having gone to the sanctuary of the temple to behold the power and glory of God (v. 2), to praise God's steadfast love (v. 3), and call on God's name (v. 4). His practice of praise had become his food for living (v. 5), nurtured by a constant prayer life (v. 6). This continual placing of self in the presence of God had allowed him to keep reality in perspective. Now, when in dire physical distress, the reality of the majesty of God gave him confidence in the future (vv. 8-11). The psalm becomes a prayer for those threatened by a loss of control over their situation — a reminder of who is really in charge of all future — an invitation to put our most desperate situation in the context of praise.

1 Corinthians 10:1-13

For they drank from the spiritual rock that followed them, and the rock was Christ. — 1 Corinthians 10:4

Paul's exegesis of scripture is shocking in this passage. He rehearsed the major moments in Israel's escape from Egypt and crossing the wilderness, and proceeded to interpret all of these events from a Christian perspective. He saw being led by God in a cloud and crossing the Red Sea as prefiguring baptism. When God fed them manna and gave them water from a rock in the desert, he spoke of that as an act of Christ. When the people rebelled, he spoke of that as testing Christ. Paul puts what we refer to as the Old and New Testaments together as one seamless garment. Christ is God made visible in the flesh, and this is the same God who was revealed in the early experiences of Israel.

The gospel of John spoke in a similar way when it spoke of Christ as present at creation (John 1:1 ff). What this suggests is that Christ is the experience of God acting in the midst of time. Such an approach to the gospel breaks the bonds of exclusivism. The gospel of John reports in 14:6, "No one comes to the Father except through me." Paul suggested that this way was embedded in Judaism long before Jesus was born. To follow Christ's way did not require naming Jesus but rather being open to Christ's Spirit that can be manifested even in an inanimate object like a rock. Failure to trust God as God has been revealed to them and complaining about the conditions of their lives was putting "Christ to the test."

The real issue of following Christ is trusting in God as one encounters the challenges of life. It is a form of idolatry to allow the conditions of life to overwhelm you. It suggests you think those conditions are more powerful than God who is faithful and will not let you be tested beyond your strength. This was revealed to us specifically in Jesus' life, but Paul saw it as having been manifested long before Jesus was born. It certainly sheds a different light on the contemporary issue of the exclusive way to salvation.

Luke 13:1-9

> *... do you think that they were worse offenders than all the others living in Jerusalem?* — Luke 13:4

It is common in our culture when the media interviews someone who narrowly escaped some natural disaster to suggest that God was looking out for him or her. While it is natural to feel a need to thank someone for such good fortune, when one hears it, one wants to ask why those who were injured or killed were not looked out for as well. There is the implicit suggestion that somehow they were being punished for some reason or another. Jesus gave two examples of people who suffered a tragedy. The first example was a group of people who were the victims of a political conflict: "Galileans whose blood Pilate had mingled with their sacrifices." The other example was of a group who had been killed when "the tower of Siloam fell on them."

In each case, one the result of a political incident and the other of a natural variety, Jesus asked whether those who had suffered were worse sinners than those who had escaped suffering. His response to his own question was an emphatic denial that suffering was indicative of their sinfulness. While individuals can suffer because of their sinfulness, there is also something called fate or just the accident of time and place. Death, Jesus seemed to suggest, comes to all of us. There is an uncertainty to life that we cannot guard against. What we can do is choose our response: "Unless you repent, you will all perish just as they did." To repent is to turn and redirect our lives.

Jesus' parable about the man with the barren fig tree suggests that we are given more time to live not as a reflection of our superior life but as a gracious opportunity to bear more fruit. Some who have had a near encounter with death have been shocked into the realization that they need to reprioritize their lives. Often that reorientation suggests a need to pay attention to the relationships they have been given. Lent is perhaps a good time to reflect on whether we have been giving enough attention to those with whom we are most closely related.

Lent 4

Joshua 5:9-12

> *Today I have rolled away from you the disgrace of Egypt.*
> — Joshua 5:9

In Egypt, the Hebrews had been slaves whose lives were dependent on their masters. The bounty of the land was not theirs to enjoy. They belonged to others as property. The act of circumcision, according to the traditions of Abraham, was a sign of their covenant relationship with God. They belonged, but it was not to the Egyptians. God demonstrated who had proper authority over their lives and the lives of the Egyptians, although it was unacknowledged, by sparing the Hebrews on the night that the angel of death passed over Egypt. Enslavement can be an emotional as well as a political reality. To remove the political bonds of oppression from a group of people does not mean that they are truly free. In the case of the Hebrews, God provided for them for a whole generation through the gift of manna as they journeyed through the wilderness. This "disgrace of Egypt" was not a light thing.

Slowly over the life of an entire generation, the Hebrews had to be led to freedom. At Gilgal the next generation was circumcised and celebrated the Passover. They were then ready to exercise their freedom by eating of the produce of the land. "The manna ceased on the day they ate the produce of the land." God's intention for humanity was never that they be slaves of anyone, politically or emotionally. From a spiritual perspective, there is a journey away from slavery that we all must take.

Frequently that requires an experience of a total dependence on God for a time. It is with the maturity that comes from such an experience that God can set us free to again experience the freedom that God intends in our covenantal relationship. The danger occurs when we have not truly been liberated from emotional or political freedom. As Paul said in Galatians 5:1, "For freedom Christ has set us free. Stand firm, therefore, and do not submit again to a yoke of slavery."

Psalm 32

For day and night thy hand was heavy upon me ...
— Psalm 32:4

There is a weight to sin that burdens us. It feels like the hand of God pressing down on our soul trying to squeeze out the impurity that has contaminated us. Perhaps we would be better off if we considered guilt not as a punishment for having done wrong but as the probing hands of a skilled surgeon trying to cleanse us of a cancer that is eating away at us. The psalmist declares, "Happy are those whose transgression is forgiven, whose sin is covered."

The two dimensions of sin are social and personal. The word "iniquity" is derived from "inequity" meaning unequal. The social dimension of sin is that we make ourselves unequal to others. The personal dimension is that our inner spirit becomes one of deceit (v. 2). The spirit of alienation eats away at the vitality of our life (v. 4). Yet, when we stop trying to deceive ourselves and acknowledge our sin before God, we receive forgiveness (v. 5). God becomes our refuge against the chaos that threatens to engulf us. "At a time of distress, in the rush of mighty waters, shall not reach them" (v. 6). Our prayer is that we might rise above that protective pride and stubbornness that prevents us from being truly open to God's blessing: "Do not be like a horse or a mule, without understanding, whose temper must be curbed with a bit and bridle, else it will not stay near you" (v. 9).

The state of blessedness or true joy is discovered in fully trusting God even with our sins and transgressions. By refusing to acknowledge our sins, we diminish God because we declare that our sins are more powerful than God's steadfast love (v. 10). Each time we discover the opposite to be true, we are released from our alienation from God and neighbor, and we are healed within ourselves. Then we can be glad, rejoice, and shout for joy (v. 11).

2 Corinthians 5:16-21

> *So we are ambassadors for Christ, since God is making his appeal through us ...* — 2 Corinthians 5:20

Our lives begin with the experience of forgiveness. God takes the initiative to offer us forgiveness before we have done anything to deserve it. Yet forgiveness comes with a price. We who are made a new creation in Christ are given the responsibility of being ambassadors of that reconciliation for the world. Like God's treatment of us, we are not to count people's sins as some debt that must be repaid. This is a dramatic step forward from the assumption that forgiveness is offered only after someone has demonstrated repentance and done penance.

In recent years there has been much debate in our society as to whether a person is sufficiently remorseful to deserve the forgiveness of society. Politicians and religious figures who have been publicly exposed have been central to this debate. To offer forgiveness only after a person has demonstrated remorse is a very human way of doing things, but "we regard no one from a human point of view." By taking the initiative to offer forgiveness, we allow God to shine through us. There will always be sin in the church and the world, and believers and nonbelievers will be tempted to judge others harshly. Jesus himself was subject to the judgmentalism of his peers. "He made him to be sin who knew no sin."

It was "in Christ God was reconciling the world to himself, not counting their trespasses against them." The difficult challenge for Christians is to move beyond the world's simplistic capacity to judge the wrongs of others and to become ambassadors of God's amazing grace. "For our sake he made him to be sin who knew no sin, so that in him we might become the righteousness of God."

Luke 15:1-3, 11b-32

> *And the Pharisees and the scribes were grumbling and saying, "This fellow welcomes sinners and eats with them."* — Luke 15:2

It is in this context that Jesus tells the parable of the prodigal son. It is a much beloved parable but sometimes to truly hear the impact of what Jesus is saying, we have to ask ourselves with which character we identify in the parable. Do we identify with the father who was so willing to share all that he had with his younger son even when his son behaved in such a disrespectful way? After we have worked and saved our resources, would we be willing for a member of our family, let alone a member of our church, to say to us, "Give me half of what you have because I want to leave the family and live free of its constraints"? Or do we identify with the younger son who was so self-centered that all he could think about was how to focus on pleasuring himself? Yes, he came to his senses eventually, but do we really identify with the path he took to get there? Or do we identify with the older brother who seemingly had nursed anger at both his father and his younger brother for so long that he could not be open to the possibility that his brother had truly returned?

Each of the figures in the story has some characteristics that we would not like to emulate. If we suggest that a reflection of God is seen in the father, are we comfortable in recognizing that God would give humanity such freedom and then be so gracious in receiving them home again without asking them to do anything to prove their repentance? As religious people who strive to practice the faith that we have received, don't we almost have more empathy for the older brother who feels shortchanged by God's generosity of forgiveness? Isn't this why as a society we are so quick to want to judge the public figures that betray our trust? Perhaps the most comforting part of the parable for many of us is the ending. While the father has thrown the party for his son who has returned, the parable ends with the father standing outside the party, as he previously had watched for the younger son, waiting for the older, self-righteous brother to repent as well. It raises the question as to who is preventing God from enjoying the joy of his creation the most?

Lent 5

Isaiah 43:16-21

Do not remember the former things, or consider the things of old. I am about to do a new thing....
— Isaiah 43:18-19a

It is the radical freedom of God that makes the journey of faith such an ambiguous thing. You have to learn to trust the one who made the promise rather than your understanding of the promise. The faith of Israel that carried them through their turbulent history always centered on their memory of the miracle of the escape from Egypt. Who could have guessed that a ragtag bunch of slaves could escape the control of the most powerful army of the time? Now they were in exile and all the trappings of power and identity had been stripped from them. But they remembered. "Thus says the Lord, who makes a way in the sea, a path in the mighty waters, who brings out chariot and horse, army and warrior; they lie down, they cannot rise, they are extinguished, quenched like a wick...." It was the memory that God could not be contained by the logic of the world that kept hope alive. It was against all logical calculations that Israel could ever emerge from Egypt.

Later the same incredible set of events released them from exile. Not all of Israel believed that God would accomplish such a miracle but the memory was preserved in the traditions and rituals. We live in a world in which power seems to determine the future. Wars seem endless. Our own complicity in the economy that devours the resources of the world and perpetuates violence through our sale of military might makes hope for peace seem a hopeless dream. Yet we continue to speak of a Prince of Peace who embodies a God who says, "I am about to do a new thing; now it springs forth, do you not perceive it?" The freedom of God makes it impossible to predict the shape in which this new hope will be manifest. The task of the Christian is to maintain hope in the future by remembering how God has fulfilled his promises in the past. As we near the end of Lent when the impossible will become a reality, what signs of hope do you see?

Psalm 126

May those who sow in tears reap with shouts of joy.
— Psalm 126:5

Psalm 126 is an almost giddy response to the totally unexpected experience of good fortune. Israel had been in exile and though they yearned for the land of Israel, the political realities made that seem an impossible dream. Then in one of those impossible twists of fate, they were free to return to Israel. It all seemed so unreal — like a dream (v. 1). The only response possible was sort of a giddy laughter and the deep joy of being confirmed in the eyes of the nations (v. 2). The response to God's blessing was joy (v. 3). Like the water in the Negeb that in a flood seemed so out of control and then was returned to the banks that control its flow, so Israel had direction returned to their lives (v. 4). The lesson in life was one of patient trust in God's care. Those who sowed in tears but patiently trusted in God's faithfulness reaped with shouts of joy (v. 5).

The agricultural metaphor of the sweat and tears of planting and cultivating with only the silent trust that such effort would bear fruit would later be used by the church to understand the cross and the resurrection (1 Corinthians 15:35 ff). Like the farmer, one has a responsibility to plant the seed, but it is an offering to God. There is an interval between planting and harvesting that we do not control (Matthew 13:1-9), but at the harvest we are glad (v. 6). It is in remembering how God has been faithful in our past that we gain courage to trust God for our future.

Philippians 3:4b-14

If anyone else has reason to be confident in the flesh, I have more....   — Philippians 3:4

Christ does strange things to our pride. Paul could point to all of the reasons for religious pride. He could demonstrate the right background, practice, and commitment. "Circumcised on the eighth day, a member of the people of Israel, of the tribe of Benjamin, a Hebrew born of Hebrews; as to the law, a Pharisee; as to zeal, a persecutor of the church; as to righteousness under the law, blameless." The list is pretty impressive. "Yet whatever gains I had, these I have come to regard as loss because of Christ."

When we are insulted, mocked, or dismissed in getting our way in the church, our temptation is to want to rehearse all the reasons why our opinion should bear weight. We hold on to our "Doctor of Ministry," let people know how hard we work, and allow others to see our devotion to the faith. Each of these can be of great value in shaping our ministry. After Paul cited all of this, he said, "For his sake I have suffered the loss of all things, and I regard them as rubbish, in order that I may gain Christ...." When we look at the life of Christ, he suffered the loss of pride, possessions, and dignity in his journey to the cross. When we feel our existence threatened either as an individual or as a church, we are faced with the choice of protecting what we have or being open to what new thing God is doing (Isaiah 43:19). What Christ revealed and Paul experienced is that the death of pride is sometimes the price we must pay to experience the resurrection of God in our lives.

John 12:1-8

Mary took a pound of costly perfume made of pure nard, anointed Jesus' feet, and wiped them with her hair.   — John 12:3

It was a lavish and costly gesture. Whatever Judas' motives, he did have a point. The money could have been given to the poor.

Jesus was continually emphasizing God's compassion for the poor. The characters present in this story each have their own history. There is Martha who was busy performing a service, lavishing her love on Jesus. There was Lazarus who was the bearer of a miracle in his own being. There was Judas who could make the most logical sounding argument but used such high-sounding words to cover his own hidden agenda. In this group was reflected the continuing conversation of the church.

We have those among us who have been brought back from the dead. Their lives were going nowhere, and now they live in wonder of what God has done for them. Their very existence in the church is a living testimony to the power of God's redeeming love. There are also those like Martha who quietly work in service for Christ. The church is a vital community because of the loving service they offer often behind the scenes.

Because we know the end of the story about Judas, we may not want to admit that there are many of us within the church who also act out of mixed motives. And sometimes, like Judas, we can marshal some very logical and even idealistic arguments to support our positions. Certainly we have those who are almost foolishly extravagant in spending their wealth on Christ. How foolish to spend so much on a building when we could have given more to help the poor. Jesus' story does not allow any of us within the church to be comfortable. Jesus said, "You will always have the poor with you, but you do not always have me." In Deuteronomy 15:4-11, it is said that the reason we will always have the poor with us is that we are not faithfully obedient to God.

Jesus recognized in Mary's gesture a renewed devotion to God that would lead to a response to the poor. Our response to the poor is not a way to gain faith, but our response is the fruit of our devotion to God in Christ.

Passion/Palm Sunday

Isaiah 50:4-9a

*The Lord God has given me the tongue of a teacher,
that I may know how to sustain the weary with a word.*
— Isaiah 50:4

This passage is often considered one of the servant songs of Isaiah. There is continual debate as to whether the servant referred to is an individual or the whole community of Israel. If you assume that the servant is a corporate expression for the community of Israel, it provides an interesting reflection on the church as a called community of God. If, as Jesus suggested in Matthew 28:19-20, the responsibility of the church is to teach the whole world, then the unique vision of the teacher Israel is instructive. Isaiah saw Israel's humiliation in exile as God's instruction by which they may learn how "to sustain the weary with a word." It was by their experiencing what it meant to be powerless, abused, and insulted that they could understand the victims of the world.

This is a particularly appropriate scripture for this final Sunday in Lent that marks Jesus' entry into Jerusalem and his final steps toward the cross. One can hear the echo of what Jesus experienced in the words of the prophet: "I gave my back to those who struck me, and my cheeks to those who pulled my beard; I did not hide my face from insult and spitting." For the church to hear this not just about what Jesus, the individual, experienced but what the called community of God experienced, helps give meaning not only to Jesus' experience but also to the experience of the church when it is beleaguered.

When a church community suffers from the forces around it, the suffering can become a means by which God prepares it for ministry. There is no disgrace in suffering if it is a result of faithfulness. "The Lord God helps me; therefore I have not been disgraced...." By our suffering, we learn how to be supportive of those who also suffer in this world because of forces too great for them.

"Morning by morning he wakens — wakens my ear to listen as those who are taught." Because of our trust in the faithfulness of God, like Jesus our Lord, we can face our adversaries unafraid. When we do that, we offer hope to the hopeless around us. It is no fun to experience suffering at the hands of others in this world, but how we respond to that suffering may be our most effective witness to the world around us.

Psalm 118:1-2, 19-29

> *Open to me the gates of righteousness, that I may enter through them and give thanks to the Lord.*
> — Psalm 118:19

Psalm 118 is thought to be one of the hymns that Jesus and the disciples sang as they completed the Passover meal and prepared to make their way to the Mount of Olives. If so, its rehearsal of the faith and the steadfast love of God may well have been a source of strength for Jesus in that final journey. It is apparently one of the psalms that the early church turned to in order to understand the tragedy of Jesus' death. From the perspective of the other side of the cross and resurrection, it is easy to read the psalm in light of Jesus' experience. His triumphal entry could be seen as his invitation to the people of Jerusalem to respond to the grace of God made visible through him. "Open to me the gates of righteousness, that I may enter through them and give thanks to the Lord."

As those first Christians struggled to understand the events that followed, they could draw strength from the psalmist's words: "The stone that the builders rejected has become the chief cornerstone." Jesus became the embodiment of the whole experience of rejection that Israel had experienced and the steadfast hope in the faithfulness of God that sustained Israel. Now Jesus' rejection became not an unmitigated disaster but a further revelation of the mysterious way of God to triumph over darkness. Even in the midst of what appeared to be a tragic turn of events, both Israel before, and then Jesus, and finally his disciples could say, "This is the day that the Lord has made; let us rejoice and be glad in it." For the contemporary church, as they recognize themselves as the body of Christ, they can draw strength from this same psalm as the psalm celebrates the triumph of God over historical circumstances. "The Lord is God, and he has given us light."

Philippians 2:5-11

Let the same mind be in you that was in Christ Jesus....
— Philippians 2:5

The world looks different if we strive to see it through the eyes of Christ. If the church is the body and Christ is the head, then Christ transforms the way in which we approach decision-making. To affirm that God has established the church to be the extension of Christ's body on earth could lead to a sense of pride and feelings of superiority. Then we hear Paul's words about Jesus. He "who, though he was in the form of God, did not regard equality with God as something to be exploited, but emptied himself, taking the form of a slave, being born in human likeness." Have we accepted advantages that society offers us as benefits that belong to us? What would it mean for a church to refuse to exploit any advantages that might accrue to it as a Christian community? If the church deliberately set out to be a slave for the world, how would it affect its behavior and decision-making? Masters see slaves as existing totally for the master's benefit. The idea of slaves acting in a manner that benefited themselves or even protected themselves, if such behavior was to the detriment of the master, was not conceivable.

Paul said of Jesus: "He humbled himself and became obedient to the point of death — even death on a cross." For the church to have the same mind in themselves as was in Christ Jesus would be to defy the normal wisdom of the world that suggests that institutions and people will always act first to protect and benefit themselves. The church has suffered many conflicts both internally and externally in its history, but rarely does that conflict occur because the church was truly seeking to be a servant willing to focus on the needs of others around it. It is only by faith that we can challenge the wisdom of the world "so that at the name of Jesus every knee should bend, in heaven and on earth and under the earth, and every tongue should confess that Jesus Christ is Lord, to the glory of God the Father." It seems to be sheer foolishness until one recognizes that Easter celebrates God's triumph over the wisdom of the world. If you look through the eyes of Christ, what do you see?

Luke 19:28-40

Blessed is the king who comes in the name of the Lord!
Peace in heaven, and glory in the highest heaven!
— Luke 19:38

The Pharisees' response to this acclamation was to say, "Teacher, order your disciples to stop." Why did they want Jesus to silence his disciples? The Jewish leadership and the Roman government had reached an accord in which the Romans would take care of civil law and the religious leaders would rule in the area of religion. It was a cozy arrangement not unlike what we speak of as separation of church and state. Now Jesus' followers were disturbing the peace. They were talking politics and shouting for a king. There are always some who refuse to accept the dividing wall between private faith and public life. The disciples kept shouting, "Blessed is the king who comes in the name of the Lord!"

They refused to play by the carefully worked out rules. They heard Jesus asking them to prepare his entry into their public lives. This Jesus, they said, could break down the dividing walls of hostility, so they wanted to become involved in volatile social issues. This Jesus challenged a wealthy man not to be a slave to his money, so they wanted to speak on economic issues. This Jesus insisted that little children showed us how to enter the kingdom of God, so they wanted to become involved in public education.

Jesus responded that you could not stop such a witness because God was sovereign over all the world. The normal assumption was that the civil leaders held the real power, and they permitted an area of religious authority. The gospel proclaimed the opposite. That which could really effect change, that to which even the king would bow, that to which even nature was obedient was God whose voice Jesus' disciples expressed. If they were silenced, then nature would shout out.

Easter Day

Isaiah 65:17-25

> *For I am about to create new heavens and a new earth; the former things shall not be remembered or come to mind.* — Isaiah 65:17

Isaiah had been reflecting on the death of Israel and their life in exile. He had explored the righteous judgment of God that had resulted in the destruction of God's people. What happens when God has formed a people and done everything for them but still they have failed to be obedient? Isaiah had been unrelenting in his description of the righteous judgment of Israel. It might be a question that some would ask about the church. What happens when God has formed a people to be his witness on earth and they are utter failures in their testimony? Should we give up in despair?

Isaiah harkened back to the creation story when everything was formless and void. Hope lies in the power of God to overcome that chaos. God does what humans cannot do. God brings into being that which does not exist. When God creates a new heaven and earth, it will not be soiled by the memory of past failures. The picture of God's creation is an expression of God's unstoppable grace. Nothing that humans can do will deter God from accomplishing the divine purpose. Even nature's natural enemies will be reconciled. "The wolf and the lamb shall feed together...." The vision seems hopelessly idealistic unless one remembers how God seems to have a habit of creating light out of darkness. Easter is a celebration of the impossible possibility of God triumphing over all that seeks to defeat the divine desire for the whole world to be reconciled to God's purpose. "They shall not hurt or destroy on all my holy mountain, says the Lord."

Psalm 118:1-2, 14-24

The stone that the builders rejected has become the chief cornerstone. — Psalm 118:22

Because of the resurrection, this psalm has become a celebration of the faith confirmed by the experience of Easter. You can hear believers throughout the centuries, having relived the stories of the passion throughout Holy Week, coming into the sanctuary singing, "O give thanks to the Lord, for he is good, his steadfast love endures forever!" It is out of Jesus having been raised from the dead that Christians know that God, not death, has the final word in this world. Our universe is not a closed system but is open to the attention of a power from outside our time-constrained reality. This power is not an abstract reality but a personal God.

Jesus' message that God can be addressed as Abba, or daddy, means that God pays attention to our condition. "The Lord is my strength and my might; he has become my salvation." The universe in which we exist is not circumscribed by death but is open to a further reality. So the believer can say, "I shall not die, but I shall live, and recount the deeds of the Lord." Recall that in scripture the term righteousness has its root meaning in right relationships. We connect with this power from beyond through worship that addresses eternity. "Open to me the gates of righteousness, that I may enter through them and give thanks to the Lord." God has responded to our prayer through Jesus' resurrection by which the rest of his ministry is validated. "I thank you that you have answered me and have become my salvation. The stone that the builders rejected has become the chief cornerstone."

While this psalm was originally meant to address the history of God's relationship with Israel, who also is the "stone that the builders rejected" that will be God's cornerstone in recreating the world, for Christians the firstfruits of that reality is experienced in the resurrection of Christ. Therefore, as Christians gather for worship on Easter Day, they can sing out with bold confidence: "This is the day that the Lord has made; let us rejoice and be glad in it."

1 Corinthians 15:19-26

> *For since death came through a human being, the resurrection of the dead has also come through a human being....*   — 1 Corinthians 15:21

God's experiment with time begins and ends with the human experience. In contrast to those who would suggest that God will finally get fed up with the human condition and intervene with angels to destroy evil, Paul believed that God's purpose was expressed in the lives of human beings. Adam became the archetype of our experience of life defined by death. Jesus becomes the revelation of our life being defined by God. Jesus' ministry was the incarnation or enfleshment of God's purpose in the lives of human beings. But if that life and its relationships were totally defined by the parameters set by birth and death, then the cynic who cries out "Let us eat and drink, for tomorrow we die," speaks the truth. "If for this life only we have hoped in Christ, we are of all people most to be pitied." It was their confidence that death did not have the last word that enabled the early Christians to face the lions. By their lack of fear, they overcame every attempt by the empire to crush them.

The rulers and authorities exercise power through the application of various forms of death. Today, corporations define death as the loss of economic resources. Clubs and communities often define death by loss of relationships or exclusion. Religions can define death through shame and guilt. Politics defines death as the loss of reputation and respect. The health community defines death through illness and deformity. The state defines death through incarceration. Each community seeks to command attention to its agenda through the threat of death in one of its many forms.

"Then comes the end, when he hands over the kingdom to God the Father, after he has destroyed every ruler and every authority and power." Each of these authorities was created by God as a servant of God, but each has chosen to establish itself in place of God. In their distorted forms, each has become an enemy of the Christ who proclaims the grace of God as the prominent reality to which we can respond. Since death in its many forms seeks to distort our obedience, Christ must intervene on our behalf. "For he must reign until he has put all his enemies under his feet. The last enemy to be destroyed is death." Easter is a celebration of and a recommitment to the Christ who has overcome death and set us free to reflect the image of God in our lives.

John 20:1-18

> *Early on the first day of the week, while it was still dark....* — John 20:1a

Mary came as the inadequate disciple. The world judged her as unworthy. She was said to have been possessed by seven devils before Jesus had healed her, and tradition suggests that perhaps she had been a prostitute. Yet John describes her as the first one to come to the tomb while it was still dark. She stumbled toward faith in the darkness. She did not come with a purpose or a plan. She did not even understand what she saw when she got there. She saw two angels, and yet she only saw them as potential sources of information. "She said to them, 'They have taken away my Lord, out of the tomb, and we do not know where they have laid him.'" An empty tomb suggested to her that the body had been stolen.

Of all the possible candidates to witness Jesus' resurrection, she was the one God chose as the first witness. She was claimed by faith before she could claim faith. She did not even recognize Jesus when she saw him. To her, he was but a stranger, perhaps the gardener. She asked if he had taken the body away. It was not an affirmation of faith but only a plea for compassion from the powerless to the powerful. But then she was addressed by name. Hearing God in Christ call out her name filled her with a message of hope. She left the tomb not seeking news but prepared to announce the good news. She was the key witness to the earthquake of faith. Jesus had risen; the finite reality of death was no match for God. The powerless one became the primary witness to hope for the entire world. We come in the dark, weeping for what we have lost, and without any clear sense of direction, God addresses us by name, lifts us up, and fills our lives with new purpose.

Easter 2

Acts 5:27-32

We must obey God rather than any human authority.
— Acts 5:29

Our whole life consists of obeying some form of human authority. Most likely you are told by those who employ you the hours that you are expected to be at work. The legislature enacts laws that we are expected to obey as we live in our society. We are expected to stop at stoplights and travel within a predefined rate of speed. Our teachers expect us to complete our homework and attend the majority of our classes.

In most cases, we can think of exceptional circumstances that would encourage us to act in ways that were contrary to what the authority had defined for us. It is possible that if you told a policeman, who had stopped you for speeding, that you were rushing to visit your dying mother in the hospital, he might assist you in your journey. Even if you were an obvious member of the clergy, what would you expect the reaction to be if you told a policeman who had stopped you for speeding that you must obey God rather than human authority?

As Christians, we believe that God should be the ultimate authority in our lives, but we rarely assume that applies to the practical everyday events in our lives. If we believe that they are sincere, we can admire those who are, in the name of God, willing to defy their government in protest against some horrendous policy of the country. We often fear the results if such an attitude would become general policy. As they grew in numbers, this radical freedom of Christians became a threat to the power of governments.

What would it mean for you to continually ask yourself if this is what God would want of you in this situation? Peter was willing to defy his nation and its religious authorities rather than disobey Jesus who he believed had been exalted by God and called the people to repentance. Would a Christian church respond differently to the issues of our society than the general populace? Is the fact that many polls suggest little difference between the response of Christians and non-Christians to the issues of our society evidence of the fact that we have chosen to obey human authority rather than God in the everyday decisions of our lives? Does our Easter faith call us to a more radical obedience?

Psalm 118:14-29

> *O give thanks to the Lord, for he is good, for his steadfast love endures forever.* — Psalm 118:29

The lectionary offers us parts of Psalm 118 for Palm Sunday, Easter Sunday, and Easter 2. You are referred to those Sundays for other reflections on this psalm that became so central to early Christians' understanding of this Easter event. The additional verses that are added here, 26-29, were a hymn of praise to this God who had done such a marvelous thing. If you listen to the psalm as a dialogue between those pilgrims who came for worship and the priests who awaited their arrival, you can hear the dialogue that brings us to worship. The people said, "Blessed is the one who comes in the name of the Lord." We come to worship seeking God's blessing. The priests responded, "We bless you from the house of the Lord." It is the responsibility of the clergy to offer God's blessing to a hungry people.

The people continued, "The Lord is God, and he has given us light." At the heart of faith is the recognition that our faith is a gift from God. Even our yearning to worship is the experience of the grace of God in our hearts. Many other good people felt no urging in their lives. The priest celebrated the saving grace of that gift planted in the hearts of the people. "Bind the festal procession with branches, up to the horns of the altar." Then the people addressed God directly. "You are my God, and I will give thanks to you; you are my God, I will extol you."

The priests joined in that thanksgiving as a testimony to the steadfast love of God as they invited the people to continue their worship. "O give thanks to the Lord, for he is good, for his steadfast love endures forever." This could make an effective call to worship on this second Sunday of Easter.

Revelation 1:4-8

> *To him who loves us and freed us from our sins by his blood, and made us to be a kingdom, priests serving his God and Father, to him be glory and dominion forever and ever. Amen.* — Revelation 1:5b-6

If you want to know where the image of being washed in the blood of Jesus originated, please check your footnote on verse 5b. The NRSV chooses the manuscript that is translated "freed us" rather than "washed us" and thus is consistent with the overall image of the passage. The image that is central to the message of the Hebrew scriptures is that of the exodus from Egypt. That God would hear the cry of a suffering people and be concerned enough to effect their liberation from slavery defined the character of God. Revelation built on that image to interpret the work of Christ. While the Jews continued to marvel at the mystery of why God chose the Jews, they were confident that in doing so, God defined the divine self as one who loves and one who acts out of that love to free people from that which oppresses them.

Revelation understood that which oppresses us to be our sins. After God had freed the children of Israel, God also made clear at Sinai God's intentions for this people. "You shall be for me a priestly kingdom and a holy nation" (Exodus 19:6a). Revelation also saw God's intention through Christ to make us "to be a kingdom, priests serving his God and Father...." If through Christ we have been invited into Israel, it, nonetheless, is Israel about which the author is talking. In Genesis 12:3, the universal intention of God was announced. Abram and Sarai were to be the parents of a great nation, but the vocation of the nation was for the sake of the rest of the world. "And by you all the nations of the earth shall be blessed." Revelation echoed that call with a slight emendation. "And on his account all the tribes of the earth will wail." They would wail not because they were lost but because they finally recognized their sinfulness and their need to be saved.

Christ was the embodiment of Israel in a single person and, as followers of Christ, we have the same calling. As the cloud led the children of Israel by day through the wilderness, so now Christ comes with the cloud to lead us, and even the most resistant, those who pierced him, will recognize that his way is indeed God's way. This Jesus Christ was not only the faithful witness during his life, and the firstborn of the dead at his resurrection, but also the future ruler of the kings of the earth.

John 20:19-31

> *Jesus came and stood among them and said, "Peace be with you."* — John 20:19

Three times in this passage Jesus greeted his disciples with "Peace be with you." The first time, they were hidden behind locked doors in fear. The second time, he offered these words in the process of his commissioning them for their ministry. The third time, he said "Peace be with you" was in response to Thomas' doubts. What is this peace that calms our fears, empowers us for ministry, and overcomes our doubts? How do we receive the peace of Christ in our lives?

In the first instance, though they were filled with fear, they gathered together. When we are filled with fear, we need to come together. It is when two or three are gathered together that Christ promises to be present. It is in community that our fears are overcome. The second time was when they heard what God was asking of them. Too often our lives are aimless or have goals that diminish us. If we want the peace of Christ, we need to again take time to hear the call of God in our lives. Vocation is far more important than simply holding a job. We need to feel our lives filled with a God-given purpose.

The third time Jesus spoke his peace was when Thomas was honest about his doubts with other believers. Our doubts are the cutting edge of our faith journey. The church needs to be a place where people feel safe to voice their doubts. When we voice our doubts not in arrogance but in honest seeking, Christ shows us the wounds by which we are healed and convicted. It is in such healing that we experience the blessing of God. "Blessed are those who have not seen and yet have come to believe."

Easter 3

Acts 9:1-6 (7-20)

> *He asked, "Who are you, Lord?" The reply came, "I am Jesus, whom you are persecuting. But get up and enter the city, and you will be told what you are to do."*
> — Acts 9:5-6

While the church is locked in a battle about ordination standards and who is acceptable and who is not, it is instructive to reflect on this famous story of God's call to Paul. Paul could be appropriately called a zealot in his efforts to destroy the segment of Judaism that called themselves the *people of the way*. If Jesus was indeed the Christ, then despite his sincerity, it is clear that Paul was in direct opposition to the way of God. Being honest and sincere can simply mean that you are honestly and sincerely in the wrong.

The second aspect of this story that is so shocking is the strange way of God. God seems to have a habit of choosing people that, for all the appropriate reasons, we would be forced to conclude are unacceptable. It should cause us to be cautious about being too certain about who God calls to the ministry. Third, there is no evidence to suggest that Paul was questioning his understanding of the truth. When the light struck him down, he recognized a power in his presence, but he showed no recognition of who it might be. " 'Who are you, Lord?' The reply came, 'I am Jesus, whom you are persecuting.' " Once Jesus had announced who he was, he did not ask for belief but only obedience. "But get up and enter the city, and you will be told what you are to do."

Sometimes it is only through obedience that we come to faith. This is reinforced by the response of Ananias who was called to go and meet Saul. While Ananias did not understand and even objected to the assignment, the important thing was that he obeyed. Is it part of Luke's irony that Saul was staying at the house of Judas? This is not to suggest that it was the same Judas who betrayed Jesus, but the name may have been intentionally used to remind the hearer of that betrayal. In the same way that God could use the betrayal of Jesus for salvation, so now he could use this fierce opponent of *the way* to expand *the way* out into the world.

Finally, it is important to note that Saul's ability to proclaim the gospel occurred only after he was shown the hospitality of the faith community. "For several days he was with the disciples in Damascus, and immediately he began to proclaim Jesus in the synagogues, saying, 'He is the Son of God.' " Perhaps the issue of ordination will best be resolved through the exercise of hospitality.

Psalm 30

> *O Lord, you brought up my soul from Sheol, restored me to life from among those gone down to the Pit.*
> — Psalm 30:3

The lectionary places this psalm as a response to the story of Saul's conversion. It is enlightening to read it as a prayer that Saul may have uttered following his experience. During the several days that Saul stayed in Damascus with the disciples, you can imagine this familiar psalm being prayed in a new context. Recognizing what had happened to him, Paul could have prayed, "I will extol you, O Lord, for you have drawn me up." In light of what had happened to him, could he not see his own zealotry as a cry for help, and so he would have prayed, "O Lord my God, I cried to you for help, and you have healed me." His very fanaticism was leading his soul to destruction, and God had saved him. "O Lord, you brought up my soul from Sheol, restored me to life from among those gone down to the Pit." While God would have had every reason to judge Paul harshly for his actions, Saul experienced that the judgment of God is for salvation. "For his anger is but for a moment; his favor is for a lifetime. Weeping may linger for the night, but joy comes with the morning."

Saul could freely acknowledge his self-righteous confidence that he was executing God's judgment by persecuting those new believers. In retrospect, he could now see that God had used that very confidence to turn him around. "As for me, I said in my prosperity, 'I shall never be moved.' By your favor, O Lord, you had established me as a strong mountain; you hid your face; I was dismayed." In the shattering moment on the road to Damascus, he discovered that God had not abandoned him (v. 8), and Saul chose a life rescued by forgiveness rather than some abstract judgment that could only result in death (v. 9). Out of Saul's experience of death and resurrection he could pray, "You have turned my mourning into dancing; you have taken off my sackcloth and clothed me with joy, so that my soul may praise you and not be silent."

Psalm 30, when prayed in the light of Saul's experience, can become our prayer when we become overwhelmed by our own betrayal and wonder at the forgiving grace of God.

Revelation 5:11-14

> *Worthy is the Lamb that was slaughtered to receive power and wealth and wisdom and might and honor and glory and blessing!* — Revelation 5:12b

The history of the violent fringe of the church indicates the extreme difficulty for even the church, let alone the nations, to receive the truth of this passage. The context is John's vision of the scroll that contained God's secret plan for the unfolding of the kingdom of God on earth. This was the scroll that unveiled the future and tells us how it will all turn out. The problem for John was that at first no one was able to open the scroll so that he could see it. When he was about to give up in despair, an elder said to him, "Do not weep. See, the Lion of the tribe of Judah, the Root of David, has conquered, so that he can open the scroll and its seven seals" (Revelation 5:5). Here was the image of the militant messiah that believers had longed for. The world was convinced that history was controlled by the powerful and that only the conquering messiah could overcome evil in this world. But then came the surprise.

The lion of Judah was celebrated as the Lamb that was slaughtered. The one who was able to open up the future was the one who was willing to sacrifice himself for the sake of the world. This same Christ that Matthew recorded as being able to call upon God to bring twelve legions of angels to his rescue if necessary (Matthew 26:53), chose instead to willingly go to the cross. The future would unfold not in the hands of those who sought to use force but to those who recognized the power of sacrificial love. The early Christians lived out this truth in their life together. In a world that often excluded the diseased and crippled out of fear, they went willingly into the streets to minister to them. In a world that sought to control the world through achieving status, they lived an equality that overcame the divisions of the world. They faced down an empire that used the fear of death, even crucifixion, to control the populace by being unafraid to offer their lives on behalf of others.

It is a haunting challenge to the church that often is seduced into measuring its worth by its size and strength, to realize that the most powerful witness of the church throughout history has been a witness in which God's power was made perfect in our weakness (2 Corinthians 12:9).

John 21:1-19

Come and have breakfast. — John 21:12b

What would it mean for Jesus to invite us to have breakfast with him? The first thing we recognize is that the breakfast for these disciples was made up of the fruits of their own labors. "Jesus said to them, 'Bring some of the fish that you have just caught.'" While it was true that there was already some fish on the fire when the disciples arrived, the disciples were asked also to provide some of the fish. Of course we also recognize that even the product of our own labors ultimately are a product of God's blessing. The disciples caught the fish because they followed the instructions that were shouted to them from the shore.

Our labor is empty without Christ's blessing. It is also important to recognize that the product of their labor occurred because the disciples obeyed Jesus even before they recognized him. Sometimes we obey Christ who comes to us incognito. Perhaps he comes in the form of a stranger or a colleague at work or just the impulse that emerges from a life of faithfulness. It is important that we begin our day recognizing that that which nourishes us is a combination of Christ's blessing and our labor. As the disciples consumed their breakfast with Christ, Peter was confronted with the question, "Do you love me?"

It is important to recognize that the three times that Peter was asked the question corresponded to the three times that he denied Christ. It is part of Christ's love for us that he provides for us ways to be healed of our denials. The historic practice of the church assigning a penance for the sinner to offer in light of his sins recognized that our human nature needs to act as a response to our forgiveness. No matter how much we say we love Jesus, he asks us to demonstrate the fruits of that love by tending to his sheep. We know from the prophet Ezekiel that God was very harsh on the leaders who did not care for the flock (Ezekiel 34:1 ff). In this story, Jesus provided the bread, fish, and fire for breakfast.

Breakfast begins the day. With the proper nourishment, we have the energy to minister to the world. If the sheep are fed, they will go forth in ministry and bring a light to the world. Our love of Jesus must be demonstrated in actions that nourish the flock for the journey.

Easter 4

Acts 9:36-43

> *Now in Joppa there was a disciple whose name was Tabitha ... She was devoted to good works and acts of charity.* — Acts 9:36

Luke, the author of Acts, made it a point throughout the gospel of Luke to match stories about men with stories about women. As we leave the story of Saul's conversion and return to the Jerusalem church and the ministry of Peter, we again hear of the ministry of a woman disciple in the early church. This Tabitha, or Dorcas, had developed a ministry of charity in the city of Joppa. Reflecting Jesus' own ministry, she had chosen to focus her ministry on the vulnerable of society. "All the widows stood beside him, weeping and showing tunics and other clothing that Dorcas had made while she was with them."

In a strongly patriarchal society that had no formal social security system, widows could quickly find themselves in severe financial difficulty. Her clothes closet had apparently addressed some of those needs. In capsule form, this short story reflects the experience of the early church. While they were a vulnerable minority within society, rather than choosing to expend their efforts on protecting themselves, they deliberately went out into the streets and ministered to the really needy of their community. Because they were ministering to the poor and the diseased of society, they exposed themselves to the unsanitary conditions of their community. Like Dorcas, they were not immune to contracting diseases themselves in the process of exercising their ministry. When they did so, they drew upon the healing power of the faith community and the power of God's Spirit to assist them.

Peter, who symbolizes the church leadership, responded to their need in the same way that they were responding to the needs of others. As the life of Christ demonstrated, and the early church constantly experienced, while believers were not immune to pain and suffering, God was faithful to them in often-miraculous ways. Even today, a church that is attentive to signs of the presence of God's Spirit will notice ample signs of God's healing presence among them.

Psalm 23

> *The Lord is my shepherd, I shall not want.*
> — Psalm 23:1

Psalm 23 is likely the most famous of all the psalms. Its words of trust have sustained people throughout generations. You can imagine Jesus claiming God as shepherd (v. 1) and being restored in his times of retreat in prayer (v. 2). He could feel God leading him in the path of righteousness as he pursued the course of his ministry (v. 3). As conflict increases and the shadow of death loomed larger in Jesus' life, would he not be comforted by God's sense of protection (v. 4)? You can picture him as he sat at the table with his disciples, knowing that his enemies were preparing to arrest him, being strengthened by the psalmist's words, "You prepare a table before me in the presence of my enemies...." Yet that same Passover meal was a reminder of the hospitality of God throughout the lives of his people (v. 5). Even in the midst of conflicts, he experienced God's goodness and mercy (v. 6).

It has become important for the body of Christ to pray this prayer so that they might feel God as the shepherd who fills their every need. The church also needs to avail itself of the green pastures and still waters that God provides her even as she attempts to follow God in the path of righteousness. It should not be a surprise when the church's pursuit of righteousness in our society includes experiencing dark valleys. Yet it is the repeated experience of the church that the regular sharing of the table together opens them to the hospitality of God even in the midst of their enemies. It is a reminder that true goodness and mercy are part of dwelling in God's house even when that means being bold in the face of the opposition that exists in the world. Psalm 23 continues to be a community prayer of trust.

Revelation 7:9-17

> ... *the Lamb at the center of the throne will be their shepherd, and he will guide them to springs of the water of life, and God will wipe away every tear from their eyes.* — Revelation 7:17

One of the questions that continues to haunt the faithful over the centuries is if Christ has come, why is the world not a better place? Earlier in Revelation 6:10, "They cried out with a loud voice, 'Sovereign Lord, holy and true, how long will it be before you judge and avenge our blood....' " In chapter 7 it is made clear that God was deliberately holding back a final judgment in order for God to accomplish the divine purpose. "Do not damage the earth or the sea or the trees, until we have marked the servants of our God with a seal on their foreheads" (7:3). True to the promise to Abram in Genesis 12:3b, "... there was a great multitude that no one could count, from every nation...."

While the delay was divinely intended, the vision of heaven declared that the sacrifices of the believers had not been in vain. "These are they who have come out of the great ordeal; they have washed their robes and made them white in the blood of the Lamb." The message to believers was that no faithful act was ever lost. Each act of faithfulness, even when it appeared to be futile in its effect, was in reality an act of praise.

It is easy to become discouraged when one measures the worth of an act in terms of its measurable results. What provides Christians with the courage to continue making their witness even in seemingly hopeless situations is the confidence that what they are doing is truly an act of worship. If liturgy is the work of the people lifted in praise to God, then what happens in gathered worship is a focusing of what has been happening all week long. Like the angels in heaven, the gathered congregation reflects back on its past week and looks forward to the coming week and sings, "Amen! Blessing and glory and wisdom and thanksgiving and honor and power and might be to our God forever and ever! Amen."

John 10:22-30

> *How long will you keep us in suspense? If you are the Messiah, tell us plainly.* — John 10:24b

Is faith taught or caught? While we expend great resources in trying to convey the truth of Christianity and while many have come to an intellectual understanding of the faith, there is still the mystery of what brings a person to the faith. The religious leaders challenged Jesus to declare who he thought he was so that they could decide how they wanted to respond. Jesus was not interested in engaging in an intellectual debate.

The real declaration of who Jesus is comes first from experience rather than intellectual knowledge. It is the person who has experienced the power of Jesus personally who first comes to belief and then seeks to understand that belief. "I have told you, and you do not believe." They could have responded, "When have you told us whether you are the Messiah or not?" But he was not talking about words but experience. "The works that I do in my Father's name testify to me." Yet in that great mystery of faith, many people knew what Jesus had done, but only some of them were moved to experience God's presence in those works. "My sheep hear my voice. I know them, and they follow me."

Faith is not an intellectual understanding but a mysterious gift of inner transformation that enables one to hear the voice of God in the ordinary events of life. It is what in Celtic spirituality is spoken of as "thin moments" or moments when the eternal seeps into our time-constrained reality and the moment is transformed. In verse 30, Jesus stated unambiguously, "The Father and I are one." But the words did not generate awe and faith among those who heard him. Rather they were angered and wanted to stone him.

The truth of Christ seeps into our lives only when we suddenly become aware of the work of God in our lives. It happens all the time, but we cannot simply be told about it. We must experience it in a way that allows us to hear Christ's voice. Having heard, we want to follow him.

Easter 5

Acts 11:1-18

> *Why did you go to uncircumcised men and eat with them?* — Acts 11:3

Even Peter was accountable for his actions by the community of faith. He may have been the leader of the early church but he was subject to the criticism of others who also felt they had a legitimate claim on and an understanding of the faith. It is hard for us from this distance to appreciate what an earthshaking event it was for this Jewish sect to accept Gentiles into their community. Conversion of Gentiles to Judaism was a familiar experience but it required the inquirer to go through the procedure of becoming a full-fledged Jew. For males, this included the process of being circumcised. Acts records that it was the circumcised believers who raised the criticism for Peter. They were of the firm belief, backed by their clear understanding of Torah, that Jews should not associate with Gentiles. Peter reflected that belief in his own resistance to God's invitation to eat unclean food.

As the church currently struggles with the acceptance of homosexuals into the community of faith, we get some sense of the depth of their concern. This was not some casual expansion of tolerance. Rather, it seemed to those who raised the issue that Peter was violating a clear directive from God in sharing table with these outsiders. One can hear the scripture and theology that is brought to bear on criticizing those who want to make space for homosexuals as full members of the faith. For Peter, there was a critical experience that caused him to reinterpret his understanding of the faith.

In his association with these Gentiles, he experienced the power of God's Spirit working in their lives. That caused him to hear Jesus' words in a new light. "John baptized with water, but you will be baptized with the Holy Spirit." He then recalled the Pentecostal experience of receiving the Spirit in a way that enabled them to speak to people from every nation (Acts 2:1-12).

Throughout Christian history as it has adapted to new circumstances and new challenges, it was when believers experienced the power of God's Spirit working in someone's life that they allowed themselves to reevaluate their understanding of scripture in a new way. Perhaps as we sit at table with each other, we will be able to sense the power of the Spirit working among us. Then we, too, will be faced with God's challenge: "What God has made clean, you must not call profane."

Psalm 148

> *Let them praise the name of the Lord, for his name alone is exalted; his glory is above earth and heaven.*
> — Psalm 148:13

Psalm 148 is a psalm of praise that includes every facet of existence. It is a psalm that belongs at the end of the hymn of creation when God "saw everything he had made, and indeed, it was very good" (Genesis 1:31). You can imagine God having completed his work on the seventh day and suddenly the whole creation bursting forth in praise. It comes from the heavens, the angels, and the hosts (vv. 1-2). It springs forth from the sun, moon, and stars (v. 3) and from the waters that were left above the firmament on the second day of creation (v. 4). This watery chaos, whose bounds were fixed by God, gives testimony to the sovereignty of God over all the forces of chaos (vv. 5-6). That same praise echoes from the mystery of the forces within the created world. The sea monsters, deeps, fire and hail, snow and frost, and stormy winds all obey God's commands (vv. 7-8).

From the mountains to the hills, from fruit trees to cedars, and all forms of animal life the praise of God springs forth (vv. 9-10). All classes, sexes, and ages of people from kings to children are invited to praise God (vv. 11-12). Praise is at the center of all creation because every facet of the jewel reflects God's continuing glory (v. 13). It is this same God who has chosen to raise the sign for a chosen people as a sign of God's love for all people. The ultimate symbol of God's glory is God's capacity to love a particular people (v. 14). It is clear that the creator of all that exists can also personally care for the few and even the individual.

Revelation 21:1-6

> *See, the home of God is among mortals. He will dwell with them as their God; they will be his peoples, and God himself will be with them....* — Revelation 21:3

The book of Revelation offered a vision of the completion of God's intention that had been working itself out since the beginning of creation. In contrast to those who would suggest that God will carry off the faithful to heaven and leave the evil earth behind, Revelation saw an earthly fulfillment of God's purposes. The home of God was among mortals and not vice versa. It began in Genesis with God overcoming chaos, symbolized by the waters, and ends with a time when chaos will be ended — "and the sea was no more."

The promise of God from the beginning was for all peoples, and, though for a time, God chose a special people, it was always for the purpose that "in you all the families of the earth shall be blessed" (Genesis 12:3b). Despite periods of intense nationalism, the Hebrew prophets continued to proclaim a vision of universalism as God's intent. While Israel wrote the history of God's vision, they were not seen as the only people whom God claimed. "Blessed be Egypt my people, and Assyria the work of my hands, and Israel my heritage" (Isaiah 19:25; see also Isaiah 56:7; Amos 9:12). John made clear that Christians also must not lose sight of God's love for all peoples and all nations. The prophecy of Isaiah 65:17, "For I am about to create new heavens and a new earth; the former things shall not be remembered or come to mind," is echoed in Revelation as a reminder that God has been in charge all along and will complete the divine intention by bringing history to a fulfillment.

The seemingly chaotic path that we have traveled was necessary for God to preserve our dignity and freedom, but it was never beyond God's ultimate control. In Genesis 1:7 some of the waters that symbolized chaos were deliberately left to be part of creation but were prevented from overwhelming creation. "So God made the dome and separated the waters that were under the dome from the waters that were above the dome." Such chaos, though it was necessary for our development, did result in pain, suffering, and death. Finally, however, God "will wipe every tear from their eyes. Death will be no more; mourning and crying and pain will be no more, for the first things have passed away." Our hope lies, not in the avoidance of pain and suffering, but in our trust in God who has ordered this creation for us. This hope is not for us alone but for all of creation, which from the beginning God pronounced "very good" (Genesis 1:31).

John 13:31-35

> *By this everyone will know that you are my disciples, if you have love for one another.* — John 13:35

Jesus had just demonstrated the type of servanthood that he commanded his disciples to offer one another by himself washing their feet (John 13:1-20). He then acknowledged that "one of you will betray me" and the reader, not the disciples, was told that it was Judas. In this manner, we are made aware that Jesus' love was offered even to Judas who would betray him. Immediately upon Judas' departure, Jesus said, "Now the Son of Man has been glorified, and God has been glorified in him." In the Hebrew scriptures, to speak of the glory of God was to speak of signs of God's presence. As Jesus prepared his disciples for his coming crucifixion, he demonstrated that the glory or presence of God was revealed through a love that extended even to those who rebel against God's purposes.

Following this demonstration, Jesus said to his disciples, "I give you a new commandment, that you love one another. Just as I have loved you, you also should love one another." We have been given our marching orders. We are to demonstrate to the world a capacity to love others in a manner that even transcends betrayal.

God's glory is made manifest when enemies are reconciled. As John's readers are fully aware, such a demonstration of love will not always be joyously received by the world around us. Jesus was about to pay the cost of such love, and his disciples should be under no illusion that the path of faith would be easy.

While the church will continue to tell the rest of the world about Jesus and seek to help others in obedience to Jesus, their most powerful witness will be a demonstration of their capacity to love one another. Churches are made up of humans with all the foibles of the rest of the world. As such, the church will experience conflict, tension, fights, and even betrayals. None of this will surprise anyone. What will surprise them is when we demonstrate the capacity to love each other despite such human foibles. When churches demonstrate how to love each other in such situations, then the world will know that we are Jesus' disciples.

Easter 6

Acts 16:9-15

> *During the night Paul had a vision: there stood a man of Macedonia pleading with him and saying, "Come over to Macedonia and help us."* — Acts 16:9

There is a mystery to the work of God that continues to challenge our rational minds. This story begins with Paul having a vision of a man pleading with him to come to Macedonia. While the church will often seek to do long-range planning and set goals for itself, we are not particularly inclined to set everything aside and follow a vision. Someone may suggest an inspirational idea, but frequently, it is smothered in questions and pragmatic concerns about possible consequences.

Those who were with Paul became convinced that his vision was a genuine call from God. This followed upon two experiences in which they believed that God was forbidding them to "speak the word" in Asia and in Bithynia. While it is not made clear how they knew this, it is clear that they believed their mission was being directed from beyond themselves. Yet, having come to Philippi, in Macedonia, they did not have any clear direction about what to do next. It is reported that they "remained in this city for some days. On the sabbath day we went outside the gate by the river, where we supposed there was a place of prayer...." If you do not know what to do, then it is time to gather in prayer.

Paul, in contrast to the reputation modern people have of his being anti-woman, found a group of women there and began to speak to them. Even here, the mystery of God continued to work in ways that surprise us. It was not these women, but another woman, Lydia, who God had moved to listen to what Paul was saying. "The Lord opened her heart to listen eagerly to what was said by Paul." She was a merchant who had obviously done quite well in her business, and she brought her household to be baptized and then invited Paul and his companions to take up residence in her house.

Paul came to Philippi, not as a result of carefully laid plans but in response to a vision. When he got there, he did know what to do; so he waited expectantly. When nothing seemed to be developing, he sought a place of prayer. It was God who opened the heart of one who heard him and established the church at Philippi. As a church, we continue to make plans and set goals for our ministry, but it is the mystery of God that determines who happens to overhear us. It is the Spirit of God that directs us. The challenge for us is to learn to trust the Spirit of God when our carefully laid plans are frustrated.

Psalm 67

> *May God be gracious to us and bless us and make his face to shine upon us....* — Psalm 67:1

Psalm 67 is a harvest thanksgiving psalm. What the worshipers experienced was a bountiful harvest (v. 6) that they saw as a reflection of God's blessing. They celebrated that blessing, not only as a way of thanking God, but also because they believed that as others saw how God had blessed them, they, too, would revere God (v. 7). The psalm begins and ends by blessing God in the third person. "May God be gracious to us and bless us and make his face to shine upon us ..." (v. 1) and "May God continue to bless us ..." (v. 7). In verses 2 through 5, God is addressed directly in the second person. It is as if prayer draws us into a personal relationship with God and then moves us back out into the world in which we live.

Even in our intimacy, the focus of our prayer is still on the world around us. In our prayers of thanksgiving is a recognition that God's very blessings in our lives can become a source of testimony to the world around us. "May God be gracious to us and bless us and make his face to shine upon us, Selah that your way may be known upon earth, your saving power among all nations" (vv. 1-2). The movement is always outward even though we have experienced it personally. Be gracious to us (v. 1) that others might know (v. 2) and respond with joy and obedience (v. 4). The prayer guides us in an authentic thanksgiving that escapes the temptation of self-congratulations that somehow we are blessed because we are better than others.

Imagine a church regularly giving thanks for how God has richly blessed the church but always keeping in mind that these blessings are for the purpose of witnessing to the world about the graciousness of God. Perhaps for the church, it is a prayer in response to Luke's admonition: "From everyone to whom much has been given, much will be required; and from the one to whom much has been entrusted, even more will be demanded" (Luke 12:48).

Revelation 21:10, 22—22:5

> *... and the leaves of the tree are for the healing of the nations.* — Revelation 22:2d

This image of the culmination of history has some challenging aspects to it. First, it was clearly earth-centered. If other scriptures spoke of believers being caught up into the clouds, here Jerusalem came down to earth. In contrast to gnostic belief that salvation was in escaping the material world, which they believed was evil, Revelation saw salvation as including the material reality of our life here on earth. Second, this passage suggested that Jerusalem was still only part of the whole world. Other nations would continue to exist and there would still be those who practiced falsehood. Such nations could not enter Jerusalem and despoil God's saved community, but they still existed. There was continuity with what had gone before as pictured in the fact that both the river and the tree of life from the Garden of Eden were again present. The tree of life produced twelve kinds of fruit, and its leaves were for the healing of the nations. This would only be important if there were nations that still needed to be healed.

If there were still nations in need of healing and there were still those who practiced falsehood, what was different about this image of the culmination of history? It would appear that life continued on in its diversity but that the people of faith finally had a clear and certain relationship with God. Perhaps we never arrive at a place where all of creation is fixed in perfection. Maybe life is always evolving and progressing in some manner. Those who arrive at a secure faith and trusting relationship with God are not content within themselves but are still directed outward toward the nations that need healing. As with the promise to Abraham in Genesis 12:3, by the faith of the people, all the nations of the earth will be blessed.

John 14:23-29

> *Peace I leave with you; my peace I give to you. I do not give to you as the world gives. Do not let your hearts be troubled, and do not let them be afraid.*
> — John 14:27

What is the peace of Christ and how does it differ from the peace that the world offers us? Clearly the peace of Christ does not mean the absence of suffering, conflict, or death. Christ suffered all of these. What the world offers as peace is often seen as the absence of conflict. It is secured by the use of force in a way that prevents a person from inflicting harm on another. The problem with such peace is that it is secured by fear and does nothing to address the envy and lust that exists within all of us. As the book of James suggests, "Those conflicts and disputes among you, where do they come from? Do they not come from your cravings that are at war with you?" (James 4:1).

Jesus, in preparing his disciples for his departure, was seeking to open them to a power that would transform their inner cravings and redirect them in a manner that would bring a true peace to the believer. Such peace was centered in a selfless love that Jesus had attempted to demonstrate to them. Yet it is more than an idea or virtue that we must achieve through an effort of the will. Rather, it is openness to the Spirit of God that seeks to work that transformation within us. "But the Advocate, the Holy Spirit, whom the

Father will send in my name, will teach you everything, and remind you of all that I have said to you."

Jesus sought to demonstrate that peace as he began to move toward the cross. He would not resist the events that sought to cause him harm but rather would look for the transforming possibilities that existed in each new circumstance. Each act was approached as a means of demonstrating his love for God. The ruler of this world "has no power over me; but I do as the Father has commanded me, so that the world may know that I love the Father." The peace of Christ is discovered as we approach each circumstance as an opportunity to demonstrate the love of God. Many a conflict within the church could be transformed if each of the believers was seeking to demonstrate the love of God in his or her behavior.

The Ascension Of Our Lord

Acts 1:1-11

> *They asked him, "Lord, is this the time when you will restore the kingdom to Israel?" He replied, "It is not for you to know the times or periods that the Father has set by his own authority."* — Acts 1:6b-7

Humanity is mesmerized with the concept of time. The future tantalizes us with its myriad of possibilities. Jesus' advice in Matthew 6:34 about not being anxious about what will happen tomorrow seems to fall on deaf ears. We desperately want to know what will happen in the future.

Several times in the gospels the disciples, representing thoughts that we also have, tried to get Jesus to reveal the future to them. While Jesus would speak about the future in terms of the faithfulness of God, he refused to put a timetable on God's fulfillment of those promises. "It is not for you to know the times or periods that the Father has set by his own authority." There are some things that need to be left up to God. Our task is to trust that God is faithful and to shape our lives in light of that trust.

The history of the church suggests how difficult it is to follow that advice. Some preachers have made enormous profits by predicting the timing of God's ending of the world. The fact that this contradicts the words of Jesus as recorded in the gospels, for example Mark 13:32, does not seem to deter their confident predictions. It is easy to become self-righteous in criticizing them, but in the local church we also let our anxiety about the future shape our decisions and actions.

The ascension of Jesus took him out of one particular moment in time and space and made him present in all times and all places. The disciples saw him ascending and "while he was going they were gazing up toward heaven, suddenly two men in white robes stood by them. They said, 'Men of Galilee, why do you stand looking up toward heaven?' "

Jesus is now of the future and of the present as he once was of the past. Like the disciples, we can no longer fix him in one place or time. Because he is of all time, all time is sacred, and we can trust him for the future and not be anxious. Our hope does not rest in our knowledge of the future but in who is waiting for us in the future.

We have celebrated the evidence that God will not be defeated by the evils of the world. The cross that was meant to be a sign of the world's violent rejection of the love and grace of God has been transformed into a sign of God's redemptive love. Now that we know that God, not death, will have the final word, let us live our lives in hope.

Psalm 47

> *He chose our heritage for us, the pride of Jacob whom he loves. Selah* — Psalm 47:4

It is curious that the psalmist refers to Jacob, his old name, rather than Israel, the name God gave him when he blessed him at the Jabbok (Genesis 32:24-32). Up until that moment, while Jacob showed flashes of faith, the dominant feature of his personality was that of a conniver, or as his name suggested, a striver who was quite willing to trick and take advantage of others in order to better himself. Yet, like David at a later date, God seems to have a fondness for rascals.

Perhaps it is a sign of God's patient work at redemption. The psalmist celebrates the anticipated future of God's triumph. "Clap your hands, all you people; shout to God with loud songs of joy.... He subdued peoples under us, and nations under our feet." The fact that this psalm is read as we celebrate the ascension recognizes that God's triumph over evil does not come in a manner that most people expect. His victory is brought about by a slain lamb (Revelation 5:9) who chose to rule as a servant.

The rascals of the world, including churches that act like rascals occasionally, are not beyond hope. Jacob became Israel, one who wrestled with God and man and prevailed (Genesis 32:28). We frequently do not understand how God's purposes can be accomplished in a world that is so resistant by a church that frequently is more interested in survival than faithfulness. Yet that same church hears the scriptures, sings the songs, and prays the prayers through which God can work redemptive miracles.

"God is king over the nations; God sits on his holy throne. The princes of the peoples gather as the people of the God of Abraham. For the shields of the earth belong to God; he is highly exalted."

Ephesians 1:15-23

> *And he has put all things under his feet and has made him the head over all things for the church, which is his body, the fullness of him who fills all in all.*
> — Ephesians 1:22-23

Consider what it means to affirm that God has placed Christ "far above all rule and authority and power and dominion, and above every name that is named, not only in this age but also in the age to come." And this same Christ is the head of the church, "which is his body." If Christ is above all that exists and is also the head of the church, what does that mean for how we function as a church?

Consider what it means for decision-making within the church. Our question should not be what action will be least offensive to the majority or even how we avoid controversy. Can you imagine a conversation within the body that has the hand saying, "We dare not do that because the legs and the feet will be offended or might want to leave the body." Of course that happens at times. Sometimes the result is paralysis or even amputation. Yet a decision within the body is healthiest when it is made by the head of the body.

When the leadership of the church is trying to make a decision, the criteria should be what Christ wants. Since Christ also is head of all the other forces in the universe, all the rule, power, authority, and dominion that exists, it is right that the church should also be concerned with what Christ would want in other areas of the world as well. The issue becomes how we discern the wishes of Christ as we make our decisions and take our actions.

This is why Ephesians recorded Paul wanting the church to receive "the spirit of wisdom and revelation as you come to know him." Our first window into that wisdom is the scripture's testimony about the pattern of Jesus' life. We see Jesus use power, for example, but never to protect himself. That was one of the temptations that he faced and rejected (Matthew 4:1-10). The church, his body, when exercising power and influence, should do so for the sake of others. While Jesus did judge the self-righteousness of religious leaders, he was quick to extend the grace and forgiveness of God to others who sinned. The church should have a far stronger reputation for graciousness than for being judgmental. Jesus invited believers to look to the fruits of people's lives and at times found powerful fruit in people who did not share his faith such as the Roman centurion. The church should demonstrate an ability to listen to God speaking to them through people of other faiths.

When a human body rejects the direction of its head, we speak of mental illness or physical malfunctions. That can also happen to Christ's body. As with the human body, the church needs to be encouraged to practice healthy living and seek help when it demonstrates signs of mental illness. What are the practices that could contribute to the health of your church?

Luke 24:44-53

> *And see, I am sending upon you what my Father promised; so stay here in the city until you have been clothed with power from on high.*   — Luke 24:49

There are times when our most important and faithful task is to wait. Actions are an important part of the faith, but being too quick to act can cause poor results. As Luke recorded Jesus' ascension, Jesus reminded his disciples of what they had already learned. "These are my words that I spoke to you while I was still with you." He also told them of the responsibility that they carried into the future. "Repentance and forgiveness of sins is to be proclaimed in his name to all nations, beginning from Jerusalem."

If they had any idea that he was about to leave them, to be told that they had the task of preaching repentance and remission of sins among all the nations must have seemed an overwhelming task. Perhaps in recognition of those feelings, he promised them that God would give them the power. But to receive that power, they must first wait. They were not told how long they had to wait. They were simply to wait until they received the power from on high.

A church may sense a call to a particular mission but feel overwhelmed by the size of the task and the meagerness of their resources. Some would urge that they should change the mission to more nearly fit the resources available. Others would urge them to proceed and trust that the Lord would provide. A third possibility, as suggested by this passage, is that the church should engage in a season of prayerful waiting. This is not passive inactivity but an active seeking of God's guidance and blessing for the task at hand. "They worshiped him, and returned to Jerusalem with great joy; and were continually in the temple blessing God." The disciples knew the outlines of their call but demonstrated the patient trust that God would provide them the power to carry it out according to God's timing.

Without God, even with the best of intentions, our ministry is not effective. With God all things are possible.

Easter 7

Acts 16:16-34

> *One day, as we were going to the place of prayer, we met a slave girl who had a spirit of divination and brought her owners a great deal of money by fortune-telling.* — Acts 16:16

The strange thing about this incident is that the slave girl told the truth about Paul and his companions. "These men are slaves of the Most High God, who proclaim to you a way of salvation." She was the mass media of the day, and she was giving Paul plenty of publicity. While a contemporary evangelist might shun bad publicity, most would be pleased to receive good publicity that raised their profile among the people whom they desired to reach. What possibly could be wrong with a spirit of truth giving an evangelist lots of publicity? Paul was annoyed and in response to her behavior he turned and healed her of this spirit that possessed her. Was he annoyed that her owners were using her to make money or that even truth-telling can be disturbing if it is no respecter of persons?

By his healing her, he was removing this strange spirit from her by which her owners had made a profit. Whatever Paul's original motivation, the result of his healing the girl was that she was no longer valuable to her owners. When the gospel interfered with the economics of the market place, not only were her owners disturbed but also so was the crowd. If truth can be used for profit, people are pleased. But sometimes even truth can exploit people in the process. Truth must be blended with compassion if its message is to be healthy. Paul's healing of the girl cost her owners a profit and the crowd a good show. The result was that Paul was not only flogged but also thrown into prison. Rather than being disturbed by the injustice of his punishment for doing good, Paul used it as an opportunity to witness to the jailer that resulted in his conversion.

The church will always find itself in the conflict between truth and economics, and at times it will suffer injustice in the process.

However, regardless of the fairness of the world around us, how we choose to respond can become an opportunity for God to work through us.

Psalm 97

> *The heavens proclaim his righteousness; and all the peoples behold his glory.* — Psalm 97:6

Our normal use of the word righteousness often carries the sense of a cold, unbending perfection that is not particularly sensitive to human feelings or frailties. We speak of a self-righteous person as someone who is self-assured of his or her own rightness. We speak of righteous anger as an anger that is not open to being questioned or reasoned with. When the Bible speaks of righteousness, however, it carries the sense of right relationships rather than the imposition of a cold, impersonal set of laws.

When the heavens proclaimed God's righteousness, they were speaking of God's right relationships. When Jesus summed up all of life in terms of love of God and love of neighbor, he was subsuming all of the law and the prophets under the framework of right relationships. When God has placed all of creation in right relationship with God and each other, "all the peoples behold his glory." Once again, the psalmist holds up a vision of universalism. It is not just the chosen people but the whole earth that will rejoice. The foundation of God's throne is righteousness or right relationships and its close companion, justice. Our own experience makes clear that not everyone in the world wishes for a universal establishment of right relationships. If we were in right relationship with all of our neighbors, we could not rationalize the disparity between the rich and the poor.

In the psalm, the coming of God was pictured like a terrible thunderstorm that swept across the land. "Fire goes before him, and consumes his adversaries on every side. His lightnings light up the world; the earth sees and trembles. The mountains melt like wax before the Lord, before the Lord of all the earth." The struggle between good and evil is not a struggle of laws but a struggle of right relationships. Those who are willing to continue through the storm will experience the dawn. "Light dawns for the righteous, and joy for the upright in heart." The struggle for the church is to resist the temptation of self-righteousness and continue to seek right relationships with all our neighbors and with God.

Revelation 22:12-14, 16-17, 20-21

> *See, I am coming soon; my reward is with me, to repay according to everyone's work.* — Revelation 22:12

This final vision, near the end of the book of Revelation, is a striking one on several counts. First, it is positive. There is no threat of punishment. One is not judged according to sins but repaid according to one's work. Is there a suggestion here that though we are saved by grace, there is a sense in which we are rewarded by our deeds? Is this another way of saying, "You will know them by their fruits" (Matthew 7:20)? Second, this event takes place on the earth. People are not lifted up to heaven. Rather Jesus comes to establish a city for the righteous or those in right relationships. There is even the suggestion that there will continue to be others living outside the city who are not allowed to enter the city. "Blessed are those who wash their robes, so that they will have the right to the tree of life and may enter the city by the gates."

What we are offered is an urban vision of the Garden of Eden. The river and the tree of life that were once a part of the garden are now this new Jerusalem. Third, what God brings about is not a total break from the past but has continuity with what has gone before it. "I am the root and the descendent of David, the bright morning star." The human saga is not some hopeless disaster that finally must be replaced. What we are experiencing now is part of what will finally come to be through the grace of God. Finally, our humanity retains its physical aspect. One still is thirsty and needs water and food, and we still have the freedom of choice. "And let everyone who is thirsty come. Let anyone who wishes take the water of life as a gift."

For the church that continues to live and strive within an ambiguous world, we are told that our past matters, our efforts count, and the future holds promise. "Come, Lord Jesus! The grace of the Lord Jesus be with all the saints. Amen."

John 17:20-26

> *The glory that you have given me I have given them, so that they may be one, as we are one....* — John 17:22

John offers these words as part of Jesus' prayer before he was arrested and crucified. If we have ever wondered about unanswered prayer, then here we have Jesus' prayer that the church will be one even as Jesus and God are one, and 2,000 years later it appears that we are still waiting for God's answer to that prayer. Not only did the early disciples fight among themselves, but also, there has never been a chapter in church history where the fighting and quarreling has disappeared. Jesus offered an image of the unity for which he prayed in his own relationship with God. When one examines that image, one is struck by its own seeming contradiction. If God and Jesus are one, why was Jesus allowed to die on the cross? Because we look back on the cross through the perspective of the resurrection, we may fail to grasp the full power of Jesus' cry of abandonment reported from the cross. At the same time, perhaps it is in the cross that we see a resolution to the seeming contradiction between Jesus' prayer and the continued experience of the conflicted church.

If God and Jesus are one despite the appearance of the contradiction of the cross, then is it possible that there is a unity to the church that also transcends appearances? Jesus suggested that his disciples would see his glory that God had given him out of love. That glory was revealed in the brokenness of the cross. Is the glory of God hidden in the brokenness of the church as well? Jesus suggested that God's indwelling in him was like his indwelling in the church. When Jesus was crucified, the disciples, while temporarily running away, came back together to try to understand what had happened. Some of them, the most vulnerable among them, went to the tomb without a clear understanding of what they were looking for. It was in that frightened, almost desperate, clinging to their Lord that they experienced the resurrection.

The conflicts in the church also cause many to run away but still they gather, and it is often the most vulnerable among us that go to the tomb out of desperation. Yet time and again, we experience the resurrected Christ reconnecting us with each other. Perhaps the answer to Jesus' prayer must first be experienced among the faithful as an experience of Christ that transcends all their expectations. When we have experienced this unity that transcends all that seeks to separate us, the world may come to believe that, indeed, Jesus is the Son of God.

The Day Of Pentecost

Acts 2:1-21

> *When the day of Pentecost had come, they were all together in one place.* — Acts 2:1

Too often Gentile Christians forget that Pentecost was a Jewish celebration of the renewal of the covenant that they had with God. Fifty days after Passover, Jews renewed the covenant that they had with God. The symbol of fire resting on the disciples' heads recalled the symbol of fire that was part of the original covenant-making process in Genesis 15:17. When Abram had laid out the divided animals, it was God who passed between them symbolizing the remarkable testimony of the Jewish faith that it was God, in the form of a smoking fire pot and a flaming torch, who accepted responsibility for keeping this covenant that God had made with Abram.

As has been frequently noted, this story also becomes the mirror image of the story of the tower of Babel in Genesis 11:1-9, where the arrogance of humanity resulted in their being divided into many tribes that spoke different languages. As they gather, the disciples experience the possibility of the reversal of this division. Through the power of the Holy Spirit they began to speak in other languages. This was not a reference to *glossolalia*. They were not speaking a heavenly language. The report made clear that Jews from all around the world heard them speaking "in the native language of each." This further astonished them because these speakers were not from some intellectual class but people from the rural province of Galilee. Not only are the divisions of language overcome but also the divisions of class, age, sex, and nationality. This is emphasized by Peter's interpretation of the event. Peter recalled the prophecy of Joel where the Spirit of God was poured out on young and old, male and female, slave and free.

Pentecost was a renewal of hope that God would heal the divisions that seek to tear our world apart. For the church, Pentecost is a time to openly acknowledge the divisions that exist even within the church that reflect the arrogance of the tower of Babel. The mirror images of Babel and Pentecost offer us a challenge and a hope for the future. By the Holy Spirit, we are given a word that not only respects our differences (each heard in their own language) but also unites us in a common testimony to the reconciling love of God. As it was with Abram, it is clear that it is God who will accomplish this reconciliation, but it is by our faith that we will respond to what God is doing.

Psalm 104:24-34, 35b

> *When you send forth your spirit, they are created; and you renew the face of the ground.* — Psalm 104:30

On Pentecost, the focus of our attention is on the Spirit of God. While our understanding of the Spirit of God is more fully developed in the New Testament, God's Spirit is fully present in the Hebrew scriptures as well. Remembering that in Hebrew the word for breath and spirit are the same, these verses recall the creation story in Genesis 2:7 where God was forming the earthling. When all of the parts had been created from the clay or elements of the earth, it was still not a living human being until God "breathed into his nostrils the breath of life; and the man became a living being." This same breath or spirit is spoken of in this psalm in a reversal of creation. "When you hide your face, they are dismayed; when you take away their breath, they die and return to their dust." However, the reference here is much broader. The psalmist was recognizing that all of creation was dependent on the breath or Spirit of God. Our entire creation, in ways that we choose to ignore, is a dependent creation.

As scientists explore other planets that have been incapable of producing life, we are made more and more aware of how fragile and exacting the conditions are that permitted life to emerge on this planet. For the believer, the miracle of life itself is cause for great awe. "O Lord, how manifold are your works! In wisdom you have made them all; the earth is full of your creatures." There is an ecological aspect to our celebration of the Spirit of God. "When you send forth your Spirit, they are created; and you renew the face of the ground." When we celebrate Pentecost, we are not only celebrating the birthday of the church but also the birth of creation. Our stewardship of the ecology of our planet is lifted up when we recognize how dependent the entire creation is on a mystery that is beyond our control. For the psalmist, such awareness could only result in songs of praise. "I will sing to the Lord as long as I live; I will sing praise to my God while I have being." For us it may result in a new respect for the sacredness of our creation.

Romans 8:14-17

For all who are led by the Spirit of God are children of God. — Romans 8:14

In the creation story of Genesis 2b ff, it is when God breathes the breath or Spirit into the earth creature that it became a living human being. Our lives depend on this Spirit enlivening us. The psalmist says, "When you take away their breath, they die and return to their dust." There are many who prefer to live in denial of that intimate and necessary connection with God. We prefer to think of ourselves as biologically determined. We are born as a result of a male sperm impregnating a female egg. We are nourished by the food of the earth and continue to grow until one day our biological frame is either cut short or is used up and we die. Such a perspective makes us slaves to the physical aspects of life.

If we are myopic enough, life is determined by the pursuit of pleasure and the avoidance of pain. Yet the human brain has always been restless with the conclusion that we are nothing more than a biological phenomenon. There is a restless spirit within us that wants to believe that we are connected with something greater than our finite selves. Most religions seek to give expression to this connection. Paul built on the Jewish belief of our connection through the Spirit of God. "For all who are led by the Spirit of God are children of God." We are touched by eternity and ennobled by this connection. As Christians affirm that Jesus was the Son of God, so we also affirm that we are all children of God. If we deny this connection, we can easily become slaves to the moment and "fall back into fear." Paul expressed this reception of God's Spirit as a spirit of adoption that makes us "heirs of God and joint heirs with Christ." To receive our inheritance, or the benefits that come with being an heir of God, requires more than just an intellectual assent.

We are joint heirs with Christ — if, in fact, "we suffer with him so that we may also be glorified with him." The path of Christ was a resistance to a life focused on one's own needs and a willingness to trust God regardless of the circumstances. To live a life like Christ is to believe that we are connected with something greater than ourselves. It is also to live our life in response to that greater reality even when doing so is at the expense of our own pleasure or safety. Pentecost is a renewal of our covenant with God so that we might live in the Spirit of Christ.

John 14:8-17 (25-27)

> *This is the Spirit of truth, whom the world cannot receive, because it neither sees him nor knows him. You know him, because he abides with you, and he will be in you.* — John 14:17

There is a mystery to the church that cannot be proven by the world's standards of proof. This is a truth that can only be experienced. Jesus promises that God will send an advocate to the church that is a Spirit of truth. Then, he warns that the world will not recognize this truth because it is not prepared to receive such truth. The church has one foot in both worlds. At times, it can feel the Spirit of God within it. At other times, it is filled with the skepticism of the world and cannot recognize the presence of God's Spirit among its members. When we find ourselves having such doubts, we are invited to strengthen our faith by intentionally doing some of the works of Christ. Jesus told his disciples, "I am in the Father and the Father is in me."

Here we see the connection that holds the universe together. God is in Jesus, and the Spirit of that same God is in us. Acting in a consciously Christian manner draws us closer to Christ and strengthens our connection with God. When our spirits connect, we are drawn away from fear and made aware of our adoption as children of God. When we do the works of Christ, we will produce the fruits of Christ, and these fruits will become their own verification. As we do the works, we will experience the Spirit, and the truth shall be made known to us. By the church doing the works of Christ, even when we are not confident of our own faith, we experience a different kind of peace than that which the world offers. We know the peace of realizing that we are not alone but are connected to the God who in Christ is healing the world.

The Holy Trinity

Proverbs 8:1-4, 22-31

> *The Lord created me at the beginning of his work, the first of his acts of long ago.*   — Proverbs 8:22

On Trinity Sunday, when the church acknowledges the three-in-one aspect of the Godhead, the lectionary reaches back into the wisdom literature for its reading from the Hebrew scriptures. One can hear the word that will be echoed in the beginning of the gospel of John. To paraphrase John 1 only slightly, "In the beginning was wisdom and wisdom was with God and she was God." Later in John 16:13, this third part of the Trinity will be referred to as the Spirit of truth. Proverbs suggests that this wisdom precedes all other aspects of creation. "In the beginning when God created the heavens and the earth, the earth was a formless void and darkness covered the face of the deep, while a wind from God swept over the face of the waters" (Genesis 1:1-2). God began to set limits on the chaos through wisdom as expressed in God's speaking a word. The fact that wisdom is seen as feminine in Proverbs (8:1) and uses a feminine tense in Hebrew enlarges our understanding of the feminine side of God. God will be experienced as masculine through the images of the Father and the Son, but God as wisdom or the Spirit of truth is experienced as feminine.

For the Hebrews to recognize that the feminine side of God existed from the very beginning was to crack open the rigidity of the patriarchal faith and allow our understanding of God to evolve. While the Eastern church has had more experience in understanding God as Sophia, it is not absent from our traditions as well. While the Wisdom literature is often a neglected part of the Bible, it is probably the most natural expression of faith in our age. It approaches faith from the perspective of common sense. For Presbyterians, the ancient saying that we cannot reason our way to faith, but our faith should be reasonable is an expression of the importance that we place on the gift of reason. As we celebrate the

Trinity, it is important to call to mind this feminine aspect of God that helped set divine boundaries to the chaos that continually threatens to engulf us.

Psalm 8

> *O Lord, our Sovereign, how majestic is your name in*
> *all the earth!* — Psalm 8:1a

The structure of this psalm gives a clue to its meaning. It begins and ends with words of praise: "O Lord, our Sovereign, how majestic is your name in all the earth!" In the context of that praise, at the center of the psalm, is a statement of praise of humanity: "Yet you have made them a little lower than God, and crowned them with glory and honor" (v. 5). The psalmist reflects in wonder at why so majestic a God should take time out and be so gracious to humans. The attributes normally reserved for God — glory, honor, dominion — have been granted to humans. The fact that such qualities, naturally belonging to God who created the whole universe (v. 3), have been gifted to people, not only suggested the generous love of God but also suggested how people should exercise these gifts. Their model for exercising honor, glory, and dominion is God who does not hesitate to give these qualities away. Later Christians will see this same quality given concrete expression in the "Son of Man came not to be served but to serve" (Mark 10:45). Dominion, honor, and glory for humans have often meant an exercise of control over and, all too frequently, exploitation of both the natural creation and other peoples.

The church has the opportunity to offer an alternate vision of such qualities as first seen in God. Now these qualities are capable of being expressed in the community of faith. As followers of Christ, the church can show the world a dominion that comes out of service, honor that does not avoid suffering on behalf of others, and a glory that finds expression in the appreciation and care for both the natural world and the stranger that is within their gate.

Romans 5:1-5

And not only that, but we also boast in our sufferings....
— Romans 5:3a

What a strange phrase. It appears so masochistic. If it were taken out of context, it could easily lead to a distorted practice of seeking out suffering in an unhealthy manner. The context of this phrase is the hope made possible by the grace in which we have been saved. While the Christian does not seek out suffering, Christians do not see the first objective of life as the avoidance of suffering either. There is full recognition that being saved does not offer you some magical protection from the woes of life. Clearly the experience of Jesus should suggest to believers that faith may very well lead to suffering rather than avoid it. Why, then, would anyone want to be a Christian? Surely there must be some alternate wisdom, some power of positive thinking, or some life philosophy that holds better promise of success. Rather than seeing suffering as one of the great negatives of life, Paul approached suffering as a possibility for something positive.

"... suffering produces endurance, and endurance produces character, and character produces hope, and hope does not disappoint us, because God's love has been poured into our hearts...." For Paul, because he knew that God was not defeated by death or pain, he could approach the difficult moments in life not from fear but from hope. When his own people rejected him, he recognized it as an opportunity to reach out to the Gentiles. When he was beaten and physically abused, he saw it as a sharing in the sufferings of Christ. When he was thrown into prison, he saw it as an opportunity to testify to the praetorian guards. Because of God's love that filled his heart, his suffering was not a threat to who he was but an opportunity to witness to the same redemptive activity of God that Jesus demonstrated on the cross.

For churches that often experience set backs in their attempts to offer ministry, Paul's understanding of the gospel provides a means by which the church might rediscover a hope that does not disappoint and testify to a redemptive gospel that offers hope to others.

John 16:12-15

> *I still have many things to say to you, but you cannot bear them now.*   — John 16:12

Perhaps this cryptic statement of Jesus underlies the reformed faith's foundational statement that the church is "reformed and always reforming." In the gospel of John, Jesus seemed to be always hinting at the fact that the truth he proclaimed was larger than that which was comprehended. In 10:16 he said, "I have other sheep that do not belong to this fold." Early on the church assumed that he was referring to the mission to the Gentiles that Paul would champion.

In contemporary times, theologians have begun to wonder if this does not apply to our relationship with people of other faiths as well. When Jesus said, "In my Father's house there are many dwelling places," the seeds were also planted for a broader understanding of how Christ works in this pluralistic world. When the church seeks to use its understanding of scripture to resist the inclusion of some category of peoples that have been traditionally excluded from the community of faith, it has to confront the possibility that such openness may be the nudging of the Spirit of truth. "When the Spirit of truth comes, he will guide you into all the truth...."

As one reads the history of the church, it becomes clear that God is often out ahead of the church inviting it to open itself to some new need or reality that confronts it. It is hard now to understand the resistance of the church to the concept of democracy on the basis that the Bible only spoke of kingdoms. It is clear that our understanding of scripture was clouded by a culture that accepted slavery or the exclusion of women from positions of church leadership.

Each time the church faces a new challenge, it fears that it may be compromising the faith. Yet, at the same time, its own faith raises the question of whether not facing the challenge may be resisting the working of the Holy Spirit. The Spirit of truth is not something that can be codified and restricted. "The Spirit blows where it chooses, and you hear the sound of it, but you do not know where it comes from or where it goes" (John 3:8).

Proper 4
Pentecost 2
Ordinary Time 9

1 Kings 18:20-21 (22-29) 30-39

> *How long will you go limping with two different opinions? If the Lord is God, follow him; but if Baal, then follow him.* — 1 Kings 18:21b

This story is so dramatic that it is easy to get caught up in the details that we escape hearing the critical issue. This was a clash of cultures that was depicted in a single contest between the prophets of Baal and the prophet Elijah. In the particular drama, Ahab's wife, Jezebel, had been politically adept at undermining the faith of Israel and replacing it with her own religion. The worship of Baal was very appealing to these essentially agricultural people because Baal was a fertility god. Prior to this event, Israel had experienced a drought, and people would be very vulnerable to the appeal of any help that was offered.

The story becomes our story when we recognize the tension between any philosophy of success challenging a faith that often calls for sacrifice. Undoubtedly the people of Israel had not really rejected the worship of Yahweh but simply blended elements of Baalism with the practice of their faith. Christians are always struggling with the blending of their faith with elements of nationalism, commercialism, and a variety of self-help philosophies. In many cases, we justify such approaches as harmless efforts to speak to the culture around us. Rarely is the choice put so bluntly as Elijah does in this story. Occasionally, however, we need a prophet to confront us with the many little compromises that we have made. There comes a moment in which we have to decide whom or what we really trust for our future. In the story, Elijah clearly has some fun with the contest as he taunts the prophets of Baal. "Cry aloud! Surely he is a god; either he is meditating, or he has wandered away, or he is on a journey, or perhaps he is asleep and must be awakened."

When it comes Elijah's turn, the clear sense of the story is that all possibility of trickery or even chance was removed. His offering and the wood for it is so thoroughly soaked in water that no one but God could consume it with fire. In contrast to the strenuous efforts of the priests of Baal, Elijah simply voiced his prayer to God that God would respond as a clear testimony to the truth of his prophet. For our contemporary society, the contest may best be engaged with humor rather than demonstrations of intense religious fervor. When we turn to God in trust, we do not need special techniques of prayer but only the simple trust that the God of our ancestors will continue to be faithful to us.

Psalm 96

> *Say among the nations, "The Lord is king!"*
> — Psalm 96:10a

There is probably no more powerful affirmation that believers could make in whatever nation they reside than this declaration. There is always an uneasy tension between loyalty to one's nation and loyalty to one's God. That tension often exists under the radar of our awareness until we are forced by circumstances to make a choice between the two. In Elijah's story in the previous reading, Baal was a god of the land and its fertility. It could easily be translated into a language of patriotism because its main focus was securing the prosperity of the land and its people. It was only at a time of drought, or perhaps in our time an incident of war or terrorism that we are confronted with the question of whom we really trust.

For the psalmist, the central cause of the divisions among the nations was the failure to recognize God as the God of all the nations (v. 3). It is in worship that we come to recognize that we are part of something that is greater than that which is part of any nation or ideology. By our failure to "ascribe to the Lord the glory due his name...." we slip into worshiping other idols within our individual societies. Even our ecological imbalance that increasingly threatens the future of our planet is the consequence of human arrogance that fails to recognize that we are all children of the same God. When humanity begins to "sing to the Lord, bless his name; [and] tell of his salvation from day to day" (v. 2), then that same song of praise will be echoed by nature as well. "Then shall all the trees of the forest sing for joy before the Lord; for he is coming, for he is coming to judge the earth" (vv. 12-13a).

It is in worship that we recognize that we are not God and are restored to our proper place in creation. While we cannot impose worship on others, we should not forget that it is one of the most powerful acts that we participate in on behalf of the future of the world.

Galatians 1:1-12

> *Or am I still trying to please people? If I were still pleasing people, I would not be a servant of Christ.*
> — Galatians 1:10b

When Paul spoke of the gift of Christ "who gave himself for our sins to set us free from the present evil age ..." he was speaking of the mystery of our own experience in the church. When we remember that sin is an act, attitude, or condition that distorts our ability to love God fully and our neighbor as ourselves, we recognize that our faith has not shielded us from the tensions and distractions that separate us from God and neighbor even in the church. When Paul spoke of the present evil age, he was speaking of the outer conditions and inner urges that result in our acting in such a way as to cause separation from God or neighbor. Can you hear yourself saying, "I would like to pray more often but I just do not have the time"? Can you hear yourself saying, "If I knew that beggar was really in need, I would be glad to help, but there are so many people who just want to take advantage of our kindness"?

When Paul spoke of an evil world, he was speaking of more than those who intentionally set out to harm others. He was also speaking of all the ways in which we contribute to distancing ourselves from God or neighbor even in the church. There is a freedom that Paul believed Christ has offered us that can set us free from living in response to "the present evil age." To live this freedom, one must focus on being a servant or slave of Christ. The church cannot proclaim this freedom and, at the same time, direct its energies toward pleasing others. A church that is driven by the consumer mentality of our society continues to seek ways to be attractive to its "potential customers."

While it is hardly wrong to want to reach out to outsiders, the most powerful message we have is the witness of our own lives. When we, in the church, demonstrate the power to live together as servants of Christ free from the selfishness of the world, we will be proclaiming a message that speaks to the hunger of our world.

Luke 7:1-10

A centurion there had a slave whom he valued highly, and who was ill and close to death. — Luke 7:2

Jesus is someone who turns our world upside down. In this story, the key figure was a Roman centurion. He was a member of the occupation forces that demonstrated an unusually compassionate manner in exercising Roman rule. While he had shown respect for the Jewish people, there was no evidence that he had any interest in becoming a Jew. Nor does the story suggest that the centurion wanted to become a follower of Jesus. He was risking embarrassment by asking the Jewish elders to go to Jesus to ask him to do the centurion a favor. What if Jesus mocked his request or demanded of him some action that would undermine his capacity to govern the people of whom he was in charge?

While we do not know a great deal about the treatment of slaves by the Romans, it is also interesting that the centurion was willing to risk this on behalf of a slave in his household. Jesus' willingness to respond to the centurion's request was a clear demonstration of the grace of God that is not restricted to a people of a particular belief. The real turning point of the story, however, came at the point when Jesus came near to the centurion's house. We learn why the centurion sent the elders rather than going to Jesus himself. He sent friends to explain, and they said to Jesus, "Lord, do not trouble yourself, for I am not worthy to have you come under my roof; therefore I did not presume to come to you." Then the centurion demonstrated his trust in the power of Jesus to heal his servant by saying, "But only speak the word, and let my servant be healed."

The centurion went on to explain that he knew this because he knew how authority operated in his own context. There is a certain universal dimension to faith that transcends particular religious expressions. Peter would speak of this same truth when later in Acts he was in the presence of another centurion and said, "I truly understand that God shows no partiality, but in every nation anyone who fears him and does what is right is acceptable to him" (Acts 10:34-35). The challenge for the church is to be willing to recognize and respond to this aspect of faith in the lives of others even when they show no interest in becoming part of our faith.

Proper 5
Pentecost 3
Ordinary Time 10

1 Kings 17:8-16 (17-24)

> *Then the word of the Lord came to him, saying, "Go now to Zarephath, which belongs to Sidon, and live there; for I have commanded a widow there to feed you."*
> — 1 Kings 17:8-9

This story will later find its echo in Jesus' sermon at Nazareth in Luke 4:25-26. Jesus used the story to challenge the narrow nationalism of his people's faith and to emphasize the universal nature of God's love. Elijah was involved in challenging the faithlessness of his king, Ahab, and had predicted a famine that would bring the region to its knees. While from Elijah's perspective, the famine was for the purpose of judging the faithlessness of King Ahab, it clearly affected the surrounding region as well. When Elijah arrived at Zarephath, he encountered a widow outside the city gates. The widow soon explained to Elijah that the famine had finally defeated her, and she was preparing a final meal for her son and herself and fully expected to die soon afterward. Even in her moment of desperation, she demonstrated hospitality for a stranger and responded to Elijah's request for a drink of water.

It was only when he also asked for a morsel of bread that she revealed the desperation of her plight. Elijah's response to her situation was to ask her first to provide him with some bread and then to trust that she would have enough for herself and her son. As Luke would record later about another widow (Luke 21:1-4), the widow in 1 Kings also gave all she had to live on. In this story you see the elements that later will be embodied in what will be referred to as the Last Supper of Jesus with his disciples. In 1 Kings it was a woman of poverty who refused to deny hospitality to a stranger but was prepared to have her last supper and die. Both stories feature the symbolic importance of bread and echo the story of the Israelites' trust in God each day for their daily bread.

If you read the complete story in 1 Kings, you will read the story of the death of the son and God's restoring the son to life. Finally, as Jesus would emphasize in his sermon and later in his final instructions to his disciples (Luke 24:47), God's love broke the restrictions of nationalism and was responsive to the widow's cry. This is a communion story worthy of repetition.

Psalm 146

The Lord watches over the strangers; he upholds the orphan and the widow, but the way of the wicked he brings to ruin. — Psalm 146:9

The lectionary offers this psalm as a response to the story of Elijah's experience with the widow of Zarephath. It is a prayer of commitment to place praise at the very center of one's life (vv. 1-2). It could easily have served as the prayer of the widow in response to the restoration to life of her son when she said, "Now I know that you are a man of God, and that the word of the Lord in your mouth is truth" (1 Kings 17:24). You can hear her bursting out in song, "Praise the Lord, O my soul! I will praise the Lord as long as I live ..." (vv. 1-2).

Such praise shifts the focus of where one places trust. Praise of God exposes the pretensions of power of rulers whose plans are limited by their life span (vv. 3-4). Neither Ahab, the King of Israel, nor the one who governed Sidon was able to break the famine or feed the poor in their midst. God is able to do what rulers often fail to do. God does execute justice and feeds the hungry. It is by God's power that one can have hope to triumph over all the forces that oppress.

God rules over the politics that imprison, the physical impairment that blinds, and continually seeks to right what is wrong (vv. 7-8). All of the vulnerable in the world from sojourner to widow to orphan, all who lack a protector, can count on God (v. 9). This God cannot be defeated by the march of time that finally defeats all other rulers. Therefore generation after generation can respond to God's continual reign in their lives (v. 10).

It is by our continual praise that we call to mind the only true focus of praise in life. The prayer becomes our prayer as we recognize how truly vulnerable we are and the limited way we can protect against such vulnerability. It is with such awareness that we turn again to the God who is not defeated by the physical limits of life.

Galatians 1:11-24

> *For I want you to know, brothers and sisters, that the gospel that was proclaimed by me is not of human origin....*   — Galatians 1:11

Paul was making the astounding claim that he had talked with Jesus after the crucifixion and in a place far removed from Jerusalem or Galilee. He was claiming that the message that he was delivering was not an interpretation but was a message told directly to him by the risen Christ, whom he admitted he had never met before the crucifixion.

This was a bold claim for the truth of the resurrection that seemed to violate the boundaries of what is possible. All of the theories that people have used to explain the resurrection within the limits of our earthly life fall apart if this claim is true. Here was a person who everyone agreed had died now speaking a new message to a person who had never met him while he was alive. It is a clear and unambiguous claim that life is not terminated by death.

This was also the basis upon which Paul claimed to be an apostle or one sent by Jesus. This claim led Paul to a radically new interpretation of what had happened in his own life. Paul was quite clear that God had set him apart even before he was born. Here is the intersection of eternity with time. God's purpose is neither determined, nor frustrated, by our behavior. Paul admitted that he was a persecutor of the church. He did this out of a zealous commitment to the faith of God's own people. But when God was ready to implement what God had already determined beforehand, the grace of God transformed his life. It began on the Damascus Road but apparently also required a trip to Arabia. It is not clear what happened in Arabia but only after that trip was Paul willing to talk with any of the original apostles. In this case, he talked to Peter and to James, Jesus' brother, another latecomer as a follower of Christ.

The faith that Paul proclaimed was not one among many philosophies of life but a truth that was shaped in eternity and entered time in a manner that transformed the direction of Christianity. What other truths of God are hidden in eternity awaiting God's timing for their revelation?

Luke 7:11-17

He was his mother's only son, and she was a widow....
— Luke 7:12b

Throughout scripture a constant theme is that God is and expects us to be sensitive to the cry of the widow and the orphan. They are exemplars of the most vulnerable among us. The widow, by her marriage, had left the protection of her own family, but then, with the death of her husband, she lost the protection of her husband as well. There were few means by which a single woman could support herself. However, if she had a son, she could expect to be supported by him.

The situation in Nain was that this unnamed woman had lost both her husband and her son and therefore would become one of the vulnerable of society. In this brief description of Jesus' response to her situation, we see an image of the compassionate God who heard the cry of the widow. No one called Jesus' attention to this situation, but he was willing to interrupt his journey to respond to her. Jesus' response was direct and compassionate. He reassured the woman and told her not to weep. Then he went to the funeral bier upon which the young man was lying and restored him to life.

We see in this brief story a description of the interrupted ministry of the church. As the body of Christ, the believers seek to respond to their Lord in ministry. Occasionally, in the process of carrying out that ministry, believers are interrupted by a clear and present need of one who has become vulnerable in the society around them. Their ministry, at such times, is to compassionately respond to the feelings of the wounded and to directly address the resolution of their needs.

In the history of the early church, it is reported that one of the reasons for the church's powerful impact on the surrounding community was its willingness to attend to the needs of the most vulnerable even when it meant placing believers at risk. They went out into the streets and took the sick and the homeless into their care. This was their choice of how they were to obey Jesus' commandment that they should love one another even as Jesus had loved them (John 13:35). It was by such acts that the world came to know that they were truly Jesus' disciples.

Proper 6
Pentecost 4
Ordinary Time 11

1 Kings 21:1-10 (11-14) 15-21a

> *And Ahab said to Naboth, "Give me your vineyard, so that I may have it for a vegetable garden, because it is near my house...."* — 1 Kings 21:2a

The story of Naboth's vineyard is a carefully crafted tale of the conflict of power in the world. A primary question of faith is what would happen if you truly tried to live a life of faith in a world that only believes might makes right. King Ahab of Samaria noticed a vineyard next to his palace that would bring him pleasure to have as a garden. As do many people of wealth and power, Ahab assumed that everyone had their price; so he made an offer to buy Naboth's vineyard. He was not trying to be unfair but simply assumed that the critical issue was the issue of price. Naboth, however, operated from a different set of values. Within the traditions of ancient Israel, all land belonged to God and was entrusted to families for their use. To sell the land for money was to break that trust and violate the person's responsibility for future members of the family. So he refused to sell the land. Now Jezebel, Ahab's wife, set out to secure the vineyard for her husband. She craftily used the traditions of Israel to achieve her purpose. She enlisted the help of the elders and nobles who lived with Naboth in his city to proclaim a fast. Such fasts were generally proclaimed in times of community stress to appeal to God for relief.

During the fast, two scoundrels came in and sat opposite Naboth and accused him of cursing God and the king. Naboth had used God's name and offended the king, who was God's anointed. Since it seemed right that someone had to be at fault for the stressful conditions of the community and since, according to custom, two separate witnesses had accused Naboth, Naboth was judged guilty.

The punishment was that he would be stoned to death, and this was carried out.

It would seem that the innocent can be unjustly accused by the powerful and even the religious traditions of the community can be used against them. But God was not oblivious to what was happening. He sent Elijah to confront Ahab and pronounce judgment upon him. The story allows that the powerful can take advantage of the innocent, but God will not allow such injustice to go unpunished. Christians would later see this same scenario played out in the life of Jesus and later in the lives of his disciples. God does not shield the faithful from evil, but he does not allow evil to escape ultimate judgment.

Psalm 5:1-8

> *O Lord, in the morning you hear my voice; in the morning I plead my case to you, and watch.*
> — Psalm 5:3

As a response to the injustice portrayed in the story of Naboth's vineyard, you can hear Naboth pleading his cause to God. "Give ear to my words, O Lord; give heed to my sighing. Listen to the sound of my cry, my King and my God, for to you I pray" (vv. 1-2). When a person experiences serious injustice and is powerless to resist it, it is appropriate for that person to place his or her cause before God. In a larger sense, this psalm becomes a morning prayer in which we orient our whole day as we begin to live in a less than perfect world.

We begin our day with a plea that God might hear our innermost groaning as we present the entire day ahead of us as a sacrifice to be found acceptable to the Lord (vv. 1-3). Later Paul will speak of presenting our bodies as a living sacrifice, holy and acceptable to God, which is our spiritual worship (Romans 12:1). We are well aware that there are injustices in the world in which we live, but we do not wish our lives to contribute to that which offends God.

Despite appearances in the world, we are confident that the way of the wicked, seen in the proud and the deceitful, is not acceptable to God (vv. 4-6). Our life is sustained by the abundance of God's love, and we are dependent on God's leading if we are to follow the path of righteousness (vv. 7-8). When our world is lived in praise of God, then even the injustices which we may experience can become our offering to God.

Galatians 2:15-21

> *... yet we know that a person is justified [or reckoned as righteous] not by the works of the law but through faith in Jesus Christ [or the faith of Jesus Christ].*
> — Galatians 2:16a cf

The traditional interpretation of this verse is that we are justified not by works of the law but through faith in Jesus Christ. The difficulty is that while the verse seems to emphasize our being saved by grace and not by works, it leaves open the possible interpretation that our act of claiming faith in Jesus Christ is a work itself. A growing number of scholars are suggesting that a more accurate translation would be to say that we are justified through the faith of Jesus Christ. This would emphasize the total and unmerited grace of our salvation. It is Christ's faith that serves us and nothing that we have done to bring this about. It is almost scary to consider the radical dependence on grace that such an understanding offers.

Paul made this argument as part of his rebuke of Peter at Antioch, who he believed had reverted to accepting that one's standing before God was dependent on the carrying out of the Mosaic law. It is not an idle argument even among contemporary Christians. What are the standards by which one is found acceptable within the Christian community? Paul clearly felt there were standards and was not shy about speaking about them to those he felt violated them in the Corinthian church. Yet are those standards an expression of gratitude for what Christ has done for us or do we subtly suggest that they are the means by which we access the grace of Christ?

There may be a subtle example of how Christ's faith serves us in the story of the healing of the paralytic in Mark 2:1-12. In the story, some friends lowered a paralytic through the roof to Jesus in a room below. Then Mark says, "When Jesus saw their faith, he said to the paralytic, 'Son, your sins are forgiven.' " Nothing is said about the paralytic's faith. Could it be that the grace by which we are saved is totally free of anything that we have done? If that were so, how then, would you look on your neighbor differently?

Luke 7:36—8:3

> *I entered your house; you gave me no water for my feet, but she has bathed my feet with her tears and dried them with her hair.* — Luke 7:44b

The whole theme of this story centers on our understanding of the extent of God's forgiveness. It begins with the Pharisee's treatment of Jesus. To invite a guest to your house and then not to offer him water to bathe his dusty feet was to deliberately demean your guest. It would be somewhat like inviting a guest today but not offering to take his coat or not offering him a chair. The home was more public at the time of this story, so everyone would have seen the insult delivered and watched for Jesus' response. Was the Pharisee deliberately testing him to see if all the forgiveness he was proclaiming would be consistent with Jesus' own response to an insult?

Apparently Jesus chose not to react to this insult and was engaged in the table conversation. Then this woman, who had the reputation of being a sinner in the community, came in and stood behind Jesus and began to bathe his feet with her tears, dry them with her hair, and anoint them with an ointment that she had brought with her. It was clear that she wanted to lavish attention on Jesus and was willing to do it from the position of a servant. To wash the feet, seen as an ugly part of the body, was the task of a slave. The

Pharisee, who had invited Jesus, and insulted him by refusing to offer water or oil for his comfort, judged Jesus as being unworthy because he was so accepting of the woman's attention.

The whole scenario raises the question of why we are so afraid of forgiveness. Jesus was choosing to demonstrate love for this woman whose past behavior was judged to be unacceptable. Her present behavior toward Jesus was being judged on the basis of her unacceptable past behavior. It made a difference to the Pharisee whether the affection being lavished on Jesus was from an upright person or a prostitute. Jesus chose to see her behavior as a sign of her gratitude for being forgiven. What would it mean for the Pharisee if he acknowledged that God had forgiven her? Would it not mean that he, too, would have to accept her and respond to her actions in a different manner?

Imagine a clearly identified prostitute and an equally clearly identifiable upstanding citizen entered your sanctuary to worship God on the same day. Who would you think was most accepting of God's forgiveness and how would that affect how you responded to each?

Proper 7
Pentecost 5
Ordinary Time 12

1 Kings 19:1-4 (5-7) 8-15a

He asked that he might die: "It is enough; now, O Lord, take away my life, for I am no better than my ancestors."
— 1 Kings 19:4c

Elijah had just won a tremendous victory against the prophets of Baal on Mount Carmel. When Ahab told Jezebel about what Elijah had done, she sent a messenger to Elijah, saying, "So may the gods do to me, and more also, if I do not make your life like the life of one of them by this time tomorrow." The sweet smell of victory did not last long. His life was threatened again, and this time he ran into the desert. Like Jonah, Elijah sat under a tree and asked that he could die. There are times for many when they get weary of the challenges of living. It seems as if they are repeatedly facing the same battles, and they see no prospect of change. It is what leads many people to seek early retirement. For Elijah, an angel came and provided him food and drink for an entirely new journey that he had not yet foreseen.

Two important truths are revealed at this point in the story. First, when we are weary and think that life is going nowhere, God may have a totally new adventure to offer us. Second, it is God who provides us the necessary food and drink for the journey. It is not our discovering the food, but it is God who brings the food to us. It is not even our designing the journey, but God reveals it to us step by step. Elijah journeyed to Horeb, known as the mount of God. The purpose of the journey was not yet clear. God asked him what he was doing there and Elijah went into his litany of self-pity about what had happened in the past.

God was less interested in responding to Elijah's complaints about the past than in preparing him for the future. God told Elijah to stand on the mountain because the Lord was about to pass by. There came the famous event where a great wind, earthquake, and fire occurred but it was made clear that God was not in these events. Then came the sound of sheer silence. It was in the utter silence that Elijah stood before God, and God provided Elijah with his marching orders. What is it that allows us to stand before God and hear God's call in our lives?

Psalms 42 and 43

> *As a deer longs for flowing streams, so my soul longs for you, O God.* — Psalm 42:1

Part of the character of our times is a disquiet within us and a deep yearning to touch the mystery of God. The repeated refrain of these psalms, "Why are you cast down, O my soul, and why are you disquieted within me?" reflects the dis-ease of our time. Out of our disquiet comes an only partially articulated thirst for God. "My soul thirsts for God, for the living God. When shall I come and behold the face of God?" That thirst is expressed in our culture through all sorts of religious and spiritual quests from "new age" eclecticism to an increase of fundamentalism. Sometimes the thirst is prompted by a memory of the practice of faith in what now seems to have been a simpler past. "These things I remember, as I pour out my soul; how I went with the throng, and led them in procession to the house of God...." Sometimes the thirst is prompted by a trauma that has shattered one's present security.

"I say to God, my rock, 'Why have you forgotten me? Why must I walk about mournfully because the enemy oppresses me?'" Whatever the cause, the cry goes out, "O send out your light and your truth; let them lead me; let them bring me to your holy hill and to your dwelling." Out of our disquiet comes a yearning to praise the one sure source of creative hope in the midst of chaos. "Hope in God; for I shall again praise him, my help and my God." It is in praise that we "behold the face of God" and discover our true identity.

Galatians 3:23-29

> *There is no longer Jew or Greek, there is no longer slave or free, there is no longer male and female; for all of you are one in Christ Jesus.* — Galatians 3:28

If, as Paul declares in 2 Corinthians 5:19, "in Christ God was reconciling the world to himself, not counting their trespasses against them, and entrusting the message of reconciliation to us," then this is the picture of that reconciled world. National identity, class differences, and even gender differences are overcome in Christ. This does not mean that the world is to be homogenized but rather that those differences no longer will serve to divide us. The vision of a reconciled world that is to be demonstrated in a provisional manner within the church is a community in which differences are appreciated for their value and no longer serve to divide us. We "are one in Christ Jesus."

Paul spoke of the law once serving as a disciplinarian that protected us until Christ came. "Now that faith has come, we are no longer subject to a disciplinarian." How would our lives be different if we could free ourselves from the "oughts" of life and shape our lives as a response to Christ who has set us free? It would not be an undisciplined anarchy because we would not be operating without restraint. Our restraint, however, would be seeking to honor Christ by how we related to each other.

Try to imagine what a church would be like that was liberated from the "shoulds" of the faith and pulled forward by the grace of Christ. It is a rather exciting future for which we are called to be ambassadors.

Luke 8:26-39

> *They begged him not to order them to go back into the abyss.*   — Luke 8:31

The authority of Jesus was expressed in a striking way in this passage. Everyone recognized Jesus' authority and in their own way were disturbed by it. The man possessed with demons begged Jesus not to torment him. Was it the demons talking or the man? Why would the man suggest that Jesus might torment him? Had he grown so accustomed to his status as the village crazy that he did not want to face what it would mean to be cured?

Next, the demons twice acknowledged Jesus' authority by begging him. First, they begged him not to be sent into the abyss: "They begged him not to order them to go back into the abyss." Second, they begged him to send them into the swine that were feeding nearby. Jesus' response suggested almost a compassion for the demons. Rather than treat them as an enemy to be vanquished, he listened to their plea and allowed them to enter the swine.

Then when the demon-crazed swine rushed down the hillside and were drowned, the people in the city asked (begged) him to leave. They saw the results of his healing in the person of the man sitting beside him now restored to his sanity, but they also knew of the economic cost to their village. The swineherd was a source of income for the villagers. Finally the cured man begged to go with Jesus, but instead, Jesus told him to return and proclaim the good news of what God had done for him. There was a fear of Christ that was present in the man, the demons, and the villagers. What is the threat of recognizing and responding to the authority of Christ in your life? Would it cure you, threaten your economic well-being, or throw you into a chaos of uncertainty?

Proper 8
Pentecost 6
Ordinary Time 13

2 Kings 2:1-2, 6-14

> *You have asked a hard thing; yet, if you see me as I am being taken from you, it will be granted you; if not, it will not.* — 2 Kings 2:10

Except for a brief reference to Enoch in Genesis 5:24, Elijah was the only other figure in the Hebrew scriptures that reportedly did not die. The manner of his death and its effect on his disciple, Elisha, find their echo in the later description of Jesus' ascension in Luke 24:50-53 and Acts 1:6-11. The manner in which first Elijah and later Elisha parted the waters of the Jordan also echoes Moses' parting of the Red Sea in Exodus 14.

For Christians, this story connects the two pivotal events of the Bible. God's power over death, as first demonstrated in the Passover event and later in the resurrection of Christ, was made visible in Elijah's ascent to heaven. This mystery that we call God refuses to be under human control; yet God continues to be present in powerful ways in the journey of the people of God. God is not bound by the politics of nations, the physical challenges of nature, or the limits of our natural life. While more powerful than any force that would seek to contain God, God chooses to be personally involved with people in their lives. This ascension story allows us a glimpse of the connection between the eternal and our finite lives. Even in scripture, these glimpses are rare and serve to remind us that what we do here on earth does have significance in eternity. The church becomes a mobile window into an eternity. Through its liturgy, the church lifts up the work of our lives to God in praise. By the reading of and meditating on scripture, we are invited to hear how our story is connected with God's story. By prayer we enter into communion with God. By the work of God's

Spirit, believers are empowered to carry out God's work in a way that splits the waters of chaos and offers hope to those in despair.

Psalm 77:1-2, 11-20

> *In the day of my trouble I seek the Lord; in the night my hand is stretched out without wearying; my soul refuses to be comforted.* — Psalm 77:2

The psalms are God's gift to us to instruct us how we are to pray. It is sometimes helpful to remember that these psalms were prayed by many of the biblical figures that we look to for inspiration. To think of Jesus praying this psalm in the Garden of Gethsemane can help us understand prayer in times of deep distress. Hear Jesus praying, "I cry aloud to God, aloud to God, that he may hear me. In the day of my trouble I seek the Lord; in the night my hand is stretched out without wearying; my soul refuses to be comforted." Does this help us to understand that there is a time to "cry aloud to God" without ceasing and to refuse to simply give in to our condition? When Jesus was in deep distress in the garden, he may have prayed, "I will call to mind the deeds of the Lord; I will remember your wonders of old ... You are the God who works wonders; you have displayed your might among the peoples. With your strong arm you redeemed your people, the descendants of Jacob and Joseph. Selah"

Doesn't this instruct us as well that when we are in times of deep distress, it is the memory of how God has been faithful in the past that gives us courage for the future? For the liturgy of the church to recall the stories of Moses splitting the Red Sea reminds us of God's way. In the words of the psalmist, "Your way was through the sea, your path, through the mighty waters; yet your footprints were unseen." We face the future, not with proof, but with promise and an invitation to trust. It is in the rehearsal of God's acts through the church's liturgy that people are given permission to cry out to God and to trust God for their future.

Galatians 5:1, 13-25

> *For freedom Christ has set us free. Stand firm, therefore, and do not submit again to a yoke of slavery.*
> — Galatians 5:1

The early church, like our contemporary church, struggled with the sometimes discouraging reality of the inability of humans to live together in harmony. Fights among church members are not a new phenomenon. There are a great number of people in our society who claim Christ as their Lord and Savior but do not want to be part of the institutional church. Yet the scriptures are clear that our faith is a corporate faith rather than an individual philosophy of life. Paul was convinced that in Christ we have been set free but was equally concerned that such freedom did not become a license for a selfish lifestyle. To exercise one's freedom without concern for one's neighbor was to become a slave to passions and fears. "For you were called to freedom, brothers and sisters; only do not use your freedom as an opportunity for self-indulgence, but through love become slaves to one another."

The choice for any church is between seeking to "love your neighbor as yourself" or to "bite and devour one another" and in the process to be consumed by one another. The latter is what often discourages people in their relationship with a church. Yet in choosing to disassociate themselves from the church, they are taking the exact opposite path from that which was taken by Christ. Jesus did not choose to disassociate himself from humanity because their behavior was displeasing but rather "emptied himself, taking the form of a slave ... he humbled himself and became obedient to the point of death — even death on a cross" (Philippians 2:7-8).

When the church fails us by displaying less than Christian behavior, it is an opportunity for us to display Christian behavior toward members of the church. In doing so, we are living by the Spirit rather than by the flesh. Paul provided a suggestive list by which we can know if we are living by the flesh or by the Spirit in 5:19-23. To live by the Spirit is to not allow ourselves to "become conceited, competing against one another, envying one another" (5:26).

Luke 9:51-62

> ... *but they did not receive him, because his face was set toward Jerusalem.* — Luke 9:53

It is so hard to see beyond the politics of the moment and allow God to guide you. Jesus offered to stay in a village of Samaritans, but they did not receive him because his face was set toward Jerusalem. A long history of political rivalry reinforced by religious prejudice had separated the Samaritans from the Israelites. They had once been part of the same nation, and they still worshiped the same God. In their separation, they had developed distinctive traditions, and those traditions became more important than the faith that united them.

Many of the divisions among Christian denominations have historical causes and hotly debated theological issues that have long since been forgotten by most of the people within the denomination. Yet in their separation, they developed distinct traditions and practices that now have become sufficiently important to prevent the realization of the unity of the body of Christ. In Luke's story, God in Christ was physically present among these Samaritans, but they rejected him because he was going to Jerusalem. They had long ago rejected Jerusalem as the center of their faith. In clinging to their specific traditions, they missed the opportunity to respond to God in their midst.

Next we are told that Jesus' disciples wanted to bring down fire and punish them for their lack of hospitality. Jesus rebuked his closest disciples for their tendency to want to use divine power to force recognition of God's presence among them. Finally we are given three incidents where otherwise good concerns became a barrier to their openness to following Jesus. The first man was dissuaded from following Jesus by the apparent lack of economic security. The second and third felt a filial loyalty to their parents and family that caused them to pull back.

Each of these incidents revealed the cost of discipleship that sometimes interferes with the most understandable of responsibilities. When Jesus set his face toward Jerusalem, his entire focus was on being faithful to God no matter where it would lead. In the process, many of the same entangling loyalties that affect us were exposed.

Proper 9
Pentecost 7
Ordinary Time 14

2 Kings 5:1-14

> *"Father, if the prophet had commanded you to do something difficult, would you not have done it? How much more, when all he said to you was, 'Wash, and be clean'?"* — 2 Kings 5:13b

As we listen to this story, we should keep in mind that it was one of the two stories that Jesus chose to illustrate his sermon in Nazareth that so infuriated his countrymen (Luke 4:24-28). The story itself drops hints of an understanding of God that far transcends the concerns of Israel as a nation. From the beginning it acknowledges God's involvement in the concerns of other nations: "... because by him the Lord had given victory to Aram." It also suggests that sometimes God's work in other nations may at times come at Israel's expense. "Now the Arameans on one of their raids had taken a young girl captive from the land of Israel...."

The heart of the story centers around the army commander, Naaman, and his desire to go to Israel, based on the story of a captured servant girl, to be healed of his leprosy. Kings, being kings, assumed that anything that was important that was going to happen would be directed by a king. Therefore the king of Aram sent Naaman to the king of Samaria to be healed of his leprosy. It was such an impossible request that the king of Samaria assumed that it was a pretext by which the king of Aram would pick a quarrel with Samaria.

We can quickly see how the normal assumptions of the powerful often overlook the more subtle hand of God in the affairs of life. Elisha corrected the assumptions of his king and invited him to send Naaman to him for the cure of leprosy. The king of Samaria had already made it clear that no one but God could effect such a cure (v. 7), so he sent Naaman in response to the prophet's request. When Naaman arrived, Elisha did not even go out to greet him but sent a servant out to tell Naaman to go and wash seven times in the Jordan. This is really a story of how God works through servants and slaves rather than those who presume to have authority and power in the world. Naaman, who was accustomed to the ways of the powerful and expected to be treated with respect, was furious at the way he was handled. He left in anger, and again it was a servant who spoke the truth to power.

One of Naaman's servants spoke up and said, "Father, if the prophet had commanded you to do something difficult, would you not have done it? How much more, when all he said to you was, 'Wash, and be clean'?" And so Naaman, who was used to giving orders, took orders and washed and was made clean. Later, Christians would hear an echo of this story in a Messiah who told them that he had come to serve rather than be served. As Christians listen to the message of a servant, they hear the word of God.

Psalm 30

> *O Lord my God, I cried to you for help, and you have healed me. O Lord, you brought up my soul from Sheol, restored me to life from among those gone down to the Pit.* — Psalm 30:2-3

One could reflect on Psalm 30 in the context of Naaman's healing from the previous lesson. Leprosy was considered a disease that demonstrated the punishment of God. It also forced people into social isolation. Even though Naaman was a very successful military commander, he may have felt isolated because of his skin disease. While he was not of the Israelite faith, his healing had convinced him that the only real God was the God of Israel (2 Kings 5:15). With the psalmist, he could well have prayed, "O Lord my God, I cried to you for help, and you have healed me."

What appeared to be a life sentence to the disease had been broken. "O Lord, you brought up my soul from Sheol, restored me to life from among those gone down to the Pit." Naaman could recall the arrogance of power that had been part of his past life. "As for me, I said in my prosperity, 'I shall never be moved.' By your favor, O Lord, you had established me as a strong mountain; you hid your face; I was dismayed." He came in power seeking a magic potent that he could acquire by his wealth and power and had to learn humility in the simple act of obedience. "Hear, O Lord, and be gracious to me! O Lord, be my helper!"

Naaman's response to his healing was one of praise and a desire to continue to worship the God who had healed him. "You have turned my mourning into dancing; you have taken off my sackcloth and clothed me with joy, so that my soul may praise you and not be silent." While the connection between Naaman's cure and this psalm is entirely one of imagination, it does help us to see how this psalm can guide us in our own prayer life when we have had our self-contained life interrupted by the grace of God.

Galatians 6:(1-6) 7-16

> *My friends, if anyone is detected in a transgression, you who have received the Spirit should restore such a one in a spirit of gentleness.* — Galatians 6:1a

It is not unusual for people who have been alienated by the church at an earlier time in their life to carry an image of the church as a self-righteous, judgmental community. For a community that proclaims that we are the recipients of forgiveness by a gracious God, we have a great deal of difficulty in proclaiming that same forgiveness to those around us. While the Bible repeatedly speaks of the judgment of God, it is made clear in Christ that God's judgment is for the purpose of salvation and not condemnation. The only people that seemed to elicit real anger from Jesus were those who exercised religion in a way that harmed or excluded others. Paul recognized the necessity of holding members of the community accountable for their behavior. The purpose, however, of accountability was for that person's own sake.

Once we have called a person to account for a transgression, "you who have received the Spirit should restore such a one in a spirit of gentleness." The mutuality of ministry means that we bear the burdens of each other and cannot absolve ourselves of that responsibility because a person has been separated from the community. Sometimes, as Paul recognized, our efforts at reconciliation may seem hopeless, but the very act of seeking reconciliation has its own reward. "So let us not grow weary in doing what is right, for we will reap at harvest-time, if we do not give up."

The criteria by which we can measure our own behavior was often described by Paul as the fruits of the Spirit. Such fruits, as they are variously listed in most of Paul's letters, are acts and attitudes that build up the community. In contrast, the fruits of the flesh are those ways of living that result in friction and dissension. Frequently they are based on that which seems to meet our personal needs rather than that which considers what is best for our neighbor. "So then, whenever we have an opportunity, let us work for the good of all, and especially for those of the family of faith." Imagine that as the mission statement of your church.

Luke 10:1-11, 16-20

> *After this the Lord appointed seventy others and sent them on ahead of him in pairs to every town and place where he himself intended to go.* — Luke 10:1

The mission of the seventy prepared the church for its mission to the world. First, it echoed the Genesis 10:1-32 account of the world following the flood being made up of seventy nations. Second, there may also be an echo of the incident in Numbers where Moses was instructed by God to appoint seventy elders who would share some of God's Spirit originally given to Moses. Since Luke was telling this story for the sake of the church, it may well be intended to prepare the church for its worldwide mission in preparation for Christ's return. In that sense, the church is to go to every nation and prepare them for Christ's coming.

In an echo of the Moses' account, there is a clear suggestion that some of the Spirit by which Jesus performed his ministry was now to be shared with these missionaries. When they returned, they reported, "Lord, in your name even the demons submit to us!" In preparing today's church for its mission work, there is the full recognition that while the church possesses the power of Christ as it performs its ministry, it is also vulnerable as was Christ. "See, I am sending you out like lambs into the midst of wolves." The church is not to enter the world as some fortified occupation force but as one that is vulnerable and dependent on various people in need of ministry. "Carry no purse, no bag, no sandals," and when you enter a house eat and drink whatever they provide.

The very power of the church is its identity with the people even as it seeks to bring to them the peace of God. There is also full recognition that ministers will not always be received warmly. When they are received warmly, they should offer practical ministry to the people's needs and proclaim to them that the kingdom of God is near to them. If ministers are not received warmly, they should leave that place but not without declaring to them that the kingdom of God is very near. The instructions are very practical, but they carry with them an understanding that the church is preparing the world to receive Christ. The task of the church is an awesome task.

Proper 10
Pentecost 8
Ordinary Time 15

Amos 7:7-17

> *I am no prophet, nor a prophet's son; but I am a herdsman, and a dresser of sycamore trees....*
> — Amos 7:14b

Sometimes we want to stay within the parameters of our profession only to discover that God has other ideas. Many who have found themselves called to a second career in the ministry have experienced just such a disruption of their lives. This can even be truer when people are called to speak out against some grave injustice in their society. It would be far more comfortable to leave that task to someone else. Amos did not seek to be a prophet, but God called him from tending his flock to speak a word to the nation. Not only that but he was also called to speak to the nation in the north when he was really from the south. Sometimes it takes an outsider to help us see what is right before our eyes. The story of the northern country of Israel was the story of the good Samaritan applied to a national scope. At the time of Amos, the northern country was experiencing prosperity and appeared to be quite active in participating in religious activities, as well. Yet in the midst of their economic prosperity and active religious life, there were many wounded and needy people in Israel who were being ignored by both the religious and political authorities in the community.

Amos chose to go to the equivalent of the national cathedral of Israel and declared that God was measuring them by how they treated their neighbors in need. Amos declared that God would not be mocked by such insensitivity in the midst of a time of prosperity. In that blend of church and state that so challenges our own nation, Amos was told that Bethel was the king's sanctuary and the temple of the kingdom and that he was not welcome there. The government did not wish to hear words that challenged the legitimacy of how they were governing, and they wanted the religious symbols of the nation to support rather than challenge what they were doing.

How does one balance the priestly need to minister to the people and support them in their struggles with the prophetic call to challenge the direction of our society? How willing are we to support those who do challenge the temptation of our society to pass by on the other side of the weak and vulnerable of our society?

Psalm 82

> *How long will you judge unjustly and show partiality to the wicked?* — Psalm 82:2

The lectionary has properly seen this psalm as an appropriate addendum to Amos' sermon challenging the justice of the nation. The psalm utilizes a metaphorical context of God calling a divine council to judge the gods. A contemporary application might be made by seeing the gods as representing the impersonal structures and authorities that shape our lives. In the Torah, it is made clear that God expects a measure of impartiality in exercising justice in the courts. "You shall not render an unjust judgment; you shall not be partial to the poor or defer to the great: with justice you shall judge your neighbor" (Leviticus 19:15).

God makes it clear that that same impartiality should be part of all the structures that govern our lives. A structure that favors the rich is not in accordance with God's will. Like us, God does not like a world where the wicked prosper (v. 2) or the defenseless and the needy are ignored (vv. 3-4). At the same time, a society cannot hide behind the appearance of neutrality that actually favors the powerful over the weak. It is wrong, for example, for a court system to favor the rich over the poor simply because the rich can afford to hire the best lawyers to defend them.

The psalmist describes a society that lives in denial of such partiality in their court system. "They have neither knowledge nor understanding, they walk around in darkness; all the foundations of the earth are shaken." In the metaphor of the heavenly court, God reminds the structures of the universe that they are not eternal and that God will judge even the seemingly neutral structures by how they carry out God's intention for justice (vv. 6-7). As with Matthew 25:31-46, it is not just individuals, but societies and nations that are judged by God. "Rise up, O God, judge the earth; for all the nations belong to you!" People of faith who do not demand that their country respond to the needy undermine the very future of their country.

Colossians 1:1-14

> *Just as it is bearing fruit and growing in the whole world, so it has been bearing fruit among yourselves from the day you heard it and truly comprehended the grace of God.* — Colossians 1:6

Paul's strategy in approaching a church may be instructive for anyone who wishes to address a church. With a few exceptions, he always began by giving thanks for what they were doing well. "In our prayers for you we always thank God, the Father of our Lord Jesus Christ, for we have heard of your faith in Christ Jesus and of the love that you have for all the saints...." He also made a connection between what God was doing in the whole world and what God was doing in their particular community. "Just as it is bearing fruit and growing in the whole world, so it has been bearing fruit among yourselves...."

All churches like to be affirmed for what they are doing well, and there is dignity in seeing a connection between what is taking place in a particular place and what is happening on a larger scale. Having emphasized those two points, Paul then expressed his concern for them and his prayers that their faith would be more than just an abstraction. For Paul, the truth of faith had to be embodied in how people related to each other. He urged them to "lead lives worthy of the Lord, fully pleasing to him, as you bear fruit in every good work and as you grow in the knowledge of God." All churches need to know that their efforts are recognized and affirmed, but no church can rest on its past achievements. There are always challenges that lie in the future of all churches.

Paul prayed, "May you be made strong with all the strength that comes from his glorious power, and may you be prepared to endure everything with patience, while joyfully giving thanks to the Father...." Perhaps the key to any church's life is the ability to face the challenges while continuing to give thanks to God in all circumstances.

Luke 10:25-37

> *Which of these three, do you think, was a neighbor to the man who fell into the hands of the robbers?*
> — Luke 10:36

This story begins with a lawyer standing up and asking the question that haunts all of life. "Teacher," he said, "what must I do to inherit eternal life?" As Jesus often did, he answered the question with a question of his own. Unlike the accounts in Matthew 22:34-40 and Mark 12:28-34, the lawyer was the one who answered his own question, and he did so with Jesus' approval. The lawyer was not satisfied and responded with an additional question, "Who is my neighbor?" In response, Jesus told the story of the Good Samaritan. When Jesus finished telling the story, Jesus asked the lawyer which one of the three figures in the story had been a neighbor. If we are going to love our neighbor, which one is the neighbor that we are to love? We protect ourselves by classifying who is worthy of our response and who fails to qualify for our kindness. Jesus turned the question upside down and told the lawyer that a neighbor was one who showed mercy rather than the one who needed it. It is easy to love one who shows mercy.

The question of who deserves our love is reversed and seems to be rather do we deserve anyone else's love? Because the story deliberately casts the normally disliked Samaritan into the role of hero, we know that we are not worthy because of who we are but by the mercy we show. It also suggests that the quality of our mercy is increased when it comes to the one who least expects it. The Samaritan had ample reason to justify his not stopping because of a history of antagonism between the Jews and the Samaritans. We prove to be neighborly by being responsive to those who least deserve it because that is the way that God has loved us.

Proper 11
Pentecost 9
Ordinary Time 16

Amos 8:1-12

> *The time is surely coming, says the Lord God, when I will send a famine on the land; not a famine of bread, or a thirst for water, but of hearing the words of the Lord.* — Amos 8:11

For anyone who wants to know whether the church should be involved with the issues of economic justice, they need only to read Amos. Amos spoke to Israel at a time when the nation was economically prosperous. By every indication, it was also a time in which people were active in the practice of their religion. In the midst of this prosperity, Amos recognized a widening gap between the faith that was proclaimed and the economic realities of the society. People had become increasingly obsessed with gathering wealth and increasingly unconcerned with the plight of the poor. In Amos' words, "Hear this, you that trample on the needy, and bring to ruin the poor of the land, saying, 'When will the new moon be over so that we may sell grain; and the sabbath, so that we may offer wheat for sale?' "

The difference between this description and how it might be described today is that we no longer feel the constraint of religious days on our economic activities. The mantra of our time is expressed in the advertisements that suggest that people will be available 24/7. In Amos' time, the people still observed the rituals of religious obedience, but their spirit was focused on the gathering of wealth. The economic obsession had the result of turning people into objects rather than humans. "We will make the ephah small and the shekel great, and practice deceit with false balances, buying the poor for silver and the needy for a pair of sandals, and selling the sweepings of the wheat." The sweepings of the wheat was an urban form of leaving the edges of the field available for the poor to glean. Amos was doing more than to warn the society of their insensitivities. He was declaring that God had grown weary of waiting for them to change and would bring a harsh judgment upon them. He would send a famine, but it would not be a famine of food or drink but a famine of hearing the words of the Lord. God, who had chosen to be present to this people through their entire journey, was choosing to withdraw from their presence.

Up until this time, their faith attested to the belief that it was God who sustained them and nurtured them even when they ignored God. Now Amos was suggesting that God would ignore them. As will be later pictured in Matthew 25:31-46, the nations were judged by how they responded to the needy among them, and Samaria was found wanting. How would God judge our nation today?

Psalm 52

> *See the one who would not take refuge in God, but trusted in abundant riches, and sought refuge in wealth!*
> — Psalm 52:7

Our society is engaged in a massive debate over what you can really trust for your future. In the last fifty years, the affluence of this nation has expanded exponentially. While a large proportion of our society is active to some degree in religious activities, there is an increasing attitude of neglect for the poor and the needy. We resist the thought that our corporate responsibility could be exercised through government programs that we would pay for through taxation. At the same time, we use our affluence to create a life that is protected from contact with the most needy of our society. When the psalmist spoke of the godly, the author was often referring to the poor and the vulnerable whose lives were clearly dependent upon God. The most vulnerable of our society are under no illusion that they can take care of themselves.

The psalmist recognized that the most devastating weapon that anyone had was a deceitful tongue and words that devour. We can witness the debate of words that try to protect us from the suffering of the vulnerable. The psalmist could be speaking of much of our society's debate about the poor when he said, "You love evil more than good, and lying more than speaking the truth. You love all words that devour, O deceitful tongue." Much of our talk of compassion begins with the premise that the wealthy must guard their wealth against those who would like to take it from them.

It is rarely heard that those who have abundance have a responsibility to use it in a way that benefits the most vulnerable of our society. There is little apparent fear that "God will break you down forever; he will snatch and tear you from your tent; he will uproot you from the land of the living." In the end, as a society, we have chosen that which we believe we can most trust for our future, and it is not God.

Colossians 1:15-28

> *He is the head of the body, the church; he is the beginning, the firstborn from the dead, so that he might come to have first place in everything.*
> — Colossians 1:18

Paul's understanding of the church was that it was far more than a collection of individuals of similar belief or even an organization that attempted to perpetuate the faith. For Paul the church was, in some mysterious way, the continuance of the body of Christ on earth. This Christ was the very image of the invisible God who was the author of all that existed. Paul made a cosmic claim for Christ. "For in him all the fullness of God was pleased to dwell, and through him God was pleased to reconcile to himself all things, whether on earth or in heaven, by making peace through the blood of his cross." Christ became the very nexus of history around which everything — past, present, and future — revolved. And this Christ was the head or the source of the church.

Paul was fully aware of the frailty of the church, but he saw its suffering, and Paul's suffering as part of that body, as a continuation of the sufferings of Christ. In the same way that the first body of Christ had to suffer, so did the second or continuance of that body have to suffer if God was to be glorified. In the same way that it did not make sense to the world that God's Messiah would suffer, it also did not make sense to the world that if the church were truly the body of Christ it would suffer.

The suffering of the church was necessary to effect the reconciliation of Christ. While Paul was speaking of the Jew/Gentile division, he could be speaking of the other divisions within the religious world when he said, "And you who were once estranged and hostile in mind, doing evil deeds, he has now reconciled in his fleshly body through death, so as to present you holy and blameless and irreproachable before him...." The task of the church is far more than just to nurture its members in the traditions of the faith. The task of the church is to be God's instrument of reconciliation among all things.

Luke 10:38-42

> *Lord, do you not care that my sister has left me to do all the work by myself?*   — Luke 10:40

Many clergy could read this story with a great deal of sympathy for Martha. They know what it feels like to believe that they are carrying more than their share of the burden of making sure that all goes well in the church. There is also another small group within the church that could feel sympathy for Martha. People speak of the 80/20 rule where 20% of the people do 80% of the work, the financial support, and so forth. Yet all of us feel put on the defensive by Jesus' words: "Martha, Martha, you are worried and distracted by many things; there is need of only one thing. Mary has chosen the better part, which will not be taken away from her." The story raises questions about the practice of hospitality.

We speak of the church as God's house because we have set aside this space as a place of hospitality for God. While God cannot be contained by a physical structure, we have set aside a particular place as a special sign of what is true in all places. In this story, Martha welcomed Jesus into her home, and, in the back of believers' minds, through Jesus she welcomed God into her home. But Martha was "distracted by her many tasks." Since they were the tasks of making Jesus feel welcome, we are invited to reexamine the art of hospitality.

What was the point in time when Martha moved from feeling that she was welcoming Jesus to feeling as if her sister was letting her down? Is there a point in time when the 20% no longer feel the joy of serving God through their efforts and instead feel burdened by the task? It is tempting to compare Mary's role to the 80% who simply come to church but accept little responsibility. Yet there is a significant difference. Mary's choice was to focus her energy on "listening to the Lord." If 80%, or even 20%, of a church's membership did not allow any task to distract them from listening to the Lord, what might happen to the church?

Proper 12
Pentecost 10
Ordinary Time 17

Hosea 1:2-10

> *Go, take for yourself a wife of whoredom and have children of whoredom, for the land commits great whoredom by forsaking the Lord.*   — Hosea 1:2b

Has anybody ever listened to this story from Gomer's perspective? Here I am the wife of this prophet. It is not easy being a prophet's wife. A prophet feels driven by an inner compulsion. Prophets lives are not their own and all those around them are all part of their message. A prophet's wife never feels like a whole person. You are like a piece of a puzzle that only your husband sees in his mind's eye. He calls one of our children Jezreel after some defeat he saw coming for Israel. Another he calls "Not pitied" and a third "Not my people" because he sees God withdrawing pity and separating himself from Israel. It is not fair for children to represent their father's vision or to carry out their father's dream.

And what about me? I also begin to feel like I am just an appendage to my husband and not a real person in my own right. I made a mistake. I'll admit it. I had an affair. I know I should not have had an affair, but I was so lonely. For a moment I thought someone else could make me feel important. It was wrong, but maybe I understand how people stray from God now. Sometimes you get lonely and frightened. God seems so distant and unpredictable and something comes along that feels more real. You reach out and, only too late, do you realize that it is an illusion. I did, anyway.

I know that Hosea's God is a demanding God, and I thought there might be an easier way in the arms of a lover. I have to admit that when I realized what a fool I was, Hosea was still there ready to take me back. Like his God, Hosea still loves me and welcomes me home like a prodigal daughter. But then comes another problem. How do I accept forgiveness? Hosea sees himself acting like God acts toward Israel. But every day I look at his face, and it reminds me of my guilt. Here he is, Mr. Righteous, looking with pity on this adulteress. I think unless you have been there, you cannot understand what it means to accept forgiveness. If God wants to save his people, God will have to come and live among us.

Psalm 85

> *Steadfast love and faithfulness will meet; righteousness and peace will kiss each other. Faithfulness will spring up from the ground, and righteousness will look down from the sky.* — Psalm 85:10-11

Psalm 85 celebrates Israel's return from exile but probes the fact that upon their return all was not well. From Israel's perspective, the fact that Cyrus let them return was a sign of God's forgiveness for the sins that had gotten them into trouble in the first place. "You forgave the iniquity of your people; you pardoned all their sin." But when they returned, they found a land of abject poverty. The psalmist challenged God to complete the divine forgiveness by saving this people from the ruinous poverty in which they found themselves (vv. 4-7). This psalm invites us to boldness in our prayer life that many might at first find uncomfortable.

It is one thing to thank God for the blessings of life and quite another to challenge God. "Will you be angry with us forever? Will you prolong your anger to all generations?" The psalmist was confident that the character of God was one of steadfast love, and that the conditions of his people did not reflect this steadfast love. So he put his case before God, "Let me hear what God the Lord will speak...." We are encouraged to place our case before God because we know the character of God.

One of the intents of God in calling a people to be God's people was to make God's glory manifest on earth. While the psalmist could understand that the exile was God's punishment for the sins of the people, their restoration was a sign of God's forgiveness. That forgiveness would not be visible to the world if it meant that God's people now lived in abject poverty. "Surely his salvation is at hand for those who fear him, that his glory may dwell in our land."

To pray, "Your kingdom come, your will be done, on earth as it is in heaven," is to pray for a transformed earth. "Steadfast love [of God] and faithfulness [of people] will meet; righteousness and peace will kiss each other." By the instructions of the psalmist, we learn that our prayer life is expected to be a two-way street of shared expectations. God expects faithfulness from us, and we can expect steadfast love from God. "Faithfulness will spring up from the ground, and righteousness will look down from the sky."

Colossians 2:6-15 (16-19)

> *He disarmed the rulers and authorities and made a public example of them, triumphing over them in it.*
> — Colossians 2:15

Previously, Paul had asserted that Jesus was head of the body, the church (Colossians 1:18). In this passage, Paul expanded that claim and asserted that Christ is "head of every ruler and authority." This was not one among several competing philosophies and human traditions but the very core of reality in the universe that Paul was talking about. Circumcision was the physical act by which the Jewish people were marked as belonging to God. Paul asserted that there was a spiritual circumcision through baptism by which God claimed all peoples. Physical circumcision was restricted to males who practiced the law of Moses. This spiritual circumcision through baptism erased the barrier between males and females and that between Jews and Gentiles.

While this universal dimension to God's purpose had been glimpsed in the words of various figures in the Hebrew scriptures, it was now made abundantly clear in the crucifixion of Jesus. Jesus had challenged many of the accepted traditions of Israel in his ministry. He seemed to have violated the sabbath, eaten meals with tax collectors and sinners, presumed to speak for God in offering forgiveness of sins, and been found lacking by many of the religious leaders of the day. It had become an accepted understanding of the law, as expressed in Deuteronomy 21:22-23, that "anyone hung on a tree is under God's curse."

Therefore, by all that the best thinkers in Israel believed to be sacred, Jesus died a sinner rejected by God. Jesus, who proclaimed the steadfast love and grace of God, was seen by the law to be a sinner. Yet his resurrection revealed God's affirmation of Jesus. God allowed this law that condemned Jesus to be nailed to the cross (v. 14) and erased the record against him through the resurrection. The Roman rulers and the religious authorities had exercised their power against Jesus in a public execution. Jesus "made a public example of them, triumphing over them in it."

Luke 11:1-13

Lord, teach us to pray, as John taught his disciples.
— Luke 11:1b

While the form of the Lord's Prayer that we are accustomed to is that given in Matthew, Luke offers a stripped down version of the familiar prayer. This variation reminds us that it is not the form of the prayer but the approach to God that is important. We are to begin all our prayers with an approach to God that is both intimate and respectful. "Father, hallowed be your name." In that relationship, we recognize God is like an intimate parent and yet is also holy other. God can be depended upon but should not be trivialized. Our prayer should not begin with first focusing on our own needs but in recognizing God's rule in the world. So we pray, "Your kingdom come."

To pray for God's kingdom to come is to pray for a historical, political, global change to come about. It is in that context that we also pray for a daily trust in God to meet our personal needs. "Give us each day our daily bread." This petition reminds us of the experience of Israel in the wilderness where God provided them manna to eat. God told them that they would receive manna each day (Exodus 16), but they, being concerned about the future, decided to gather enough for several days. The extra that they hoarded for the future spoiled, and God reminded them that they must learn to trust God each day for their daily bread.

The warning in the wilderness story is that if we gather more than we need for our daily provision, it will spoil. The reality is that when we hoard too much and lose the capacity to daily trust God, it spoils us. Having placed ourselves in the hand of an intimate, yet awesome, God and committed ourselves to God's agenda, we turn and focus on our interpersonal relationships.

"And forgive us our sins, for we ourselves forgive everyone indebted to us." There seems to be an almost conditional clause in this petition. Yet it is also a recognition that our capacity to really forgive others is grounded in the forgiveness that we have received from God in our own lives. It may also suggest that for us to fully recognize God's forgiveness in our own lives, we need to offer forgiveness to our neighbor.

The prayer is concluded with a petition that God not bring us to a time of trial. While we can recognize that God often uses times of trial to strengthen our faith, we are always fearful that the next trial will overwhelm us. In this spare version of the prayer, we see an outline for all of our prayers.

Proper 13
Pentecost 11
Ordinary Time 18

Hosea 11:1-11

> *When Israel was a child, I loved him, and out of Egypt*
> *I called my son.* — Hosea 11:1

Hosea continued to use the various images of a family to envision God's relationship with Israel. As God was preparing Moses to return to Egypt to lead the children of Israel out of slavery, he told Moses to tell Pharaoh, "Israel is my firstborn son ... Let my son go that he may worship me." Now Hosea, drawing on that image, had God recall, "When Israel was a child, I loved him, and out of Egypt I called my son." With a pain that only a parent fully understands, God agonized over the fact that this child of God had gone astray after idols. Like many a parent who reflects on a child's rebellious ways, God began to recall the tender moments when the child was but an infant.

To emphasize the tenderness of God, the imagery used is that of God as a mother caring for her infant. "Yet it was I who taught Ephraim to walk, I took them up in my arms; but they did not know that I healed them." You can picture a mother who once nursed her child reflecting back on those moments of infinite tenderness. "I was to them like those who lift infants to their cheeks. I bent down to them and fed them." There is that moment of despair when a parent considers the necessity of giving up on their rebellious child. "They shall return to the land of Egypt, and Assyria shall be their king, because they have refused to return to me." But even as God considered releasing the child, Israel, to the consequences of their rebellious ways, the heart of a parent recoiled within God. "How can I give you up, Ephraim? How can I hand you over, O Israel? ... My heart recoils within me; my compassion grows warm and tender. I will not execute my fierce anger...." And God began to plan for the return of his child.

"They shall come trembling like birds from Egypt, and like doves from the land of Assyria; and I will return them to their homes, says the Lord." Whether Jesus recalled this passage from Hosea as he formed the story of the prodigal son or not, both the parable and this passage reveal the agonized pain as well as the forgiving compassion of God.

Psalm 107:1-9, 43

> *For he satisfies the thirsty, and the hungry he fills with good things.... Let those who are wise give heed to these things, and consider the steadfast love of the Lord.*
> — Psalm 107:9, 43

The entire psalm is a litany of the saving ways of God. It rehearses the various conditions of life that threaten human existence and dignity and celebrates the saving power of God in each of them. The image of God that is celebrated is of a redeemer that is particularly aware of the needy in the world and works to extricate them from their problems. God's redemptive activity is not restricted to any one location, but God gathers the needy in "from the east and from the west, from the north and from the south." Those who are lost as in a desert waste and cry out to God, God delivers them to a home in which their needs can be satisfied (vv. 4-9).

Those who are imprisoned in a life of rebellion against God's ways and find their lives consumed by a deep darkness also can cry out to God, and God will set them free as a liberator (vv. 10-16). Those who are sick and suffer affliction can cry out to God and be healed by the great healer (vv. 17-22). Those who seek their fortune in business but find they are drowning in a great storm can turn to God who stills the storm and grants them peace (vv. 23-32).

God can turn the rivers into deserts and the deserts into pools of water that feed the hungry (vv. 33-38). God is contemptuous of those who misuse their governing power, and God is a continual redeemer of the needy. The wise take note of both aspects of God's steadfast love (vv. 39-43). God gives direction to the lost, freedom to the imprisoned, healing to the sick, and calms the storm or reorders nature for the needy. The church could take note of how Jesus' life embodies these various aspects of the character of God and how this same litany can form the outline for the mission statement of the body of Christ.

Colossians 3:1-11

> *So if you have been raised with Christ, seek the things that are above, where Christ is, seated at the right hand of God.* — Colossians 3:1

Because of the dominance of our secular culture, even our churches have placed less emphasis on heavenly images and shifted their focus to the practical aspects of living out our lives here on earth. Paul used the image of Christ, sitting at the right hand of God, as a way to reorient our perspective as we respond to the practical issues of our daily living. He set up a contrast between setting our minds on things above and on things on earth. We might speak of viewing things from the animalistic aspects of our nature that is shaped by our passions and fears rather than the more spiritual perspective of what serves humanity or God. By viewing things from the perspective of Christ, who has been affirmed by God through the resurrection, we gain an eternal perspective.

This is not a denigration of the material aspects of life, which are part of God's creation, but a decision about how to respond to the choices before us. To view our behavior from what Paul referred to as this earthly perspective results in the negative behaviors of anger, wrath, malice, slander, and abusive language. It might be interesting for a church, when it gets caught up in conflict that often displays negative behavior among its members, to step back and ask if they are viewing things from the perspective of Christ. In the passage that follows, Colossians 3:12-17, Paul described the type of behavior that he believed reflected the mind of Christ.

It is by seeing things through the perspective of Christ that we are enabled to overcome the many divisions that seem to plague our society. Paul was fully aware that churches do not always behave in a Christlike manner, but he believed that we are to continually strive for a renewal of our minds that allows us to reflect Christ to the world. Paul was very conscious of the types of divisions within his society, so he painted a picture of that newly reconciled world for which the church should strive. "In that renewal there is no longer Greek and Jew, circumcised and uncircumcised, barbarian, Scythian, slave and free; but Christ is all and in all!" If you were to paraphrase Paul using contemporary divisions among us, how would you paint the picture for your church?

Luke 12:13-21

> *... for one's life does not consist in the abundance of possessions.* — Luke 12:15b

At some level, most of us know that our lives do not consist in an abundance of possessions, but we are still seduced by the possibility of gaining sufficient possessions so that we will be free to focus on other things that really count. The problem is that the measure of what is enough keeps changing. The commandment says, "You shall not covet ..." (Exodus 20:17).

In a society that is so focused on economics, that is a hard commandment to obey. No matter what we have, we are so aware of the fear of not having enough that we never feel secure. When we read this parable, it seems clear that the man in the parable was greedy, and we vow not to be that way. Is it possible that he was simply trying to be prudent with his good fortune? One year the land brought forth plentifully, but who could predict what would happen the next year? There could be a drought or blight, and there would be no crop. What should he have done? The parable does not say. Should he have given all the excess, beyond what his current barn would hold, to the poor? Is Jesus suggesting that our good fortune is never for ourselves alone?

The Bible seems to have the perspective that everything that exists belongs to God (Psalm 24:1) and that what we have is on loan to us for the sake of the whole community. In a culture that almost worships the concept of private possessions, this is a very hard concept to accept. But even if we accepted this theoretically, the problem is affected by our fears and our low concept of humanity. The theory is that if we have a lot this year, we should share it with our needy neighbors so that next year, if we are in need, our neighbor will share with us (2 Corinthians 8:13-14). Our own tendency to covet makes us fearful that our neighbor will covet as well; therefore, we enter a whole cycle of fear rather than love for our neighbor.

While we may not arrive at a state of perfect generosity, we can recognize the power of greed to distort our very nature. The alternative suggested is that we focus on being rich toward God. As we move step by step to that focus, perhaps we will feel the burden of the material lessening in our lives and our capacity to be generous without fear increasing.

Proper 14
Pentecost 12
Ordinary Time 19

Isaiah 1:1, 10-20

> *... even though you make many prayers, I will not listen; your hands are full of blood.* — Isaiah 1:15

Are there times that you feel like your experience of worship is a set of routines that you go through without any sense of spiritual depth? It is easy, at such times, to place the blame on the church or those conducting the worship. The prophet Isaiah spoke about those times when worship fails us. His emphasis was not on the structure or style of worship but the connection between what happens in worship and what happens in our daily living. Matthew made a similar connection in Matthew 5:23-24 when he quotes Jesus saying, "So when you are offering your gift at the altar, if you remember that your brother or sister has something against you, leave your gift there before the altar and go; first be reconciled to your brother or sister, and then come and offer your gift."

Isaiah made it plain that we cannot separate our acts of worship from the love and justice God expects us to offer our neighbor. He made quite a list. "Wash yourselves; make yourselves clean; remove the evil of your doings from before my eyes; cease to do evil, learn to do good; seek justice, rescue the oppressed, defend the orphan, plead for the widow." When you go to the airport, you are asked to pass through a metal detector to determine if you are carrying a weapon that might cause harm to someone. What if we had a similar device for worship, only it detected any iniquity in your life as you came before God? What if the iniquity detector measured you by your effect on your neighbor?

If your behavior, attitude, or position in life contributed to inequity, God's alarm would go off. Might we then see the connection between our worship and how we live our lives? Perhaps there is such an alarm system built into our worship experience. The alarm system is the feeling of listlessness in the act of worship. The prophet, and Jesus, said that it was by turning our compassion outward that we will again experience the love and praise of God. There is only one member of the audience when we worship and that is God. God sees worship and our daily life as intimately connected. "Remove the evil of your doings from before my eyes." We live to worship and worship to live. Worship fails us when the life we bring to God is a life that ignores those that God loves. That is why, early in the structure of reformed worship, there is a prayer of confession and assurance of forgiveness. We need that to make our worship acceptable.

Psalm 50:1-8, 22-23

> *Those who bring thanksgiving as their sacrifice honor me; to those who go the right way I will show the salvation of God.* — Psalm 50:23

Psalm 50 complements the passage from Isaiah that is critical of people who perform the acts of worship but do not allow their acts of worship to shape their daily lives. Psalm 50 is a vision of judgment centered on the relation between worship and ethics. Verses 1-6 describe the judge and his authority. God is the mighty one who summons the earth (v. 1) and the heavens (v. 4), who serve as the jury (v. 6). God is the chief witness (v. 7).

In verses 8-13, the sham of sacrifices as a religious act separated from daily life is exposed. It is not that people are neglecting the act of worship. "Not for your sacrifices do I rebuke you; your burnt offerings are continually before me." The psalmist then proceeds to mock their sacrifices. "If I were hungry, I would not tell you, for the world and all that is in it is mine." Verses 14-15 describe what God wants from the faithful as they come before him in worship. God wants them to bring a sacrifice of thanksgiving, to fulfill their commitments made in their covenant relationship, and to call on God in times of trouble. Instead, what God sees are people who are good at reciting God's law and speaking of their covenant relationship with God (v. 16) but who refuse to be disciplined by God's word in their lives (v. 17).

The parallel today would be people who quote the Bible in their speech and publicly brag about their church membership but who refuse to allow God's expectations to shape their daily lives. The psalmist suggests that their daily lives violate such commandments as those against stealing, adultery, false witness, and honoring their parents (vv. 18-20). If you were to identify which commandments are most frequently broken in our everyday lives, which ones would you choose?

God has given time for people to recognize their own evil, but they have taken God's silence as approval of separating their words of worship from the ethics of their lives (v. 21). God's judgment is now pronounced. Yet, God's judgment is always another opportunity to repent and live a life of thanksgiving and salvation. The invitation is to let the times when we are obedient to God at personal sacrifice be a sign of our worship and praise.

Hebrews 11:1-3, 8-16

> *Now faith is the assurance of things hoped for, the conviction of things not seen.*   — Hebrews 11:1

This famous definition of faith comes in the midst of the author's urging that the believers not falter in their faith during a difficult time. It would be an appropriate reminder for any church that is going through a difficult time or for any group struggling to achieve a cause against seemingly impossible odds. People who continue to advocate for peace in this war-torn world, or ethics in the midst of corruption, might find their hope in these verses. Most people seek encouragement by identifying small signs of progress.

The author of Hebrews recognized that sometimes you have to strive for those things that seem impossible even when you can see no signs of progress. To reinforce his belief that these are things worth striving for, the author reviewed the history of faith that revealed a variety of examples of the achievements of faith against all odds. He began with the creation story as a way of suggesting that acts of faith were a legitimate path from the very beginning.

In the beginning there was nothing that would give evidence that creation was even a possibility. Yet, according to the testimony of Genesis 1:1 ff, God was able, by merely speaking a word, to create the world out of nothing. This was not even a struggle for God but was simply the result of God expressing his divine self with a word. The question is how should people live in response to this mysterious power that is able to create visible reality out of invisible? The answer is that we are to live by faith.

The author offered some preliminary examples of living by faith and then came to Abraham as a primary example of living one's life through trusting in this invisible mystery that we call God. Abraham was pulled forward in life not in response to visible rewards but because of a promise made by an invisible God. It was by faith that he left everything behind to obey a God who promised a land that he had never seen. It was also by faith that he believed that God could produce progeny through his marriage to Sarai, even though it was clear that both of them were well past childbearing age.

Living in faith does not mean simply setting out for a goal and persevering until you achieve it. Rather, according to Hebrews, it means trusting against all the evidence that God can fulfill God's promises. The author of Hebrews made clear that his examples of faith all died before they "received the promises, but from a distance they saw and greeted them." To live by faith is to trust that your efforts on God's behalf are worthwhile even when you cannot see any results. We are a paragraph in God's unfolding story and none of what is written in faith is wasted.

Luke 12:32-40

> *Make purses for yourselves that do not wear out, an unfailing treasure in heaven, where no thief comes near and no moth destroys.* — Luke 12:33b

One of the realities of life is that what we treasure, we also fear we will lose. Whatever it is that we prize in life, whether it be wealth, family, strength, beauty, or recognition, we are also afraid of losing it. So it becomes our source of insecurity as well as security. We devote what we have to securing the prize, and then we become anxious about losing it. The result is that our attempt to protect ourselves separates us from neighbor and God.

When Jesus said, "Do not be afraid, little flock," he was speaking to those disciples who would make up the church. When he asked them to sell their possessions and give alms, he was challenging their source of security. The church is as subject to the anxiety of the material as anyone else. However, the church and individuals have to continually consider whether their trust for the future rests in their accumulation of possessions or in God. In Luke, Jesus offers the faithful a treasure of the kingdom that is beyond the fragility of life. No thief can steal it, and nature cannot destroy it. Jesus declared that our real security is a gift and not a possession.

God wants to give us the kingdom where neither thief nor accident of nature can threaten us. But to receive the gift, we have to detach ourselves from the many false attachments that so fill us with anxiety. "For where your treasure is, there your heart will be also." We have to live our trust in God to be able to experience God's trustworthiness. The offering in worship is not primarily a way to finance the church, but rather it is an act of worship by which we switch allegiances and attach ourselves to a treasure that will not fail us.

Proper 15
Pentecost 13
Ordinary Time 20

Isaiah 5:1-7

> *For the vineyard of the Lord of hosts is the house of Israel, and the people of Judah are his pleasant planting; he expected justice, but saw bloodshed; righteousness, but heard a cry!* — Isaiah 5:7

This parable undoubtedly provided the foundation for a parable that Jesus would tell about the wicked tenants in Luke 20:17 and parallels in other gospels. It begins almost like a folk song: "Let me sing for my beloved my love-song concerning his vineyard...." The pleasantness of the beginning is intentional. It is to suggest that the loving-kindness of God is like that of one who would carefully build a vineyard. Attention is given to each detail, and no expense is spared to make this as good a vineyard as possible. But then inexplicably, things go wrong.

Despite planting the best of vines, the grapes that were produced were not quality grapes but what Isaiah refers to as wild grapes. All of this is a buildup to explaining what the owner of the vineyard will do in response to his failed vineyard. At this point, it could simply be a sad tale of a failed agricultural experiment. The owner's reaction seems a little strong — removing the hedge, breaking down the wall, and not allowing it to be pruned or hoed. It becomes clear, however, that the owner of the vineyard is not just anyone but is actually God. This is revealed when the owner declares that he "will also command the clouds that they rain no rain upon it." This is clearly something that only God can do. Suddenly the ears of the listener perk up.

There is something more here than merely a sad tale. At this point, the meaning of the parable is made clear: "For the vineyard of the Lord of hosts is the house of Israel, and the people of Judah are his pleasant planting; he expected justice, but saw bloodshed; righteousness, but heard a cry!" Isaiah went on to denounce the growing disparity between the rich and the poor in Israel and the resulting failure of justice in the land. Since Isaiah was telling this tale as a judgment on the people of God, it becomes a haunting tale for the continuing people of God in the church. Are we risking our own destruction by the hand of God through our failure to pay attention to the justice and violence within our own communities? If we do not believe this to be so, is it because God has changed God's expectations for the people of God?

Psalm 80:1-2, 8-19

> *Why then have you broken down its walls, so that all who pass along the way pluck its fruit?*
> — Psalm 80:12

In a sense this psalm could be posing the initial question that Isaiah's parable was designed to answer. It uses the same image of Israel as the vineyard and recognizes that things have gone terribly wrong. Why, the psalmist wants to know, would God allow this to happen to the very people that God has chosen as God's own? It is the type of question that Israel might ask at any time that it has experienced disaster. It is the type of question that a church might cry out to God when it has experienced hard times. There were times that Israel's prophets would answer the question by saying that this is punishment for their unfaithfulness. Lest we be too casual in our answer, let us remember that it might have been the type of question that Jesus could have asked when his disciples abandoned him. It was the question he uttered from the cross: "My God, my God, why have you forsaken me?"

While the psalmist does not have an answer to the question of why this has happened, he is confident that God is still in charge of what will ultimately happen. "But let your hand be upon the one at your right hand, the one whom you made strong for yourself. Then we will never turn back from you; give us life, and we will call on your name." For Christians this was the answer that Jesus received through the resurrection. For churches, the question still needs to be asked as to whether their difficult times are the result of their own unfaithfulness or the impact of the faithless community around them.

Whatever their conclusion, they need to be able to affirm that the final outcome is in the hands of the one who sits at the right hand of God. Therein lies the ultimate hope of all of our problems.

Hebrews 11:29—12:2

> *Therefore, since we are surrounded by so great a cloud of witnesses, let us also lay aside every weight and the sin that clings so closely, and let us run with perseverance the race that is set before us....*
>
> — Hebrews 12:1

The author of Hebrews offered a quick survey of biblical and extra-biblical heroes who accomplished great things by faith. He also listed examples of those who suffered for their faith but did not personally see the results of their efforts. "Yet all these, though they were commended for their faith, did not receive what was promised, since God had provided something better so that they would not, apart from us, be made perfect." The assumption is that one must be perfect to enter the presence of God and, apart from Christ, that is impossible. Therefore these heroes of the past, for the fulfillment of the promise, had to wait for "Jesus the pioneer and perfecter of our faith...." Their very ability to persevere, despite the lack of any signs of achieving their goal, was offered as encouragement to believers who were now engaged in the struggle.

"Therefore, since we are surrounded by so great a cloud of witnesses, let us also lay aside every weight and the sin that clings so closely, and let us run with perseverance the race that is set before us...." It is not uncommon for dedicated Christians to grow weary in the face of the failure of the world to respond to God's offer of a better way of life. It is particularly discouraging when the failure of humanity is especially visible within the church itself. It is important, at such times, to recall the many patient saints that have toiled faithfully in our past.

Like the heroes that were mentioned in Hebrews, many of the saints' names have been lost to the pages of history and yet they are the reason that we are here. It might be ennobling for a church to occasionally research their minutes and identify some of the faithful efforts of people in their history. It is particularly humbling for individuals to identify people in their own personal history that have been significant in the shaping of their faith. Many may not even be aware of the impact that their lives had, they are the foundation on which we build.

A litany of such people who have toiled in a church's past could be shared in a worship service as part of that great cloud of witnesses that surround us and encourage us to "run with perseverance the race that is set before us...." And when we are discouraged at the effectiveness of our efforts, we should also recall "Jesus the pioneer and perfecter of our faith, who for the sake of the joy that was set before him endured the cross, disregarding its shame, and has taken his seat at the right hand of the throne of God."

Luke 12:49-56

> *I have a baptism with which to be baptized, and what stress I am under until it is completed! Do you think that I have come to bring peace to the earth? No, I tell you, but rather division!* — Luke 12:50-51

These are hard sayings for the church. In many churches the emphasis is on not upsetting people rather than challenging them with the urgency of the gospel. Many a pastor has felt the pressure of the church to not say any words that might be considered controversial and certainly not to engage in any activity that might upset some of the members. Most mainline denominations are repeatedly criticized for taking positions that have upset people and are urged to adopt policies that will be more acceptable to their membership.

None of us like to have our assumptions about life challenged, and yet the gospel described Jesus as having repeatedly challenged the mores of his society and the accommodations that many of the religious leaders of his day had made with the society within which they lived. One can imagine the response in a church if the pastor said, as Jesus did, "Now you [church officers] clean the outside of the cup and of the dish, but inside you are full of greed and wickedness" (Luke 11:39) or "Woe also to you lawyers! For you load people with burdens hard to bear, and you yourselves do not lift a finger to ease them" (Luke 11:46). While Jesus was referring to scribal lawyers, it might apply to our members who are secular lawyers as well.

The danger, of course, is that we will justify every conflict as a sign of our righteousness and fail to listen to anyone who disagrees with the wisdom of our behavior. While the gospel recognized that faithfulness might well cause division within the church as it challenged people's comfortable accommodations with society, the gospel also lifted up Jesus' life as the guide for our behavior. The baptism with which Jesus was baptized was a life that continually was lived out in compassion for others. While Jesus lost some disciples because the good news he proclaimed was too upsetting for them, he did not lose any because he lacked compassion for them.

In the story of the rich man who wanted to inherit eternal life, Luke 18:18-26, Jesus was clear about the false attachments that separated the man from what he wanted and compassionate in urging him to take steps that would bring him closer to God. No one should take delight in causing division among believers or in upsetting those who hunger for the gospel, but one must also recognize the urgency of the time and not be afraid to speak the words or exercise the ministry that the gospels make plain.

Proper 16
Pentecost 14
Ordinary Time 21

Jeremiah 1:4-10

> ... *I appointed you a prophet to the nations.*
> — Jeremiah 1:5c

While the earlier prophets focused their words on God's people, Jeremiah was called to be a prophet to the nations. As the threat to the existence of Israel and Judah became critical, their faith expanded their understanding of the sovereignty of God. It is natural at times of uncertainty and chaos to want to narrow your focus, but Israel did the opposite. They began to ask what it was that God was doing among the other nations and what their role was in God's work. At the same time, Jeremiah expanded his understanding of his call backward to before he was born. The sovereignty of God encompassed both time and space and was not to be defined by national boundaries or the limits of time. When we sense the call of God in our lives, we are invited to ask what God's intentions are for our lives in the larger context of God's work. What was the purpose God intended in our birth? We are asked to look beyond our personal and private lives and seek to understand where we belong in the larger context of history.

It is so tempting to keep silent in the faith and to feel inadequate in the face of the complex issues of our society. There is always someone who knows the Bible better than we do or has a better argument about the issues. Jeremiah was called by God to proclaim the faith at a time when society was falling apart. He was called to challenge the experts of faith and politics and boldly interpret what God was saying in the midst of chaos. His first response was to resist the call and point out his youth as an excuse. Like Moses before him, he felt overwhelmed by the challenge.

God's response was that God would be present and provide him the words and the courage to respond.

Many Christians have withdrawn into a private faith and have refused to provide our society with a framework to understand what God is doing in our midst. While it takes courage to speak in the midst of our chaos, Christ has promised to be with us as we teach the nations (Matthew 28:19-20), and God touches our mouths so that we might provide understanding in the midst of confusion.

Psalm 71:1-6

> *Upon you I have leaned from my birth; it was you who took me from my mother's womb. My praise is continually of you.* — Psalm 71:6

There is an axiom of the reformed faith that vocation, or the call of God, is part of each of our lives. Some are called to be pastors but all of us are called to be ministers of the faith. This is reflected not only in the practice of ordaining elders and deacons as part of our church governance but also in the belief that God's call shapes what we do in the world outside of the church. There is a certain dignity to the belief that our lives have a God-chosen purpose that is greater than the immediate moment.

In moments of discouragement, it is easy to conclude that our lives are useless and our efforts to make a difference in the world are futile. At times when we feel surrounded by problems, it is easy to wonder whether anyone really cares about what happens to us. Psalm 71 becomes a framework for our prayers at such times. Because we are called by God, we are invited to call upon this God in times of distress. "Rescue me, O my God, from the hand of the wicked, from the grasp of the unjust and cruel." When we are feeling overburdened by the stresses and challenges, we are encouraged to pray, "Be to me a rock of refuge, a strong fortress, to save me, for you are my rock and my fortress."

If we were but a meaningless collection of atoms in an impersonal universe, such prayers would seem to be a delusion. If, however, we believe that God has called us and personally cares about us, then it is appropriate to pray, "In your righteousness deliver me and rescue me; incline your ear to me and save me." We make such a prayer not simply from a position of self-interest but because we have some understanding of the very character of God.

If God has called us and intends for our lives to contribute to the fulfillment of God's purpose, then it is consistent with the character of God to provide for us the means to fulfill our call. While we do not pretend to understand fully the mystery of God's call in our lives, when we reflect back on the many twists and turns of our lives, we can sense the invisible hand guiding us. Our lives have meaning. Our "praise is continually of you."

Hebrews 12:18-29

> *Therefore, since we are receiving a kingdom that cannot be shaken, let us give thanks, by which we offer to God an acceptable worship with reverence and awe....*
> — Hebrews 12:28

The author of Hebrews drew a sharp contrast between previous manifestations of God in the lives of God's people and what has happened in Jesus Christ. Recalling the theophany of God on Mount Sinai when Moses received the Ten Commandments, he noted that God's presence was accompanied by "a blazing fire, and darkness, and gloom, and a tempest, and the sound of a trumpet, and a voice whose words made the hearers beg that not another word be spoken to them." While not denying that God was and continued to be "a consuming fire," the author of Hebrews described the new covenant made possible through Jesus as something that enabled people to approach God without fear.

The first blood that attracted God's attention was the blood of Abel that cried out to God from the ground (Genesis 4:10), but now, the blood of Christ has enabled us to attract God's attention before disaster strikes. The problem, as Hebrews saw it, was that we might reject this incredibly graceful invitation to be received by God through Christ. The author reminded his hearers that the people that refused to obey God after the first theophany were punished. God was not to be mocked.

God was trying to establish a people of God on earth through the giving of the Ten Commandments and the sprinkling of blood on them in the formation of the first covenant. Now God, through the blood of Jesus, was trying to bring about the kingdom of God that would unite heaven and earth. Could we expect God's response to be any less intense if we rejected this heavenly gift purchased at such a price? By this harsh imagery, the writer tried to awaken his people to the reverence and thanksgiving due God in worship. Because so many of our contemporary members approach worship so casually, it is perhaps appropriate to remind them that God is more than an abstract idea. There is an awesome presence and a consuming fire that has been mediated to us through the compassionate Christ. We should approach such a God with a profound sense of thanksgiving and awe in our hearts.

Luke 13:10-17

When he laid his hand on her, immediately she stood up straight and began praising God. — Luke 13:13

As you picture this story taking place in your own mind, you almost feel the weight of eighteen years of illness departing from the woman who Jesus touched. Can you imagine encountering someone who could relieve you of the accumulated stress of eighteen years that had bent you over? Note that the illness that afflicted her was described as a spirit. Whatever the spirit was in her body, there are lots of spirits that cripple us in our time. There are the spirits of anger, envy, strife, pressure to produce, and fear of losing our jobs. It is not hard to observe how such spirits have crippled people in our own churches. Note, in the story, that the power of the spirit was broken on the sabbath.

The leaders of the synagogue wanted the woman to remain bound by her infirmity until the sabbath was completed. In

Deuteronomy 5:15, the sabbath commandment was explained in terms of God's liberating work with the Hebrew slaves in Egypt. The sabbath was a time to liberate people from the crushing load of their lives and free them to love God and neighbor. Jesus saw the sabbath as precisely the time when people should experience God's liberating, healing touch. The combination of the sabbath, the synagogue, and Jesus resulted in the relief from that which had crippled her.

Consider that which is crippling or pressing the joy out of your life. Imagine weekly permitting yourself to encounter Christ in the midst of your weariness, allowing him to break the pressure of your stress, and allowing you to stand up straight to praise God. The sabbath is a principle built into the very rhythm of life. Life finds its meaning in being productive and feeling that our gifts are valued. Life also requires the rhythm of work and rest. Even God rested on the sabbath. If we fail to participate in this rhythm and allow ourselves to be consumed by our work, we will discover a strain that can a break the relationship with God and each other that allows us to celebrate the goodness of life. The stress will eventually cripple us and make us unable to praise God.

Proper 17
Pentecost 15
Ordinary Time 22

Jeremiah 2:4-13

> *But my people have changed their glory for something that does not profit.* — Jeremiah 2:11b

Jeremiah was accusing the people of losing their memory and forgetting the God that had formed them. The people would likely have been confused at his accusation. He was one of their priests, and he would likely have been speaking to them in a religious ceremony. It was the practice of Judaism to engage in what we might call a living memory. They did not think of the escape from Egypt as just an ancient event that happened to their ancestors. Rather, the exodus was a memory both ancient and contemporary. They continually reworked the memory as if it happened to them. It was their continual source of renewal.

Jeremiah believed that there had been a subtle shift in this practice of living memory. Even the priests had failed to detect this subtle shift. The priests did not say, "Where is the Lord...?" The faith had adapted to fit the culture and no longer challenged the culture to remind them of the God who had shaped them. "... The prophets prophesied by Baal, and went after things that do not profit." Baal was a god of fertility. It was a god of personal gain. Were the prophets becoming prophets of success and pragmatic religion and forgetting the God who had led them through bad times and good?

The people, said Jeremiah, have forsaken the "fountain of living waters" and pursued a life of "cracked cisterns that can hold no water." Water was the symbol of the source of life. The fountain of living water was a source of life that came from outside themselves. Israel wanted to be its own source of life. It built cisterns that it could control to gather its own water. But they were cracked cisterns that could not hold on to the very life-giving water that they gathered. This foolish choice had happened because they failed to recite the memory of the true fountain of life. For Christians, our core living memory is given focus in the Last Supper. It is the fountain of living water that God offers to refresh us. Are those who try to draw on the faith, independent of the church, unlike those whom Jeremiah said had tried to substitute cracked cisterns for the fountain of living water? The water is still life-giving, but the well is often shallow and the faith grows stale. It is in the memory rehearsed by the church that we again encounter the fountain of living water.

Psalm 81:1, 10-16

> *I would feed you with the finest of wheat, and with honey from the rock I would satisfy you.* — Psalm 81:16

This psalm reminds us of a central feature of Israel's faith that has been preserved in the Christian faith as well. The center of both Israel's life and that of Christians is worship. It is in worship that we reaffirm our central identity. Psalm 81 is a call to praise by the entire worshiping community. "Sing aloud to God our strength; shout for joy to the God of Jacob." It is in worship that we reaffirm our allegiance to God who has called us forth as a people. A principle way that we do that is by a liturgy that engages us in remembering the history of God who has repeatedly heard the cry of the people (vv. 5-7a). It is also in worship that we hear God appealing to us afresh (v. 8) and reminding us of the misplaced priorities that have become gods for us (v. 9). It is by remembering how God has been faithful to God's people and to us as individuals that we are given courage to face the future. "I am the Lord your God, who brought you up out of the land of Egypt. Open your mouth wide and I will fill it." It is also by the memory rehearsed in worship that we are reminded of the consequence of our failure to listen to God in our past (vv. 11-12). Out of that memory comes an appeal to renewed faithfulness. "O that my people would listen to me, that Israel would walk in my ways!"

Without regular worship, which re-members us as a community with God and each other, we quickly forget and succumb to a world that resists God. The final line of this prayer reminds us of the desire of God to care for us. "I would feed you with the finest of wheat, and with honey from the rock I would satisfy you." The proleptic image of this messianic banquet in the future is preserved for us in the communion meal, which is also a living memory.

Hebrews 13:1-8, 15-16

> *Let mutual love continue. Do not neglect to show hospitality to strangers, for by doing that some have entertained angels without knowing it.*
> — Hebrews 13:1-2

As Hebrews drew to a close, the author exhorted them to a style of life together that would embody the faith that they proclaimed. It was centered in mutual love that continued to build up the body. It was out of that experience of loving and being loved that Christians found the power to love beyond their community. "We love because he first loved us" (1 John 4:19). The practice of Middle-Eastern hospitality was lifted to a new level by remembering when Abraham welcomed strangers at the Oak of Mamre (Genesis 18:1-15) and discovered that he was welcoming angels.

Drawing on this ancient story, Christians were urged to always welcome strangers because they might well be entertaining angels without knowing it. Christians were also urged to fulfill the commandment of loving your neighbor as yourself by trying to place themselves in the other person's situation. Particularly they were to think of prisoners and those being tortured as if it were happening for them.

This same manner of identifying with the other and allowing that to shape one's actions led the author to affirm the sacredness of the covenant of marriage. In a community of mutual love, it was important to honor the commitments that people had within the community and not allow lustful impulses to destroy the bonds of trust that were essential.

Finally, there was a warning against the love of money. Clearly the problem of wealth becoming a major factor that divides the community of faith is something that has been true from the beginning. The same instructions could be of value to any Christian community as they seek to embody the way of Christ who "is the same yesterday and today and forever."

Luke 14:1, 7-14

> *But when you give a banquet, invite the poor, the crippled, the lame, and the blind. And you will be blessed, because they cannot repay you.*
> — Luke 14:13-14a

Jesus' admonition highlights the problem of pride and self-interest that continue to plague the church in every age. Jesus talked about the position of honor at a banquet. Apparently there was a quite honored pecking order among guests within the society. He suggested that rather than presuming your position of honor and then suffering the embarrassment of being asked to move down when a more important personage arrived, you deliberately take the lowest seat in the room and let your host ask you to move up. You can imagine the effect if this type of humility was an active part of a church's ethos.

The obvious question becomes who plays host at a church and asks people to move up? Too often the pastor is placed in that position and then criticized for making the wrong choices. The essence of the parable was expressed by Paul in Romans 12:10: "... love one another with mutual affection; outdo one another in showing honor." The real challenge to our pride comes in Jesus' advice to his host. "But when you give a banquet, invite the poor, the crippled, the lame, and the blind. And you will be blessed, because they cannot repay you...."

Since this was part of Luke's advice to the church, what would the result of a church taking this advice be. Apparently the early church took this advice quite seriously. They had a reputation of going out into the streets and not only caring for but also inviting the sick and the lame to come into their community. The effect was that the church openly welcomed those that the society rejected, and the power of their witness began to spread across the Roman empire. The early Pentecostal movement employed the same strategy as they began to spread their message. Some historians suggest that this may have been the key to the remarkable growth of the Presbyterian church in Korea.

Unfortunately, as the church began to acquire more resources, the members also began to become concerned about protecting those resources. The mystery of our attachment to possessions and the way that they separate us from our trust in God still expresses itself. How do we learn to love others without expecting anything in return?

Proper 18
Pentecost 16
Ordinary Time 23

Jeremiah 18:1-11

> *Just like the clay in the potter's hand, so are you in my hand, O house of Israel.* — Jeremiah 18:6c

As a nation, we sometimes get caught up in the debate as to whether we are a Christian nation. Rarely do the advocates of such an attribution realize what an ominous path they are setting out for us as a nation. To be chosen does not mean that we have entered some special protected state. Jeremiah spoke to Israel, who did consider themselves a chosen people, and he likened them to clay in a potter's hand. The clay, here representing the nation, did have a measure of freedom.

The image suggested that the potter was finally in charge, but in the process, the potter was affected by the mysterious freedom of the clay. Sometimes the pot did not develop according to the potter's design. When the pot that was being cast turned out to violate the potter's design, the potter was free to begin again with a whole new design. Now try to apply this image to the possibility that we are a Christian nation. Because God has blessed us with such rich resources, vast fertile land, a uniquely diverse population, and an unusually stable government and economy, would it not be logical to assume that God expects much from this nation? "From everyone to whom much has been given, much will be required; and from the one to whom much has been entrusted, even more will be demanded" (Luke 12:48).

If God's intention for our nation is a people of diversity built on the mixture of a variety of immigrants and Native Americans, but in our sinfulness, the immigrants overwhelmed the Native Americans, enslaved one group of immigrants, and discriminated against several other sets of immigrants, is God free to destroy us as a nation and rework the clay into a new vessel? In both Jeremiah and the gospels, it is clear that what God expects is justice and compassion. If God is free to let us be destroyed and start again if we do not obey, perhaps those who argue against the idea that we are a Christian nation are doing so for our own protection.

Psalm 139:1-6, 13-18

> *O Lord, you have searched me and known me. You know when I sit down and when I rise up; you discern my thoughts from far away.* — Psalm 139:1-2

It is a very frightening thought to consider that God knows everything about us even to our innermost thoughts. How often have you had a lustful thought, a malicious impulse, a hateful urge that violates most of what you hope is true about yourself? How does it impact you to realize that you have never had even a fleeting thought that God did not know all about? This psalm attributed such a complete sovereignty to God that there was nothing about us that God does not know. In fact, it suggested that God knew all about us even before we were conceived. Now, consider that even though God knew everything about each of us, God still loved us enough to send Christ to redeem us. If God did that for us, knowing what God knew about us, how does that affect how we think about ourselves? Are we assuming that our judgment is superior to that of God when we start condemning ourselves? And what about our neighbor, whom God knows equally well?

When we are willing to harshly judge the person that God has redeemed at great cost, are we rejecting what God has accomplished in Christ? When we begin to think about the church and God's choice to work through the church to convey God's word, we have to be careful about being too quick to judge this expression of God's love for the church even before it was formed.

Philemon 1-21

> *I am appealing to you for my child, Onesimus, whose father I have become during my imprisonment.*
> — Philemon 10

This short letter has been a source of continuing discussion throughout Christian history. Paul has been criticized in the last century for not denouncing slavery, and he was quoted in the previous century in support of slavery. What is clear in this letter is that Onesimus was a slave who belonged to Philemon. Philemon was an active Christian who provided the meeting place for a body of Christians. Paul considered Philemon a coworker in the ministry. While it is disputed whether Onesimus was a runaway slave or a slave that Philemon had sent to support Paul during his imprisonment, it is clear that during his time with Paul, Onesimus became a Christian.

Now the question arises as to the place of a slave in a Christian home. If, as Paul said, in Christ there is neither slave nor free (Galatians 3:28), then how was Philemon supposed to treat Onesimus? Paul urged him to voluntarily receive Onesimus back, "no longer as a slave but more than a slave, a beloved brother — especially to me but how much more to you, both in the flesh and in the Lord." This faith that turned the world's values upside down and eliminated class differences now challenged Philemon to embody the faith in his relationship with Onesimus.

While we wish that we knew more, it is clear that the faith challenged the previous relationship between Philemon and Onesimus as master and slave. For the church to read this in contemporary times challenges us to recognize the impact of our Christian faith on our relationships. Where do we lock ourselves into preconceptions of people's places in the world and forget that in Christ all those relationships have been changed?

Luke 14:25-33

So therefore, none of you can become my disciple if you do not give up all your possessions.
— Luke 14:33

By the use of what is generally considered Middle-Eastern hyperbole, Jesus confronted potential disciples with the cost of discipleship. Occasionally a Christian group will try to implement this ethic as a literal prescription. What they usually discover is that some person or people enrich themselves off the devotion of the others and the community falls apart. Saint Francis of Assisi probably came closest to living out this ethic, but the community he founded increasingly found it difficult to maintain his strict adherence to the discipline of poverty. At the same time, those who seek to explain away Jesus' words quickly discover that there is a cost to true discipleship that is ignored only at one's peril. The essential truth that is conveyed through these examples and our reaction to them is that we are shaped by our attachments. While we often have a hierarchy of the attachments in our lives, and they sometimes shift in varying circumstances, we all have our personal set that shapes who we are.

To follow Jesus is to give a different priority to the attachments of our lives. Jesus recognized that the two primary sets of attachments in most people's lives were those that they have to their family and their possessions. It is not unusual for our attachment to one to loosen our loyalty to the other. Many families have had their bonds shattered because of disputes over an inheritance or some other financial decision within the family. Occasionally a sudden need within a family will cause someone to reevaluate their relationship to their possessions. To follow Jesus can challenge our loyalty to both sets of attachments. If a person is in a lucrative profession and suddenly feels a tug to serve God in a manner that means giving up their source of income, how do they handle the objection of family members who enjoy the material benefits that would be sacrificed? If people feel that their faith calls them to take an uncomfortable stand in the community that might embarrass their family, how should they choose? How are we to love God with all of our heart, soul, and mind if we are so attached to other people or things that we are not free to respond fully to the love of God? The cost of discipleship is not an easy thing to sort out, but it is not something to be taken casually.

Proper 19
Pentecost 17
Ordinary Time 24

Jeremiah 4:11-12, 22-28

> *I looked on the earth, and lo, it was waste and void; and to the heavens, and they had no light.*
> — Jeremiah 4:23

The picture that Jeremiah drew of God's judgment could easily be a description of a nuclear war followed by a nuclear winter. The earth "was waste and void; and [the heavens] had no light. I looked on the mountains, and lo, they were quaking, and the all the hills moved to and fro. I looked, and lo, there was no one at all, and all the birds of the air had fled ... the fruitful land was a desert, and all its cities were laid in ruins...."

Whether by nuclear war or global warming that destroys the ecology, the picture is of the destruction of the fragile balance that permits life on earth. In either case, it is brought about by the foolishness and greedy pride of humanity that believes they are immortal. It is almost a return to the pre-creation chaos noted in Genesis 1 before God began to speak God's creative word.

Jeremiah saw this as a global judgment in which all of humanity experienced the consequence of turning their backs on God. It was reflective of the judgment spoken in Psalm 14. Yet Jeremiah did not see this as a victory of sin over God's creative intent in creating the earth. God was still the one that measured the judgment. "The whole land shall be a desolation; yet I will not make a full end." The picture was of the arrogance of humanity running wild and, yet, God was still in charge.

The hope for humanity lies not in the progress of human knowledge. We have repeatedly seen how each new invention and each new technology holds the potential for both good and evil, and often we see its destructive edge. Our advance in knowledge will not save us from destruction. Our hope lies in the sovereignty and faithfulness of God who measures judgment and will not give up.

Psalm 14

> *Fools say in their hearts, "There is no God."*
> — Psalm 14:1a

It helps add context to this psalm if you read it with the story of Israel's slavery in Egypt in mind. When the psalmist prayed, "Fools say in their hearts, 'There is no God,' " you can see him viewing the Egyptian society that seemed to enslave and oppress the Hebrews without any remorse. As a society, he could say, "They are corrupt, they do abominable deeds; there is no one who does good." In such a society that had no accountability to a God who transcended them, the people lacked the necessary impetus to do good when doing good required any sacrifice of personal comfort and security. The society was undergirded up by the free labor of the slaves and to suddenly set them free would cause an economic disruption costly to those who had benefited from this arrangement.

"They have all gone astray, they are all alike perverse; there is no one who does good, no, not one." When a society treats people like objects whose well-being is measured by their economic worth, then it can be said of them that the society eats up people like they eat bread (v. 4). The psalmist believed that we could not treat the poor and the needy in society with disdain or neglect without experiencing the terror of God who was the refuge of the weak (vv. 5-6; Matthew 25:31 ff). The psalmist's prayer was that deliverance would come out of Zion (v. 7), that people would look again to the source of God's revelation for a way out of the morass in which they found themselves.

The struggle for the church is how to witness to such a faith in an increasingly secular society in which people at many levels are treated like objects. The people are discarded by the economic machinery when they are no longer functional for the making of profit. If the fool, and the pragmatic wisdom of our economic machinery, says in his heart there is no God, how does the community of faith demonstrate by our lives that indeed God reigns?

1 Timothy 1:12-17

> *But I received mercy because I had acted ignorantly in unbelief, and the grace of our Lord overflowed for me with the faith and love that are in Christ Jesus.*
> — 1 Timothy 1:13b-14

The clear and undeniable fact is that the church is made up of liars, thieves, adulterers, and hypocrites. Our behavior toward each other is often full of pettiness and small-mindedness. Our attitude toward others is often self-righteous and intolerant. In a corporate sense, we could join with Paul in saying that we are "blasphemers, persecutors, and people of violence." Usually when this is said of us, we grow defensive and want to point out that we are no worse, and often better, than most people. Yet it is only as we lose our defensiveness that we can grasp the truth of the gospel and recognize with Paul that our very weaknesses are the basis of our most powerful witness. It is precisely in us with all of our weaknesses that "Jesus Christ might display the utmost patience."

The ability of Christ to effect salvation through people and churches like ours is demonstration that the power of God is made perfect in our weakness. The very fact that God approved us, like Paul, for God's service is testimony to God's amazing love. This is not a reason for us to continue in our sins, but it is reason for us not to be defensive in confessing them.

To paraphrase Paul, if God can choose scoundrels like us for service to God's cause, then this is an example of hope for the world. When we can freely confess to the struggle that we have had in living up to God's love and how God is working through us despite our weaknesses, others in the world can see hope for themselves as well.

Luke 15:1-10

> Now all the tax collectors and sinners were coming near to listen to him. And the Pharisees and the scribes were grumbling and saying, "This fellow welcomes sinners and eats with them." — Luke 15:1-2

Even before we get to the stories that attract our interest we are confronted with two questions. First, why were the tax collectors and sinners attracted to Jesus? Second, why did the fact of their attraction seem so offensive to the Pharisees and scribes? Or to put it in contemporary terms, what would the church have to do to be attractive to the sinners of our day and would such behavior seem offensive to the leaders of our churches? In typical Lucan fashion, the parables that Jesus told alternate between featuring a man and a woman.

The first parable, which featured a shepherd, raises a question of its own. It began with a question: "Which one of you, having a hundred sheep and losing one of them, does not leave the ninety-nine in the wilderness and go after the one that is lost until he finds it?" Members of Jesus' audience might want to respond, "Who would be so foolish as to risk leaving the ninety-nine vulnerable in the wilderness to go after the lost one? Better to cut your losses and protect the majority." Isn't that what contributes to the grumbling among church leaders if too much time is spent associating with outsiders and not tending to the members of the church? Jesus suggested that from a heavenly perspective, it is the lost one that merits our attention and effort.

The second parable featured a woman who lost a coin in her house. While the coin was of similar value to the other nine, she was willing to set aside her other duties and focus her attention on recovering that coin. A major thrust of Jesus' ministry was reaching out to those who were excluded and restoring them to the community of faith. This may answer the question of what made Jesus attractive to sinners. He treated them as valued children of God who were worthy of attention. He also expended his energy addressing their most immediate needs.

The answer to why the Pharisees and scribes grumbled may be similar to why church members grumble when they feel others are getting more attention than they are. It is hard for us to accept Jesus' conclusion: "... there will be more joy in heaven over one sinner who repents than over ninety-nine righteous persons who need no repentance." It is our resistance to Jesus' message that causes us to recognize our own need for repentance.

Proper 20
Pentecost 18
Ordinary Time 25

Jeremiah 8:18—9:1

> *For the hurt of my poor people I am hurt, I mourn, and dismay has taken hold of me.* — Jeremiah 8:21

Perhaps more attention needs to be given to the pain in the heart of God. Mostly we focus on human suffering, our own or that of others. Occasionally we may speak of God's anger at our behavior. How often do we speak of God's pain? Jeremiah lifted up God's grief over the condition of God's people: "My joy is gone, grief is upon me, my heart is sick," said God.

Why was God in such despair? It was because God had heard the cry of his people for spiritual sustenance and no one was responding. He had heard them cry, "Is the Lord not in Zion? ... The harvest is past, the summer is ended, and we are not saved." It is one of the striking features of our culture that there is great evidence of spiritual hunger among our population, but many people are turning to everywhere but the church to get their spiritual needs met. God's question, then and now, becomes an indictment on the church to address the spiritual needs of the people. "Is there no balm in Gilead? Is there no physician there? Why then has the health of my poor people not been restored?" The many experiments that churches are making now to discover how to reach out to the alienated and the lost often cause grumbling among others in the church. Yet the question remains as to how we are to feed the obvious spiritual hunger of the population.

Perhaps all of us need to recognize the pain that such a condition causes in God's heart. "O that my head were a spring of water, and my eyes a fountain of tears, so that I might weep day and night for the slain of my poor people!" Perhaps if we shared God's tears we might be more open to God's possibilities.

Psalm 79:1-9

> *We have become a taunt to our neighbors, mocked and derided by those around us.* — Psalm 79:4

Psalm 79 is a psalm of community lament. Unlike most individual lament psalms, the community lament psalm contains no answer from God. The psalm ends with the people having poured out their agony and now they wait for God's answer. Dr. Patrick Miller refers to these as holocaust psalms. Because of our general awareness of the horror that Jewish people suffered in concentration camps, we can hear them praying this psalm from those camps. Defiled, killed, taunted by neighbors (vv. 1-4), they cried, "How long, O Lord?" (v. 5).

As bad as they might have been, they knew that their oppressors were even worse, and they asked the natural question of "Why us?" (vv. 6-7). They appealed to God's compassion against any sins of their ancestors for which they might now be suffering (v. 8). They appealed to the character and reputation of God as a basis of their salvation (v. 9). The entire psalm becomes a prayer of any people who have felt their faith mocked by their experience of injustice.

In a less dramatic fashion, it could also be the prayer of many faithful Christian communities that feel themselves mocked and derided by the secular culture around them. It is natural for the psalms to use hyperbole in their description of people's condition. Within that framework, many churches have felt the derision of society. They, too, can pray, "We have become a taunt to our neighbors, mocked and derided by those around us." They plea for mercy, and then they have to wait for God's answer.

1 Timothy 2:1-7

> *First of all, then, I urge that supplications, prayers, intercessions, and thanksgivings be made for everyone, for kings and all who are in high positions....*
> — 1 Timothy 2:1-2a

How many people pray regularly for President Obama and for former presidents Bush and Clinton? How many pray for their current senators and congressmen? How many pray for their local politicians who hold offices within their community? We have arrived at a time in our culture when we tend to hold all politicians in disdain unless they happen to be those with whom we personally agree.

When Paul urged the people to pray for the leaders in high places, he was not suggesting that they pray only for those with whom they agreed. Tertullian once said that the emperor belongs to us even more than to the pagans because God allowed him to rule. This does not mean that everything our politicians do is right or God ordained. It does mean that they need our prayers. Those who are in government need our prayers "so that we may lead a quiet and peaceable life in all godliness and dignity." Recall that Paul was saying this at a time when Christians were very much in the minority and often considered little more than resident aliens within the larger society.

The second reason that politicians need our prayers is that God does desire that everyone be saved and come to the knowledge of truth. Regardless of how you feel about a given set of office holders, Christ died for presidents, current and former, senators, and members of Congress as clearly as he died for us. We are all in need of the knowledge of truth and dependent on God for its revealing. We should protest when we feel that office holders are in error, but we should also offer intercessions on their behalf. It may be by our prayers that they will be transformed. It may also be by our prayers that the offices that they hold will be dignified and respected by the citizens that these positions serve.

Luke 16:1-13

> *No slave can serve two masters; for a slave will either hate the one and love the other, or be devoted to the one and despise the other. You cannot serve God and wealth.* —Luke 16:13

Jesus gave his final summation to this strangely disturbing parable. You have to choose whether your devotion to God will shape your attitude toward wealth or whether your devotion to wealth will shape your attitude toward God. Repeated studies have shown that poor believers are willing to give a higher percentage of their income to their church than are wealthy believers. Could it be true that as people grow wealthier they determine that a tithe is far too much money to give to their church, so they keep it for themselves.

The parable began with the premise that a servant had been squandering his master's wealth. If all that we have belongs to God, then we are accountable for how we manage what we have been loaned by God. The servant, fearful for his future, used his position as manager or steward to build relationships with others. While it appears dishonest, the master, when he discovered what his manager had done, actually praised him for his shrewdness.

Jesus seemed to be saying that if wealth is your master, then at least use it to build your future. Do not fool yourself as to what is shaping your life. While your wealth is only on loan to you, there is a soul that belongs to you. This is the possession that really matters. You need to be practical in recognizing who can really help you with what matters. You cannot serve two masters. Is it the gift or the giver that you trust for your future? While this parable is told about an individual and his use of the wealth that is entrusted to his care, the truth of the parable could be applied to churches as well. All that we receive in a church is entrusted to us to be used as directed by the head of the church. Financial meetings should be profoundly spiritual experiences.

Proper 21
Pentecost 19
Ordinary Time 26

Jeremiah 32:1-3a, 6-15

> *Take these deeds, both this sealed deed of purchase and this open deed, and put them in an earthenware jar, in order that they may last for a long time.*
> — Jeremiah 32:14b

Prophets in the Bible were always contextual in the content of their proclamations. Early in Jeremiah's career, he pointed out with devastating accuracy the failure of Israel to fulfill their covenant with God. As with most of the prophets, the signs of their failure that he noted were frequently in the areas of justice and compassion for the most needy in the society.

Because Jeremiah believed that God was a God of justice, he believed that the nation would experience the judgment of God for their failure to care for the most vulnerable within their society. Because he also believed that God was sovereign over all nations, he, along with other prophets, often saw the movement of international politics as reflecting God's judgments. In this case, he saw the siege of Jerusalem by the king of Babylon as the judgment of God and prophesied that Jerusalem would fall. Then the nature of Jeremiah's prophecies changed from judgment to hope. Because he believed that the judgment of God was always for the sake of salvation; he did not believe that God would allow God's people to be utterly destroyed. As a sign of hope, he publicly purchased a plot of land and buried the deed in an earthenware jar.

God's judgment would be executed by the king of Babylon, but there would be a time in the future when God would restore his people to their home. It is the challenge of the church to discern when they need to proclaim the justice of God to the people and when they need to provide the word of hope that will lift them out of despair. God is both a God of justice and a God of mercy.

Psalm 91:1-6, 14-16

Those who love me, I will deliver; I will protect those who know my name. — Psalm 91:14

While the lectionary does not offer the verses for reading, it is important to remember that it is from this psalm that Satan drew the verses that he used to tempt Jesus in the wilderness (Matthew 4:6). Verses 11 and 12 read, "For he will command his angels concerning you to guard you in all your ways. On their hands they will bear you up, so that you will not dash your foot against a stone."

The whole psalm was an assurance of God's protection. Satan's use of the psalm alerts us to how scripture can be misused even when it reflects a central core of our belief. The belief that God protects the faithful has been a cause of great guilt for those who suffer traumas or disease in their lives. They are tempted to conclude that their condition is a reflection of their own lack of faithfulness. As Jesus' life clearly demonstrated, the most faithful of people can become victims of horrible fates.

A central belief is that we can trust God (v. 8) who has the power to deliver us from human or natural threats (v. 3). Like a mother bird protects her young, God's faithfulness can be counted on (v. 4). That firm trust in the faithfulness of God can, and often does, ease the terror of the night and the threat in the day (vv. 5-6).

This does not say that no threats will come to the believer. It does say that God will hear the cry of the faithful, be present in time of trouble, and rescue and honor the ones who cling to God in love and call on God's name (v. 14). It is precisely when one is facing overwhelming odds that one is tempted to place self, rather than God, at the center of one's belief. The temptation for Jesus was the same as our temptation. We want to make God our personal instrument, rather than the source of our salvation (v. 16).

1 Timothy 6:6-19

> *They are to do good, to be rich in good works, generous, and ready to share, thus storing up for themselves the treasure of a good foundation for the future, so that they may take hold of the life that really is life.*
> — 1 Timothy 6:18-19

The Christian faith always lives in uneasy tension with wealth. On the one hand, Christians recognize that wealth and good fortune can be seen as a blessing from God. On the other hand, as Jesus recognized in preaching so much about the dangers of wealth, it can be a devious temptation in one's life. Paul was concerned about the envy that one who lacks wealth can have of those who possess it and the danger for those who were wealthy. He reminded those who may lack wealth, "Of course, there is great gain in godliness combined with contentment; for we brought nothing into the world, so that we can take nothing out of it; but if we have food and clothing, we will be content with these."

Paul did not condemn the wealthy but rather warned against the power of wealth to distort the lives of those who had it and those who coveted it. "For the love of money is a root of all kinds of evil, and in their eagerness to be rich some have wandered away from the faith and pierced themselves with many pains." His message to those who were wealthy was one of stewardship. "As for those who in the present age are rich, command them not to be haughty, or to set their hopes on the uncertainty of riches...."

Riches can give one a false sense of security that can quickly disappear. Riches are entrusted to people for proper use. "They are to do good, to be rich in good works, generous, and ready to share, thus storing up for themselves the treasure of a good foundation for the future, so that they may take hold of the life that really is life." It is in our generosity that we create the foundation for the future that opens us to "life that really is life."

Some are rich in skills, others in personality or wisdom, and still others in material wealth. God has provided that to us for a reason. We discover that truth as we use our wealth in a generous manner. It is in this manner that we discover godliness and contentment that leads to true joy.

Luke 16:19-31

> *There was a rich man who was dressed in purple and fine linen ... And at his gate lay a poor man named Lazarus....* — Luke 16:19-20a

Right away we know that something is different here. In the normal world it is the rich who have names and the poor that are nameless. In the soup lines, we do not need to ask for names, but in the world of the rich, we bear a name with pride. The church was so uncomfortable with the nameless rich man that they have given him the proper name "Dives" derived from the Latin word for rich man. The rich man, though nameless in the story, dressed in purple and fine linen and ate sumptuously every day. The poor man battled with stray dogs for the crumbs that fell from the table, but he was given the name Lazarus.

When Lazarus died, he already had an identity and was carried to Abraham. The rich man, however, floated in the netherworld of Hades. Apparently there was visual and verbal contact between Hades and the place where Abraham was because the rich man saw Abraham and Lazarus together. Note that he called out to Abraham and not to Lazarus. It was not as if he was a stranger, for Abraham addressed him with a term of endearment by calling him *child*. The lesson of the parable was voiced in declaring that his prior life was seen as full of blessings and that his wealth gave him many opportunities to do good. We are not told that he was an evil man. The only clue is that he had the opportunity to care for Lazarus and did not even recognize his existence.

The gulf between the rich man and Lazarus was emphasized in the story as the rich man spoke only to Abraham and asked him to send Lazarus, like a servant, to bring him a cup of water. The fixed gulf between them may well have been a gulf of attitude, but it was not one that could be changed after death. The rich man was not without some measure of compassion. When he was told that he could not be helped, he immediately turned his attention to his five brothers that were still alive. It is significant that he still treated Lazarus as a servant. He asked Abraham to send Lazarus to warn his brothers before it was too late for them as well. The warning was that the power of wealth to blind one to simple human realities is so powerful that it is almost impossible to overcome.

Proper 22
Pentecost 20
Ordinary Time 27

Lamentations 1:1-6

How lonely sits the city that once was full of people!
— Lamentations 1:1a

Lamentations is a communal lament over the disaster of Jerusalem being captured and destroyed by the enemy. Jeremiah's terrible prophecy had come true and the impact on the faith of the people was devastating. Israel had learned that when disaster had overtaken them, they still had the power of lament. This community was formed when God heard the cry of people in slavery and was moved to act (Exodus 3:7), and so, when all else failed, they could always cry out again in hopes of moving God to action.

The lament is a powerful act of faith. When disasters strike and all the structures of your life fall apart, the result is a loss of sense of self. The chaos around you leaves you feeling totally isolated and insignificant in the larger scheme of things. By uttering their lament, Israel was saying that there was still a power that could give order to chaos and that this power would hear their cry. They could not imagine what the new creation would be. They did know that nothing was impossible for God, and all they had to do was to cry out and then await God's response.

This, above all, helps make sense of Jesus' cry of lament from the cross in the form of Psalm 22. In the face of utter disaster, there was one that could make sense out of the chaos. There is a sense in which this particular lament could form the framework for a people's lament at the decline of a once proud and prosperous church. "How lonely sits the [church] that once was full of people! How like a widow she has become, she that was great among the [other churches]! She that was a princess among the provinces has become a vassal. She weeps bitterly in the night, with tears on her cheeks; among all her lovers she has no one to comfort her...." The emptiness of a once-great building can be a point of despair. "The roads to [this church] mourn, for no one comes to the festivals; all her gates are desolate, her priests groan; her young girls grieve, and her lot is bitter."

What the Christian community needs to learn from their own heritage is the power of lament. There is one who hears, and that is the one that can split the darkness by merely speaking a word.

Psalm 137

> *By the rivers of Babylon — there we sat down and there we wept when we remembered Zion.*
> — Psalm 137:1

If Lamentations is a communal lament over the devastating fall of Jerusalem, Psalm 137 is an individual lament from one who was exiled in Babylon and now had returned to see the destruction of his beloved city of Jerusalem. He recalled the times when he joined other exiles in sitting by one of the rivers in Babylon and mourning as they thought of Zion, the symbol of their faith (v. 1). Almost all of the psalms are meant to be sung because the music helps carry the emotion of the prayer. Perhaps they used their harps to accompany their laments. Then the Babylonians would come along and want to hear such sacred songs as a form of entertainment. "For there our captors asked us for songs, and our tormentors asked for mirth, saying, 'Sing us one of the songs of Zion!' "

The very request mocked their faith, and so they refused. "On the willows there we hung up our harps." The songs that were meant for the praise of God could not be used to entertain those who mocked God. "How could we sing the Lord's song in a foreign land?" To accede to such a request would be a failure to hold God in awe and would deserve the crippling (v. 5) and silencing (v. 6) of the blasphemer.

As the worshiper sat in the destroyed Jerusalem with his memory of clinging to faith in Babylon, he was stirred to anger by the treachery of the Edomites that led to the city's destruction. "Remember, O Lord, against the Edomites the day of Jerusalem's fall, how they said, 'Tear it down! Tear it down! Down to its foundations!'" Such deep anger so desirous of revenge (v. 8) and a cutting off of the dynasty that caused such treachery (v. 9) can only be given to God, lest its poison destroy the victim twice over. Faith in moments of despair must have an outlet for its anger, or the anger will turn in and destroy again. Only God can receive such hate in health.

2 Timothy 1:1-14

> *I am reminded of your sincere faith, a faith that lived first in your grandmother Lois and your mother Eunice and now, I am sure, lives in you.*
> — 2 Timothy 1:5

This letter to Timothy was filled with thoughts that challenge some of our easy assumptions. Those who think that somehow Paul turned his back on Judaism as a result of his experience on the Damascus Road need to reflect on Paul's expressed continuity with that faith. "I am grateful to God — whom I worship with a clear conscience, as my ancestors did...." While it was clear that the experience of Jesus Christ on the road to Damascus transformed Paul's understanding of the meaning of his faith, he nevertheless remained a Jew in his faith.

Paul also gave evidence contradicting his reputation of being negative toward women. Whatever the cause of his admonition for women to be silent in the church (1 Corinthians 14:34), it was clear that he recognized the power of women to convey the faith to others. "I am reminded of your sincere faith, a faith that lived first in your grandmother Lois and your mother Eunice and now, I am sure, lives in you."

From the prosperous businesswoman, Lydia, who formed a church in Philippi to Lois and Eunice, the role of women was prominent in Paul's ministry. At the moment when he feared that

Timothy might be faltering in the faith, he drew on the power of generational memory to reinforce his faith. It is not unusual for people to be carried through the valleys of doubt because they do not wish to shame the family that has nurtured them in the faith.

A third thought is lifted up in this passage is Paul's intriguing understanding of Christ. Christ, who Paul clearly identifies with Jesus of Nazareth, had also preceded Jesus. In 1 Corinthians 10:4, he identified Christ as the rock from which the Israelites drank in the wilderness, and then he identified Christ as the bearer of grace even before the ages began. While Christ had been present and active all along in creation, it was only in the life of Jesus that Christ had been revealed. John Cobb, in the *Pluralistic Christ*, explored this possibility as a means of recognizing Christ in other religions and in great works of art. Finally, Paul returned to the amazing grace of God made manifest in God's having chosen someone like Paul to advance the gospel among the Gentiles. There is enough here to challenge our faith for many days of reflection.

Luke 17:5-10

> *So you also, when you have done all that you were ordered to do, say, "We are worthless slaves; we have done only what we ought to have done!"*
> — Luke 17:10

In these final instructions to his disciples as Jesus began to prepare for the events in Jerusalem, his disciples began to be anxious. He had just told them that they were to offer forgiveness to the same person even if he sinned against them 77 times in a single day. Perhaps in recognizing the difficulty of being so forgiving, they said to him, "Increase our faith!" Challenging the assumption that faith was a matter of degrees, Jesus said to them, "If you had faith the size of a mustard seed, you could say to this mulberry tree, 'Be uprooted and planted in the sea,' and it would obey you." He then proceeded to explain that faith was not some achievement about which they could feel a sense of accomplishment.

Clearly none of them decided to test out their ability to move the mulberry bush. Faith, as Jesus explained, was simply doing what was normal for you to expect that God would ask of you. They were like slaves performing their duty rather than spiritual athletes achieving some great level of faith. There is a myth that great faith is some arcane secret that must be discovered. What Jesus was suggesting, and the church needs to keep in mind, is that true faith is manifested in the ordinary living of life.

Faith is manifested in the ordinary kindnesses that one person shows to another or the common grace that is displayed in responding in a tense situation. We grow in faith as we nurture a God consciousness in our daily lives. As we keep an awareness of God's presence in each moment in our lives, we will receive the power to do what is appropriate at any given moment.

Proper 23
Pentecost 21
Ordinary Time 28

Jeremiah 29:1, 4-7

> *But seek the welfare of the city where I have sent you into exile, and pray to the Lord on its behalf, for in its welfare you will find your welfare.*
>
> — Jeremiah 29:7

There are times when God sends us into exile as God sent Judah into exile in the time of Jeremiah. Jeremiah's instructions to those living in exile can well be God's word for us at such times. Our exiles come in many different forms. We may be exiled into a job or city in which we do not feel at home. At times we may find our place of exile to be among acquaintances that hold different values than we do.

For many in the church, their exile is in a denomination that refuses to take the actions that they feel are consistent with what they believe is true. The natural human desire is to either plot to return to where we are more comfortable or to at least yearn for that which no longer exists for us. Jeremiah counseled the exiles to settle in for the long stay. "Build houses and live in them; plant gardens and eat what they produce. Take wives and have sons and daughters...."

We are so prideful in our assumptions about the rightness of our opinions that it is difficult for us to believe that God could be working in ways that we do not understand. Imagine being part of a church or denomination that has taken a position with which you strongly disagree. In a sense, you are living in exile as surely as the elders, priests, prophets, and people to whom Jeremiah wrote. If you choose to make your home in that church and listen to God's admonition to pray for their welfare, how might your welfare as a Christian be affected?

Many of the fights in churches and splits in denominations are a result of unbending pride that cannot trust that the grace of God can be operative in that situation. To trust the sovereignty of God is to trust that God can accomplish more than we ever imagine possible if we will but trust in God's faithfulness.

Psalm 66:1-12

> *Come and see what God has done: he is awesome in his deeds among mortals.* — Psalm 66:5

There are times when praise is the only proper response to our experience in life. Psalm 66 guides us in the way of praise. Praise is more than just an exclamation of joyful feelings. Praise is both a memory and a testimony. The response to answered prayer is a desire to have everyone recognize and acknowledge the faithfulness of God that you have discovered in your own experience. The psalmist called on the whole earth to praise God (vv. 1-4). Praise is not something you can do by yourself. It requires some measure of community.

The psalmist drew upon the shared memory of the congregation by reminding them of the great deed of deliverance out of Egypt through the Red Sea. "He turned the sea into dry land; they passed through the river on foot." Part of that memory was that God would not allow the rebellious Pharaoh to exalt himself (v. 7). The wilderness experience and the defeats in battle as they entered the land were all seen as God's testing and refining them (vv. 8-12), which reminded the worshipers of the meaning of any current trials that they were experiencing. The psalmist suggested that in a similar manner to those historic memories of deliverance, so in any current experience of deliverance, the response of the worshiper was both an offering to God (vv. 13-15) and a witness to others (v. 16) of God's faithful response to one's troubles (vv. 17-19).

The psalmist recognized that the praise of God did not include the social struggle against iniquity was empty praise

(v. 18), but in this world of troubles, God did listen to prayers (v. 19). Sometimes our struggles do become a time of testing in our lives, but we must never think that they mean the absence of God's steadfast love (v. 20).

2 Timothy 2:8-15

> *Remind them of this, and warn them before God that they are to avoid wrangling over words, which does no good but only ruins those who are listening.*
> — 2 Timothy 2:14

Imagine how many church fights and denominational splits could be avoided if such a warning were heeded. There is little that damages a church more than the bickering and arguing that arises among the faithful. For Paul, there were some rock bottom truths that were essential. "Remember Jesus Christ, raised from the dead, a descendant of David — that is my gospel...." It was those key issues of resurrection and continuity with the promises of God to Israel that Paul saw as critical to the faith. He warned that we could ruin our witness by becoming too focused on debates about various ideas of the faith.

Doctrine can be important in clarifying what we believe, but all the beliefs in the world will mean little if they do not result in effective fruits of the faith. While there can be some growth in our faith through the debating of various issues within the faith, we are foolish to let the lesser issues divide us. Today it is Bible inerrancy, and yesterday it was the virgin birth. Today it is moving the piano, and yesterday it was the color of the carpet. Our witness, in such instances, is that we allow little things to separate us while we remain unconcerned about critical issues of the world.

Sometimes people leave churches because something that is happening there makes them uncomfortable. It is for the core gospel that we should be willing to go to jail and suffer hardships. Paul did not have some masochistic desire to be "chained like a criminal," but he recognized that the "word of God is not chained" and that any circumstance can be a setting for the proclamation of the gospel. If we are committed to that gospel, then regardless of the circumstances, there will be an opportunity to produce effective fruits.

Luke 17:11-19

> *He prostrated himself at Jesus' feet and thanked him. And he was a Samaritan.* — Luke 17:16

Sometimes we see better signs of faith outside the church than from within the community of faith. In the story there were ten lepers among whom one was a Samaritan. As lepers, they were outcasts. In their leprosy, they had come together in ways that their faith, nationality, and culture had separated them. Their shared crisis had united them. When they saw Jesus, they cried out for mercy. He directed them back to the resources of their faith tradition. " 'Go and show yourselves to the priests.' And as they went, they were made clean."

The community of faith that had rejected them was still their source of healing. It was the foreigner who recognized this as the mercy of God and returned to give Jesus thanks. We do not know what happened to the other nine. We are only told that they were healed as they went as Jesus had instructed them. We do know that this outsider demonstrated the power of gratitude. His faith was demonstrated by his gratitude, and his faith made him well.

When your faith is shaky and you feel cut off from the church as if you are living in a foreign territory, you are invited to turn and give thanks and be healed. It is by the power of our thanksgiving to God that we are restored to the harmony of life.

Proper 24
Pentecost 22
Ordinary Time 29

Jeremiah 31:27-34

> *The days are surely coming, says the Lord, when I will make a new covenant with the house of Israel and the house of Judah.* — Jeremiah 31:31

It is important to recognize both the continuity and discontinuity of this new covenant that God was promising. The promise was to Israel and Judah. The nation of Israel had been destroyed almost 120 years before Judah was captured. Yet God's promise included Israel and not just the remaining part of it that was called Judah. God never seemed to break continuity with the original people that he had chosen. Even in the time of the flood, Noah was related to those who had gone before him. This was not a new people that God was beginning with but the same people that he brought out of Egypt. Judah could not even claim that they were relatively better than Israel so God would just work with them.

God worked with the whole people that broke the covenant. This has implications for the Christian church's relationship with the Jewish community and our relationship with any part of the church that we may feel has betrayed its calling. While Christians do believe this new covenant that was promised was realized in the person of Jesus Christ, we are not free to break faith with those of the first covenant.

However, there also is a discontinuity. This new covenant, or new testament, was to be internalized in each individual's life. "I will put my law within them, and I will write it on their hearts." It was not a set of external standards by which they were constrained. Rather the very core of a Christian's life would find meaning and purpose in exhibiting the character of God. The obvious question is whether there is any evidence that this new covenant has come about. We continue to attempt to measure ourselves by the externals of what we do and what we can accomplish. Such frantic behavior often leaves us lonely, exhausted, and dispirited. The promise of Christ is that the Spirit will dwell with us and invites us to cultivate the fruits of the Spirit in all of our lives. When we submit to the Lord and accept God's forgiveness, we can experience love, joy, peace, patience, and so forth. This is the new covenant that God offers us.

Psalm 119:97-104

Oh, how I love your law! It is my meditation all day long.   — Psalm 119:97

This psalm is the longest in the book of Psalms. We miss in our English translations that this is an elaborate acrostic psalm. It consists of 22 stanzas of eight lines each. If it had been written in English, the first eight lines would all begin with the letter "a," and the next set of eight lines would begin with the letter "b." The continuing thread through all the stanzas is that they all reflect on the law of God. This particular section compares the law to all other sources of wisdom. It is wiser than one's enemies. It is wiser than one's teachers. It is wiser than the wisdom of the elderly that was so revered within the culture.

The psalm does not disparage these sources of wisdom but declares that all such wisdom must be measured against the wisdom of God that can be discovered in the Torah. For Christians, it is important to realize that the Torah is more than a set of regulations. We speak of it as the law, but it is really a reflection of the will of God that is expressed in stories, laws, poetry, and experiences. For the psalmist, God's law could not be contained in abstractions. To truly appreciate God's law, it must be experienced in one's behavior. "I hold back my feet from every evil way, in order to keep your word."

Jesus' life became a commentary on the Torah that interprets for us the way of God in our lives. There is a parallel between seeing Jesus as the bread of life and the Jew saying, "How sweet are your words to my taste, sweeter than honey to my mouth!" It may deepen our reflection on the meaning of Christ for our lives to substitute Christ for law in this psalm. If Christ taught us the way of God, then Christ is our wisdom. While we listen to the wisdom of history, science, and psychology for true wisdom, we need to see such truth through the eyes of Christ.

2 Timothy 3:14—4:5

> *All scripture is inspired by God and is useful for teaching, for reproof, for correction, and for training in righteousness.*   — 2 Timothy 3:16

In an age of confusion, it is natural for people to be attracted to churches and spiritual teachings that emphasize strict disciplines. When our life is in chaos, a very viable strategy is to accept a strong discipline to provide order. Many a distraught person has found comfort in the strict discipline of a fundamentalist church. In times of confusion, we are not good at making lots of decisions, and there is comfort in having someone else lay down the law for us. The danger is that we are tempted to believe that the disciplines themselves are a measure of our faithfulness rather than a means to restore our life to a sense of balance.

  Paul was arguing against a false form of asceticism. Apparently some had argued that the truly faithful would be celibate or accept a strict dietary program. It was not that being a vegetarian or choosing a celibate life was wrong in itself. For some it might be the best choice. What Paul was arguing against was the assumption that such behaviors were required for one to be truly faithful. He grounded his belief in the fact that both the material reality and the relationships between people were part of the goodness of God's creation, which according to Genesis 1:31 was "very good." The key is whether any of the realities of our lives are "received with thanksgiving."

There is no aspect of this world that cannot become an idol. Yet when we participate in this world with an attitude of thanksgiving, we are aware that each aspect of life is a reflection of God's love for us, and we can respond accordingly. Strong religious disciplines can be a gift of God to a person, but they should never become the measure by which we judge our neighbor.

Luke 18:1-8

> *Then Jesus told them a parable about their need to pray always and not to lose heart.* — Luke 18:1

Luke prepares us to hear Jesus' parable from a particular perspective. He had been talking about the coming of the kingdom. His parable was taken from a common life experience for people in Jesus' time. Judges were not restricted by a body of law that allowed for appeal. It was assumed that judges often ruled in favor of the person who was able to offer them the highest bribe. The widow in the parable seemed to lack both the economic means and the status to acquire a favorable decision from the judge. Her only resource was her persistence. Yet even in a less than fair world, sometimes persistence paid off.

This widow apparently had come before the judge before and received an unfavorable ruling. So convinced was she of the rightness of her cause that she returned repeatedly to ask the judge to rule in her favor. Jesus left no doubt that the reason why the judge finally relented had nothing to do with his conscience or change of heart. He ruled in the woman's favor out of his own self-interest. He was simply weary of her pestering him.

Even if one felt that life was unfair, it would be clear to all believers that God was a just and merciful God. A consistent theme of the Jewish faith was that God heard the cry of those who suffered and were oppressed. Reminding them of that central belief, Jesus urged them to be persistent in their prayers. If even unjust judges could be moved by persistence, then clearly God, who listened to the cry of the people, could be moved. Since our prayers do not inform God of something that God does not already know, then the purpose of our prayers is to build our relationship with God. The constancy of our prayers, even about the same subject, can only serve to deepen our relationship with God. As we deepen this relationship, we grow in our capacity to trust God even in the times of our distress.

Proper 25
Pentecost 23
Ordinary Time 30

Joel 2:23-32

> *... I will pour out my spirit on all flesh....*
> — Joel 2:28a

Peter drew on this scripture to interpret what was happening at Pentecost. In a similar manner to what the early Christians would later experience at Pentecost, so this early prophet experienced the Spirit of God as a force that transcended human control. It was understandable why Peter chose this passage to describe what was happening when the disciples were given the ability to communicate across language and ethnic barriers. In this passage, Joel described the Spirit as breaking through the artificial barriers imposed by humans as they sought to classify the world. The Spirit was no respecter of the barriers of age or gender. "I will pour out my spirit on all flesh; your sons and your daughters shall prophesy, your old men shall dream dreams, and your young men shall see visions." Nor was the Spirit constrained by the artificial barriers of class. "Even on the male and female slaves, in those days, I will pour out my spirit."

Earlier Joel had described the forces of nature as expressive of God's judgment and blessing. First the locusts were seen as God's army by which the people were judged. Then when the rains came, this too, was seen as God at work. The power of the Spirit released was the power of the presence of God. The injustices of the world led to a hunger for God's presence, which was often referred to as the day of the Lord. Joel suggested that the day of the Lord's coming would be preceded by cosmic signs. The infinite could not be inserted in the finite arena of time and space without severe disruption.

When we experience the infinite mystery infusing our lives, it forces a decision. For Christians, this prophecy would become the prism through which they interpreted the coming of Jesus. Jesus brought with him a bountiful harvest after a severe drought. One can see this in the feeding of the 5,000. But his presence forced a decision as to whether people would welcome God in him or turn away. All of humanity would like to see an overcoming of worldly divisions and a blossoming of peace within the world. The overcoming of such divisions was foreshadowed in Jesus' ministry to adults and children, male and female, and outsiders and insiders. Jerusalem became the critical turning point, and his disciples, those whom Jesus called, did escape.

All of this was confirmed by the Pentecost experience. During that Jewish festival of renewing the covenant with God, those who called on the name of Jesus received the Spirit that overcame all divisions. The church today has to decide whether they will allow this same Spirit to infuse their community. The reluctance of the church to open themselves to the Spirit may well be the awareness that such an experience does mean we are open to a force we cannot control.

Psalm 65

> *Praise is due to you, O God, in Zion....*
> — Psalm 65:1

Psalm 65 is a summary of our prayer life. It begins in adoration as we recognize that praise belongs to God and commit ourselves to praise (v. 1). As we engage in praise, we are aware that the end toward which all creation moves is praise (v. 2). Yet in the very experience of praise, we are made aware of our own sense of distance from God and are moved to seek forgiveness from God (v. 3).

It is God's forgiveness that invites and restores us to God's community. "Happy are those whom you choose and bring near to live in your courts" (v. 4). It is out of that experience of forgiveness that we recognize that all of our deliverance in the past, and our hope for the future, rests in God (v. 5). That experience of deliverance and hope is rooted in our understanding that God is author of all creation (vv. 6-8) and from that understanding comes our recognition of, and thanksgiving for, the rich bounty of God experienced in nature (vv. 9-11).

From nature's bounty comes its own voice of joy and praise (vv. 12-13). It is through prayer that we step beyond isolation and recognize our unity with all that is. Humans (v. 2), nature (v. 12), and animals (v. 13) find their voice of joy and praise in belonging to God (v. 1).

2 Timothy 4:6-8, 16-18

> *I have fought the good fight, I have finished the race, I have kept the faith.*   — 2 Timothy 4:7

Paul was now in prison and was apparently convinced that he would be executed. "As for me, I am already being poured out as a libation, and the time of my departure has come." It was from that perspective he was able to look back and feel at peace with his efforts on behalf of the gospel.

There are plenty of situations that call for us to continue the struggle or even strategically retreat and reconsider our tactics, but there comes a time when there are no alternatives. It is good at such times if we can review our lives and be satisfied with what we have done. Some have suggested that we should live each day as if it were the last so that, if it should suddenly become the last, we could face death with no regrets. Paul had apparently reached such a time. One of the reasons that he had that sense of contentment was that he had experienced the faithfulness of God to him in the past. This faithfulness of God was in sharp contrast to the betrayal and desertion that he had experienced from some of his colleagues in the faith (2 Timothy 4:9-15). His confidence in the future did not rest on some optimistic view of humanity and the structures that he had built but on the faithfulness of God.

He could see how God had transformed those trials into new possibilities for proclaiming the word of God. "But the Lord stood by me and gave me strength, so that through me the message might be fully proclaimed and all the Gentiles might hear it." It was this faithful God that gave Paul the confidence to face even death unafraid. In a sense, this was Paul's "last will and testament" before what he expected to be his death. He was confident that even death would not have the final word.

"The Lord will rescue me from every evil attack and save me for his heavenly kingdom." Many clergy have had to face disappointment in the visible accomplishments of their ministry. At times they have even felt the desertion of those on whom they had counted for support. Once again they were driven back to the core of their faith and asked whether they trusted the God who called them into ministry. Each of us has to ask ourselves whether we can join Paul in saying, "I have fought the good fight, I have finished the race, I have kept the faith." If we can say yes to that, then we can trust God for the results.

Luke 18:9-14

God, I thank you that I am not like other people....
— Luke 18:11b

We need to have some sympathy for the Pharisee in this story. He apparently was a very meticulous person in the practice of his faith. The problem was not in his practice of his faith but in the subtle element of pride that had infused his attitude. While his practice was directed toward God, his attention was focused on comparison with others. He would be like a lover who brought flowers and gifts to his beloved on their anniversary date but was most interested in making sure that she and others recognized what a great person he was for doing such things.

At first, the Pharisee would seem to be an excellent member for a church. He would probably serve on all the right committees and give generously of his time and energy. Over time, however, one would begin to recognize that he would want to be continually recognized for all that he did. The tax collector, on the other hand, might not be seen as such an excellent member of a church. Tax collectors were often seen as people who had compromised their integrity by working for the Romans and by making a handsome profit through overcharging their fellow countrymen.

If he were typical, others may have looked on him with contempt in the community of faith. How many church members are employed in professions that are denigrated by others? The tax collector might not have even engaged in any of the overt practices of the faith. But on that day, his attention was totally focused on God, and he was totally honest about his failure to live as God would want. The question for all of us is where our attention is focused. When we are vulnerable before God, as the tax collector was that day, there is the possibility of transformation in our lives.

Proper 26
Pentecost 24
Ordinary Time 31

Habakkuk 1:1-4; 2:1-4

> *I will stand at my watchpost, and station myself on the rampart....* — Habakkuk 2:1a

There are times when the negative reality of life seems overwhelming. We live in a world in which violence surrounds us and leadership's answer to violence is to respond with more violence. Churches also seem caught up in a destructive urge. "Strife and contention arise" all around us, and the church's response is to escalate the battle by threatening schism rather than working for reconciliation. Like Habakkuk, everywhere we look we see things falling apart and justice and fairness seem perverted. Habakkuk's response was "to keep watch and see what [God] will say...."

These are times when the response of faith is to lift our complaint to God and listen for God's response. God's response to Habakkuk was to "write the vision; make it plain on tablets, so that a runner may read it." It is important for the church to offer a vision of faithfulness in the midst of chaos. We do not have the power to impose a solution on our society. Even within a denomination, we have learned that we cannot legislate a solution to our differences. There is a powerful testimony to believing that God is not absent from our chaos. There is power in envisioning an alternative to the fearful response around us. For those who trust in God, it is important to spend time and energy waiting on God and speaking of a hope that transcends our ability to achieve. For "the righteous to live by their faith" means we do not submit to the fears that drive us apart but envision a time when God will heal our wounds.

Psalm 119:137-144

> *Your decrees are righteous forever; give me understanding that I may live.*   — Psalm 119:144

Psalm 119 is the longest of all the psalms and consists of 22 stanzas of eight verses each. Each stanza starts with a letter in the Hebrew alphabet in the fashion of an acrostic poem. The entire poem is an elaborate reflection on the law of God. This verse is the eighteenth stanza and therefore begins with the letter Tisade. It focuses on the righteousness of God as expressed in God's laws.

To distinguish between the way that our society uses the term righteous and the way it is usually intended in scripture, it is helpful to think of righteous meaning right relationships. God stands in right relationship with humanity. God's judgments are for the sake of humanity and their relationship with God. God's rightness in relationship to humanity is an everlasting rightness, and God's law is the truth (Psalm 119:45). This is true even when one's commitment to God's law seems to be met with the hostility of others. "I am small and despised, yet I do not forget your precepts," said the psalmist.

In contrast to our culture that begins to question the commands of God when they are inconvenient or costly, the psalmist was convinced that the righteous or right relationship with God would be achieved by paying attention to God's law. "Trouble and anguish have come upon me, but your commandments are my delight." Rather than assuming some contrast between God's law and God's grace, the psalmist saw the law as an expression of God's grace. He examined the various facets of the law in these 22 reflections in a manner similar to a jeweler examining the various facets of a diamond.

It would be interesting for a person or a congregation to try to compose 22 separate reflections on the law or will of God. What are the various ways that we can understand what it means for us to pray, "Thy will be done on earth as it is in heaven"?

2 Thessalonians 1:1-4, 11-12

> ... *because your faith is growing abundantly, and the love of everyone of you for one another is increasing.*
> — 2 Thessalonians 1:3b

This prayer describes the condition for which every pastor yearns. Too often, because of our intimate knowledge of the congregation, the pastor is acutely aware of the weak faith and factionalism of the congregation. Paul, who had seen his share of shallow faith and internal bickering, was able to say of this church that their faith and their love for one another was growing. This had become manifest in the face of persecution.

Sadly, the most difficult challenge for most churches is when they are prosperous and comfortable. It is when we have to suffer for our faith that we often discover its true depth. While Paul suggested that there would come a time of reckoning when those who are causing the congregation's suffering would be punished (1:5-10), in this verse Paul was marveling at the depth of faith and love that their persecution had revealed.

Because the church is the body of Christ, in the same way that Jesus was glorified through suffering, Paul prayed that Jesus would again be glorified in the suffering of his body, the church. As Jesus was tempted in the Garden of Gethsemane to deny his calling in order to avoid suffering, so the church will be tempted to do the same.

Therefore, Paul prayed that the Thessalonians' church would be worthy of God's call and fulfill "every good resolve and work of faith." It is our faith in God and love toward each other in the face of persecution that demonstrates the presence of God in our midst. When a pastor sees this in a congregation, he or she can only give thanks for the grace of God.

Luke 19:1-10

*Zacchaeus, hurry and come down; for I must stay at
your house today.* — Luke 19:5b

Why was it so urgent that Jesus stay at Zacchaeus' house? Why does Jesus, and later the body of Christ, need to associate with those the whole community deems a sinner? Notice that Zacchaeus did not deny he had done what the community assumed. It was only as a result of his encounter with Jesus that he promised to make restitution.

The community of faith was operating from a theory of pollution. If the pure comes in contact with pollution, it is spoiled. Jesus was operating from a theory of holiness. If the holy infuses our lives, we can be purified. Zacchaeus offered to give half of his possessions to the poor and to repay four times as much to any he had defrauded. Did Zacchaeus welcome Jesus into a house of sin, or did Jesus welcome Zacchaeus into a transformed life?

If Zacchaeus' life had been directed by his possessions, it was now clear that his possessions had become servant of a higher calling. Jesus' response was, "Today salvation has come to this house, because he too is a son of Abraham." Before Zacchaeus was identified as a tax collector, but now he was identified as a Jew. His true vocation had been restored; although there was no indication that he ceased to be a tax collector. It was not his vocation but his priority that was changed.

The challenge for the body of Christ is whether the members are willing to risk being soiled so that their more worldly companions might be purified. Can we, like Jesus, risk our reputation and welcome the sinner even before we know the response to our invitation? Jesus did not say, "Come down and follow me." He said, "Come down for I must stay with you."

Proper 27
Pentecost 25
Ordinary Time 32

Haggai 1:15b—2:9

> *My spirit abides among you; do not fear.*
> — Haggai 2:5b

Those who lived in exile had returned to find their land in ruins and the people living in poverty. While in exile, they clung to the hope of returning and once more living in "a land of milk and honey." How do you go on when all the visible signs of hope have been shattered? Haggai was very specific about the time of his vision. It was the second year, the seventh month, the twenty-first day of the month. There was this specific moment in the midst of the utter despair of the people when Haggai felt compelled to speak to the remnants of leadership, the governor and the high priest, and to the remnant of the people. He recalled the former glory and was blunt about the bleak image of the present.

"How does it look to you now? Is it not in your sight as nothing?" It was at the point when there was no reason to have confidence in the future that Haggai called for them to have courage. The courage was not based on anything except faith that the God who had promised to fulfill them in the past would be faithful to them in the future. A continuing theme of scripture from Abraham to Jesus is that nothing is impossible for God (Genesis 18:14; Luke 1:37).

Repeatedly the people of faith experienced the loss of all the signs of human control so that they might once again learn to find their hope in God. It was when they found themselves in utter hopelessness that they heard again, "My spirit abides among you; do not fear." It is the presence of this mystery that gives us the courage to keep moving when all around us there are only signs of despair.

Psalm 145:1-5, 17-21

> *Every day I will bless you, and praise your name forever and ever.*
> — Psalm 145:2

Psalm 145 is the first of six psalms of praise that conclude the book of Psalms in a crescendo of praise. The psalm begins with a commitment to daily praise God's name. The praise of God is based on the memory of God's faithful acts.

They are rehearsed in worship so that each succeeding generation might hear of God's faithfulness. "One generation shall laud your works to another, and shall declare your mighty acts." The book of Psalms has given expression to the entire variety of feelings that belong to human nature. Early in Psalms there is a predominance of laments but as the book progresses, the psalms of praise assert themselves over the laments until at the end it is all praise. It is as if the psalmist was giving expression to the entire journey of life.

We begin in full awareness of our limitations and give expression to our complaints and our petitions. Having given full vent to our pain and disappointment, we discover that there is someone listening. Then we notice that this God who listens also responds with steadfast love and mercy. "The Lord is near to all who call on him, to all who call on him in truth." Standing in awe of the mystery that we can neither control nor manipulate, we discover that the only response that makes sense is praise.

It is in praise that we are united with the fullness of life. It is also by praise that we convey to future generations the glorious splendor of God. "My mouth will speak the praise of the Lord, and all flesh will bless his holy name forever and ever."

2 Thessalonians 2:1-5, 13-17

> *As to the coming of our Lord Jesus Christ and our being gathered together to him....*
> — 2 Thessalonians 2:1a

The end of time or the culmination of history is always fascinating to us. Each generation has those who believe that they are living in the end times. It seems to give us a sense of importance to be there at the end. Notice the extreme popularity of the *Left Behind* series. Some in Paul's time had also become convinced that "the day of the Lord is already here."

Believing that it was here and that they were part of the elect apparently resulted in a life devoid of responsibility for the continuing conditions of the world. If the world was coming to an end soon, who had time or cared about changing the conditions around them? Paul cautioned them against such a belief: "For that day will not come unless the rebellion comes first and the lawless one is revealed...."

In an effort to hasten the end of time, people have continuously identified the "anti-Christ" with various historic figures. Instead of endless speculations about the end time, Paul tried to refocus their attention to the needs of the current moment. "... comfort your hearts and strengthen them in every good work and word." As we near the end of the church year, the scripture passages tend toward these apocalyptic images.

The temptation for the church, particularly when we are living in frightening times, is to speculate about a historical culmination of history. Paul's counterprescription was to suggest that the uneasiness and anxiety of our times is better addressed by "every good work and word." To speculate about the end time becomes a reflection of human arrogance that wants to believe we are at the center of God's work. The antidote is to reemphasize the practical living out of the faith.

Luke 20:27-38

In the resurrection, therefore, whose wife will the woman be? For the seven had married her. — Luke 20:33

The Sadducees cleverly tried to trap Jesus with this shrewd question. When the church engages in a debate about faith, people tend to choose sides and then try to trap each other with clever questions. The debate becomes a game of trying to defeat the other side and ceases to be a hunger for the truth.

Luke made clear that the Sadducees did not believe in the resurrection. Based on that premise, they devised a question that they believed showed them to be right. The scenario they built was based on a Levitical law (Deuteronomy 25:5) about preserving the family line. A brother of a man who died childless had a responsibility to marry the widow and have a child that would bear the deceased person's name. They believed that the case they had developed made the idea of resurrection look ridiculous. Jesus used their question as an opportunity to teach them about the character of the life of the resurrection.

He suggested that in the life of the resurrection people neither married nor were given in marriage. He then suggested that marriage was a product of our finite world. The capacity to love one another in eternity would be free of the issues of fear, jealousy, and insecurity that marriage customs help us cope with. While such a radical idea might make us nervous, it does transform our concept of love from needing to possess other people into the capacity to be loving toward everyone.

Proper 28
Pentecost 26
Ordinary Time 33

Isaiah 65:17-25

> *For I am about to create new heavens and a new earth; the former things shall not be remembered or come to mind.* — Isaiah 65:17

The people of Israel have come back to their homeland. It was a long anticipated return. Yet when they returned, they found poverty and a city in ruins. The prophet who wrote in the spirit of Isaiah, countered their gloom with an apocalyptic vision of what God would do. Anyone who has experienced despair knows the power of hope to lift spirits and renew energy. The vision Isaiah offered had images similar to that of the Garden of Eden. It drew on the human yearning to be free to enjoy the fruits of their own work, to enjoy a peaceful, long life, and to enjoy a world free of conflict. Notice how the vision unfolded on the earth and was void of the mention of the temple forms of worship or common actions of religion.

In this it has its parallel in Revelation 21:22 where there would be no temple as well. The picture would appeal to almost any human. It was God rejoicing in what God does for humanity rather than what humans would do for God. This was not a heavenly vision of angels and harps playing but a picture of humans engaged in a productive life on an earth that was fertile and peaceful. It reminds us that the purpose of faith is to be for life and not the reverse. For the church to live out this vision in a preliminary way, the church's focus must be on helping its members fulfill their vocation in their daily lives.

Isaiah 12

With joy you will draw water from the wells of salvation.
— Isaiah 12:3

It was a unique configuration of events that made it possible for Israel to occupy the hills of Canaan. At the time of their occupation of this land, the world had just discovered how to smelt iron. This enabled the manufacturing of axes that could take down the trees and clear the land for agriculture in the mountains. Also, the world had discovered slake lime with which they could plaster wells that could capture the rainwater for both their animals and their crops. Unlike Egypt, with the Nile River, Canaan's hill country was dependent on rainwater. Wells were essential for survival. The prophet drew upon this image of a well to speak of God as "my strength and my might; he has become my salvation."

As Judah lived on the brink of destruction as a nation, Isaiah offered an image of hope when "though you were angry with me, your anger turned away, and you comforted me." In the midst of their despair, they would discover again that the source of their salvation was God. As we come to the end of the church year, we are invited again to rediscover the source of our salvation. Like a well that collects the goodness of God that falls like rain all around us, the church becomes the collector of the water that slakes our thirst and gives us hope and joy.

A well holds the water that sustains life, but only if we let down a bucket can we taste the water. Jesus said to the woman at the well, "If you knew the gift of God, and who it is that is saying to you, 'Give me drink,' you would have asked him, and he would have given you living water" (John 4:10).

2 Thessalonians 3:6-13

> *For we hear that some of you are living in idleness, mere busybodies, not doing any work.*
> — 2 Thessalonians 3:11

There were those within the church of Thessalonica that were convinced that the Lord was coming at any time, and they, therefore, concluded that there was no point in continuing to work or make any effort at all. They not only refused to work for a living, but also they refused to work in the church. They concluded that since Jesus was returning at any moment, there was no point in focusing attention on the life of the church.

What would it mean for Christians to live in idleness within the church? Would it mean that they were withholding their gifts from the church? They are feeding off the body but not contributing to the building up of the church. If, as Paul has noted elsewhere, we are given every gift necessary to do the work of the church (1 Corinthians 1:7), it means some of the gifts are not being used if a church is weak.

For Christians to be "mere busybodies, not doing any work," means that they are simply standing around complaining about the state of the world and not busy working for its reconciliation. Paul urged us to "not be weary in doing what is right." In this time of moral confusion, there is power in people quietly demonstrating what really gives life meaning and purpose. The hard work of being a Christian is to help the church reveal God's story by living the truth of our story.

Luke 21:5-19

By your endurance you will gain your souls.

—Luke 21:19

As we near the end of the Christian year, this passage confronts us with the harsh reality of the world. Nothing is so stable that we can cling to it. The crowd was admiring the temple that was built by means of the sacrificial giving of the people. It was the holiest spot on earth and clearly reflected people's devotion to God. Surely, even as God is eternal, this would last until the end of time. Jesus, however, correctly predicted that it would not last. Traumatic change in our world often causes us to wonder if the end is near.

Many Christian groups have tried to use these words of Jesus to predict the end. A close reading of the text shows Jesus was saying just the opposite. He was warning them not to be led astray by these chaotic events. "When you hear of wars and insurrections, do not be terrified; for these things must take place first, but the end will not follow immediately." Jesus painted the gloomiest pictures of all the disasters and ruptures of relationships that we fear and suggested we must be ready to face them.

This was not a comfortable picture of the progressive expansion of the gospel until the whole world lives in peace and harmony. Rather it was a picture of a return to the wilderness where the secure trappings of civilization have fallen apart. In Deuteronomy 8:2-5, we are told that God led the community of faith through the wilderness so that they might learn to trust God in all circumstances. It is not our cleverness but God's faithfulness that enables us to endure.

Within the framework of cosmic disasters, church members often experience mini-disasters, ruptures of relationships, and crumbling of beloved structures. It is not the time to either despair or retreat to apocalyptic images of the end times. Rather it is a time to learn that God is faithful and will accompany us through all the chaos of our lives.

Christ The King
Proper 29

Jeremiah 23:1-6

> *The days are surely coming, says the Lord, when I will raise up for David a righteous Branch....*
> — Jeremiah 23:5a

The promise of a messiah from the line of David was a continuing theme of the prophets. While Jeremiah agonized over the fate of his nation, he remained confident of the power of God to save. For Jeremiah, the rulers had failed because they had been preoccupied with themselves and their own well-being and neglected the people. The parallel to the struggle within the contemporary church is unnerving. How often have we failed God because we have become so preoccupied with saving our institution or our own positions that we have neglected to feed the people? The temptation faced by Jesus on the cross was, "If you are king of the Jews, save yourself...." But the true shepherd does not manipulate the powers to serve himself but rather is willing to sacrifice himself for the sake of the people.

In this, the true messiah embodies God's righteousness. The thief on the cross in Luke 23:33-43 was like one of the scattered sheep. He recognized the righteousness of God in Jesus who was willing to suffer. By doing so, he was invited back into paradise. The body of Christ recognizes Christ as our king and follows a shepherd that was willing to lay down his life for others. This king rules by serving and invites obedience because at last we see one who is committed to our well-being.

Luke 1:68-79

*And you, child, will be called prophet of the Most High;
for you will go before the Lord to prepare his ways....*
— Luke 1:76

Zechariah's tongue was loosed as he named his child John. He sang this prophecy about his child. His prayer was about the future saving acts of God, but it was based on his recognition of the past acts of God. It was because of the faithfulness of God in the past that Zechariah was confident of what God was doing that had implications for the future.

He reread God's promise to Abraham in light of the people's present condition. "Thus he has shown the mercy promised to our ancestors ... the oath that he swore to our ancestor Abraham...." Because the future is always unknown, much of the anxiety in our life is based on our lack of confidence in that future. It is important that we also reread the story of God's faithfulness as a way to prepare for the future. Zechariah saw his son's destiny as preparing the way for Christ's coming. That preparation was accomplished by giving "knowledge of salvation to his people by the forgiveness of their sins." All this was "to guide our feet into the way of peace."

As we celebrate Christ the King Sunday, perhaps we can reread the promises of God in light of our situation and discover again the tender mercies of our God that lead us to the way of peace.

Colossians 1:11-20

... and in him all things hold together.
— Colossians 1:17b

Here may be the boldest claim in all of scripture. We are not talking about saving the good from the bad or separating the faithful from the wicked. The claim is that through Christ all things on heaven and earth are reconciled. The claim is that Hitler, Mother

Teresa, Genghis Khan, Saint Francis, earthquakes, and sunrises find their peace in Christ. Christ becomes the linchpin of history that holds it all together and prevents all creation from flying apart. Here is not the hero of the truth bravely fighting against the odds to give victory to the brave and faithful. Rather here is the answer to all of the "whys" of history that somehow redeems the most wicked of acts so that all now makes sense.

If we accept such a faith then our whole perspective on life changes. The change begins in the church where Christ is recognized as head of the body, but as we recognize Christ as the head of the living body, it flows out from there until we also see Christ as having first place in everything.

This challenges all our prejudices and shatters the boundaries by which we divide the world. We are to view all of the events of life through the spectacles of Christ. Nothing is ultimately lost because in Christ all things hold together. That does not mean tragedies are not tragic or evil deeds are not evil, but rather in and through Christ, we are to search for and proclaim their redemption. It also means that nothing in our life is beyond redemption. That which separates and alienates can only be finally resolved in Christ. We discover our peace as we recognize Christ as sovereign.

Luke 23:33-43

> *If you are the King of the Jews, save yourself!*
> — Luke 23:37

It is the way of earthly kings to place first priority on saving themselves. The soldiers' primary objective was to serve and protect the king. Here they represented the confusion of the world by mocking Jesus as king and serving as his executioners. The thieves, who were supposed to be in rebellion against proper authority, gave a mixed witness. One taunted him, "Are you not the Messiah? Save yourself and us!"

Like the soldier, he thought he was mocking, but in reality he was speaking the truth. The second criminal saw more clearly than all the others. "Do you not fear God, since you are under the same sentence of condemnation?" In Jesus the world attempted to condemn God and was itself condemned. Perhaps the worst mockery was that of the religious leaders. They were the ones who were supposed to understand the way of God and yet they demonstrated more understanding of the way of the world.

"He saved others; let him save himself if he is the Messiah of God, his chosen one!" Their witness stands as a warning to the church. Jesus' kingship was mocked by the secular authorities, represented by the soldiers, scoffed at by the religious authorities, represented by the priests and elders, and only understood by the criminal element of society.

Jesus himself defied the normal expectations of kings by not saving himself but offering himself for the sake of others. He defined that kingship by seeking the forgiveness of God for both friend and enemy. The church has to decide which of the authorities represented here it will serve.

Scriptural Index For Cycles A, B, C

We have arranged the scriptural index alphabetically for your ease in finding a particular reference.

The Cycle A book is titled *Water From The Well*, Cycle B is *Streams of Living Water*, and Cycle C is *Water From The Rock*. These titles are available from CSS Publishing. Call 1-800-537-1030 or order online at orders@csspub.com. Our website is www.csspub.com.

The Editor

Acts			17:22-31	A	154
1:1-11	B	153	19:1-7	B	66
1:1-11	C	169			
1:6-14	A	159	**Amos**		
1:15-17, 21-26	B	157	7:7-17	C	218
2:1-21	B	162	8:1-12	C	223
2:1-21	C	179			
2:14a, 22-32	A	136	**Colossians**		
2:14a, 36-41	A	140	1:1-14	C	220
2:42-47	A	145	1:11-20	C	309
3:12-19	B	137	1:15-28	C	225
4:5-12	B	141	2:6-15 (16-19)	C	230
4:32-35	B	133	3:1-4	A	133
5:27-32	C	145	3:1-11	C	235
7:55-60	A	149	3:12-17	C	57
8:14-17	C	70			
8:26-40	B	145	**1 Corinthians**		
9:1-6 (7-20)	C	150	1:1-9	A	71
9:36-43	C	155	1:3-9	B	34
10:34-43	A	67	1:10-18	A	75
10:34-43	B	129	1:18-25	B	114
10:34-43	A	131	1:18-31	A	79
10:44-48	B	149	2:1-12 (13-16)	A	83
11:1-18	C	159	3:1-9	A	86
16:9-15	C	164	3:10-11, 16-23	A	90
16:16-34	C	174	4:1-5	A	94

313

6:12-20	B	71	**Ephesians**			
7:29-31	B	74	1:3-14	A	59	
8:1-13	B	78	1:3-14	B	57	
9:16-23	B	83	1:3-14	B	197	
9:24-27	B	87	1:3-14	C	61	
10:1-13	C	124	1:15-23	A	282	
12:1-11	C	74	1:15-23	B	155	
12:3b-13	A	165	1:15-23	C	171	
12:12-31a	C	78	2:1-10	B	118	
13:1-13	C	82	2:11-22	B	202	
15:1-11	B	131	3:1-12	A	63	
15:1-11	C	87	3:1-12	B	62	
15:12-20	C	92	3:1-12	C	66	
15:19-26	C	142	3:14-21	B	207	
15:35-38, 42-50	C	97	4:1-16	B	212	
15:51-58	C	102	4:25—5:2	B	217	
			5:15-20	B	222	
2 Corinthians			5:8-14	A	120	
1:18-22	B	90	6:10-20	B	227	
3:1-6	B	94				
3:12—4:2	C	111	**Esther**			
4:3-6	B	102	7:1-6, 9-10; 9:20-22	B	248	
4:5-12	B	99				
4:5-12	B	172	**Exodus**			
4:13—5:1	B	176	1:8—2:10	A	223	
5:6-10 (11-13) 14-17	B	180	3:1-15	A	228	
5:16-21	C	128	12:1-14	A	232	
6:1-13	B	184	14:19-31	A	236	
8:7-15	B	189	16:2-15	A	241	
12:2-10	B	194	17:1-7	A	113	
13:11-13	A	168	17:1-7	A	245	
			20:1-17	B	113	
Deuteronomy			20:1-4, 7-9, 12-20	A	249	
5:12-15	B	97	24:12-18	A	101	
11:18-21, 26-28	A	97	32:1-14	A	254	
18:15-20	B	77	33:12-23	A	258	
26:1-11	C	114	34:29-35	C	109	
30:15-20	A	85				
34:1-12	A	262				

Ezekiel		
34:11-16, 20-24	A	280
37:1-14	A	122

Galatians		
1:1-12	C	106
1:1-12	C	191
1:11-24	C	196
2:15-21	C	201
3:23-29	C	206
4:4-7	B	54
5:1, 13-25	C	210
6:(1-6) 7-16	C	215

Genesis		
1:1—2:4a	A	167
1:1-5	B	65
2:15-17; 3:1-7	A	105
6:9-22; 7:24; 8:14-19	A	171
9:8-17	B	105
12:1-4a	A	109
12:1-9	A	175
15:1-12, 17-18	C	118
17:1-7, 15-16	B	109
18:1-15 (21:1-7)	A	179
21:8-21	A	183
22:1-14	A	187
24:34-38, 42-49, 58-67	A	191
25:19-34	A	196
28:10-19a	A	200
29:15-28	A	205
32:22-31	A	209
37:1-4, 12-28	A	214
45:1-15	A	218
45:3-11, 15	C	95

Habakkuk		
1:1-4; 2:1-4	C	296

Haggai		
1:15b—2:9	C	300

Hebrews		
1:1-4 (5-12)	C	52
1:1-4; 2:5-12	B	255
2:10-18	A	55
4:12-16	B	260
5:1-10	B	264
5:5-10	B	122
7:23-28	B	268
9:11-14	B	273
9:24-28	B	277
10:5-10	C	48
10:11-14 (15-18) 19-25	B	282
11:1-3, 8-16	C	240
11:29—12:2	C	245
12:18-29	C	250
13:1-8, 15-16	C	255

Hosea		
1:2-10	C	228
2:14-20	B	93
11:1-11	C	233

Isaiah		
1:1, 10-20	C	238
2:1-5	A	33
5:1-7	C	243
6:1-8	B	166
6:1-8 (9-13)	C	85
7:10-16	A	45
9:1-4	A	73
9:2-7	A	49
11:1-10	A	37
12	C	305
35:1-10	A	41
40:1-11	B	36
40:21-31	B	81

42:1-9	A	65	18:1-11	C	258
43:1-7	C	68	23:1-6	C	308
43:16-21	C	131	29:1, 4-7	C	282
43:18-25	B	89	31:7-14	B	56
49:1-7	A	69	31:7-14	C	59
49:8-16a	A	93	31:7-14	A	57
50:4-9a	A	127	31:27-34	C	286
50:4-9a	B	125	31:31-34	B	121
50:4-9a	C	135	32:1-3a, 6-15	C	272
52:7-10	C	50	33:14-16	C	33
55:1-9	C	122			
55:10-13	C	100	**Job**		
58:1-9a (9b-12)	A	81	1:1; 2:1-10	B	253
60:1-6	A	61	23:1-9, 16-17	B	258
60:1-6	B	60	38:1-7 (34-41)	B	262
60:1-6	C	64	42:1-6, 10-17	B	266
61:1-4, 8-11	B	39			
61:10—62:3	B	52	**Joel**		
62:1-5	C	72	2:23-32	C	291
62:6-12	B	47			
63:7-9	A	53	**1 John**		
64:1-9	B	33	1:1—2:2	B	134
65:17-25	C	140	3:1-7	B	138
65:17-25	C	304	3:16-24	B	143
			4:7-21	B	147
James			5:1-6	B	151
1:17-27	B	232	5:9-13	B	159
2:1-10 (11-13) 14-17	B	235			
3:1-12	B	240	**John**		
3:13—4:3, 7-8a	B	245	1:(1-9) 10-18	A	60
5:7-10	A	42	1:(1-9) 10-18	B	58
5:13-20	B	250	1:(1-9) 10-18	C	62
			1:1-14	C	53
Jeremiah			1:29-42	A	72
1:4-10	C	80	1:43-51	B	71
1:4-10	C	248	1:6-8, 19-28	B	42
2:4-13	C	253	2:1-11	C	75
4:11-12, 22-28	C	263	2:13-22	B	115
8:18—9:1	C	268	3:1-17	A	111
17:5-10	C	90	3:1-17	B	168

3:14-21	B	119	5:9-12	C	126
4:5-42	A	116	24:1-3a, 14-25	A	271
6:1-21	B	208			
6:24-35	B	213	**Judges**		
6:35, 41-51	B	218	4:1-7	A	276
6:51-58	B	223			
6:56-69	B	228	**1 Kings**		
9:1-41	A	120	2:10-12; 3:3-14	B	220
10:1-10	A	147	8:(1, 6, 10-11) 22-30,		
10:11-18	B	144	41-43	B	225
10:22-30	C	158	8:22-23, 41-43	C	104
11:1-45	A	125	17:8-16 (17-24)	C	194
12:1-8	C	133	18:20-21 (22-29)		
12:20-33	B	123	30-39	C	189
13:31-35	C	162	19:1-4 (5-7) 8-15a	C	204
14:1-14	A	152	21:1-10 (11-14)		
14:8-17 (25-27)	C	182	15-21a	C	199
14:15-21	A	157			
14:23-29	C	167	**2 Kings**		
15:1-8	B	148	2:1-2, 6-14	C	208
15:9-17	B	152	2:1-12	B	101
15:26-27; 16:4b-15	B	164	5:1-14	B	85
16:12-15	C	187	5:1-14	C	213
17:1-11	A	162			
17:6-19	B	160	**Lamentations**		
17:20-26	C	177	1:1-6	C	277
18:33-37	B	287			
20:1-18	A	133	**Leviticus**		
20:1-18	C	143	19:1-2, 9-18	A	89
20:19-23	A	166			
20:19-31	A	138	**Luke**		
20:19-31	B	135	1:26-38	B	45
20:19-31	C	148	1:39-45 (46-55)	C	49
21:1-19	C	153	1:47-55	A	42
			1:47-55	B	40
Jonah			1:68-79	C	38
3:1-5, 10	B	73	1:68-79	C	309
			2:1-14 (15-20)	A	52
Joshua			2:(1-7) 8-20	B	50
3:7-17	A	266	2:22-40	B	55

317

2:41-52	C	58	20:27-38		C	303
3:1-6	C	40	21:5-19		C	307
3:7-18	C	44	21:25-36		C	36
3:15-17, 21-22	C	71	23:33-43		C	310
4:1-13	C	117	24:13-35		A	143
4:14-21	C	79	24:36b-48		B	139
4:21-30	C	83	24:44-53		B	156
5:1-11	C	88	24:44-53		C	172
6:17-26	C	93				
6:27-38	C	98	**Malachi**			
6:39-49	C	103	3:1-4		C	37
7:1-10	C	107				
7:1-10	C	192	**Mark**			
7:11-17	C	197	1:1-8		B	38
7:36—8:3	C	202	1:14-20		B	75
8:26-39	C	207	1:21-28		B	79
9:28-36 (37-43)	C	112	1:29-39		B	83
9:51-62	C	211	1:4-11		B	67
10:1-11, 16-20	C	216	1:9-15		B	107
10:25-37	C	221	1:40-45		B	87
10:38-42	C	226	2:1-12		B	91
11:1-13	C	231	2:13-22		B	95
12:13-21	C	236	2:23—3:6		B	100
12:32-40	C	242	2:23—3:6		B	173
12:49-56	C	246	3:20-35		B	177
13:1-9	C	125	4:26-34		B	181
13:10-17	C	251	4:35-41		B	185
13:31-35	C	121	5:21-43		B	190
14:1, 7-14	C	256	6:1-13		B	195
14:25-33	C	261	6:14-29		B	198
15:1-10	C	266	6:30-34, 53-56		B	203
15:1-3, 11b-32	C	129	7:1-8, 14-15, 21-23		B	233
16:1-13	C	271	7:24-37		B	237
16:19-31	C	275	8:27-38		B	241
17:5-10	C	280	8:31-38		B	112
17:11-19	C	285	9:2-9		B	103
18:1-8	C	289	9:30-37		B	246
18:9-14	C	294	9:38-50		B	251
19:1-10	C	299	10:2-16		B	256
19:28-40	C	138	10:17-31		B	261

10:35-45	B	265	17:1-9	A	103
10:46-52	B	269	18:15-20	A	234
12:28-34	B	274	18:21-35	A	239
12:38-44	B	278	20:1-16	A	243
13:1-8	B	283	21:1-11	A	129
13:24-37	B	35	21:23-32	A	248
14:1—15:47	B	128	21:33-46	A	252
16:1-8	B	131	22:1-14	A	257
			22:15-22	A	260
Matthew			22:34-46	A	265
1:18-25	A	48	23:1-12	A	269
2:1-12	A	64	24:36-44	A	35
2:1-12	B	63	25:1-13	A	274
2:1-12	C	67	25:14-30	A	278
2:13-23	A	56	25:31-46	A	283
3:1-12	A	39	28:1-10	A	134
3:13-17	A	68	28:16-20	A	169
4:1-11	A	108			
4:12-23	A	76	**Micah**		
5:1-12	A	80	5:2-5a	C	46
5:13-20	A	84	6:1-8	A	77
5:21-37	A	88			
5:38-48	A	91	**Nehemiah**		
6:24-34	A	95	8:1-3, 5-6, 8-10	C	76
7:21-29	A	100			
7:21-29	A	173	**Numbers**		
9:9-13, 18-26	A	177	11:24-30	A	163
9:35—10:8 (9-23)	A	181	21:4-9	B	117
10:24-39	A	186			
10:40-42	A	190	**1 Peter**		
11:2-11	A	43	1:3-9	A	138
11:16-19, 25-30	A	195	1:17-23	A	142
13:1-9, 18-23	A	199	2:2-10	A	151
13:24-30, 36-43	A	203	2:19-25	A	147
13:31-33, 44-52	A	207	3:13-22	A	156
14:13-21	A	212	3:18-22	B	107
14:22-33	A	217	4:12-14; 5:6-11	A	161
15:(10-20) 21-28	A	221			
16:13-20	A	226	**2 Peter**		
16.21-28	A	231	1:16-21	A	102

3:8-15a	B	37	19	A	250
			19	B	114
Philemon			19	B	239
1-21	C	260	19	C	77
			20	B	179
Philippians			22:1-15	B	259
1:21-30	A	243	22:23-31	B	110
1:3-11	C	39	22:25-31	B	146
2:1-13	A	247	23	A	119
2:5-11	A	129	23	A	146
2:5-11	B	127	23	B	142
2:5-11	C	137	23	C	156
3:4b-14	A	251	24	B	197
3:4b-14	C	133	25:1-10	B	106
3:17—4:1	C	120	25:1-10	C	34
4:1-9	A	256	26	B	254
4:4-7	C	43	27	C	119
			27:1, 4-9	A	74
Proverbs			29	A	66
1:20-33	B	238	29	B	66
8:1-4, 22-31	C	184	29	B	167
22:1-2, 8-9, 22-23	B	234	29	C	69
31:10-31	B	243	30	B	86
			30	C	151
Psalm			30	C	214
1	B	158	31:1-5, 15-16	A	150
1	B	244	31:1-5, 19-24	A	98
1	C	91	31:9-16	B	126
2	A	102	32	A	106
4	B	138	32	C	127
5:1-8	C	200	33:1-12	A	176
8	A	168	34:1-8 (19-22)	B	267
8	C	185	36:5-10	C	73
9:9-20	B	183	37:1-11, 39-40	C	96
13	A	188	40:1-11	A	70
14	B	206	41	B	90
14	C	264	42 and 43	C	205
15	A	78	45:10-17	A	192
16	A	137	45:1-2, 6-9	B	231
17:1-7, 15	A	210	46	A	172

47	B	154	91:1-6, 14-16	C	273	
47	C	170	92:1-4, 12-15	C	101	
48	B	193	95	A	114	
50:1-6	B	102	96	A	50	
50:1-8, 22-23	C	239	96	C	190	
51:1-12	B	122	96:1-9	C	105	
51:1-12	B	211	97	B	48	
52	C	224	97	C	175	
62:5-12	B	74	98	B	150	
63:1-8	C	123	98	C	51	
65	C	292	99	A	259	
66:1-12	C	283	99	C	110	
66:8-20	A	155	100	A	281	
67	C	165	103:1-13, 22	B	94	
68:1-10, 32-35	A	160	104:1-9, 24, 35c	B	263	
71:1-6	C	81	104:24-34, 35b	A	164	
71:1-6	C	249	104:24-34, 35b	B	163	
72:1-7, 10-14	B	61	104:24-34, 35b	C	180	
72:1-7, 10-14	C	65	105:1-11, 45b	A	206	
72:1-7, 10-14	A	62	105:1-6, 16-22, 45b	A	215	
72:1-7, 18-19	A	38	105:1-6, 23-26, 45c	A	229	
77:1-2, 11-20	C	209	105:1-6, 37-45	A	242	
78:1-4, 12-16	A	246	106:1-6, 19-23	A	255	
78:1-7	A	272	107:1-3, 17-22	B	118	
79:1-9	C	269	107:1-7, 33-37	A	267	
80:1-2, 8-13	B	34	107:1-9, 43	C	234	
80:1-2, 8-19	C	244	111	B	78	
80:1-7	C	47	111	B	221	
80:1-7, 17-19	A	46	112:1-9 (10)	A	82	
81:1, 10-16	C	254	114	A	237	
81:1-10	B	98	116:1-2, 12-19	A	180	
82	C	219	116:1-4, 12-19	A	141	
84	B	226	118:1-2, 14-24	A	132	
85	C	229	118:1-2, 14-24	B	130	
85:1-2, 8-13	B	36	118:1-2, 14-24	C	141	
86:1-10, 16-17	A	184	118:1-2, 19-29	A	128	
89:1-4, 19-26	B	44	118:1-2, 19-29	C	136	
89:20-37	B	201	118:14-29	C	146	
90:1-6, 13-17	A	263	119:105-112	A	197	
91:1-2, 9-16	C	115	119:137-144	C	297	

119:1-8	A	86	1:4b-8	B	286	
119:33-40	A	90	5:11-14	C	152	
119:97-104	C	287	7:9-17	C	157	
121	A	110	21:1-6	C	161	
122	A	34	21:10, 22—22:5	C	166	
123	A	277	22:12-14, 16-17,			
124	A	224	20-21	C	176	
124	B	249				
125	B	235	**Romans**			
126	B	39	1:1-7	A	46	
126	C	132	1:16-17; 3:22b-28			
127	B	276	(29-31)	A	99	
130	A	123	1:16-17; 3:22b-28			
130	B	188	(29-31)	A	172	
130	B	216	4:1-5, 13-17	A	110	
131	A	94	4:13-25	A	176	
132:1-12 (13-18)	B	285	4:13-25	B	111	
133	A	219	5:1-5	C	186	
133	B	134	5:1-8	A	180	
137	C	278	5:1-11	A	115	
138	B	175	5:12-19	A	107	
138	C	86	6:1b-11	A	185	
139:1-12, 23-24	A	201	6:12-23	A	189	
139:1-6, 13-18	B	70	7:15-25a	A	194	
139:1-6, 13-18	B	171	8:1-11	A	198	
139:1-6, 13-18	C	259	8:6-11	A	124	
145:1-5, 17-21	C	301	8:12-17	B	168	
146	B	272	8:12-25	A	202	
146	C	195	8:14-17	C	181	
147:1-11, 20c	B	82	8:22-27	B	163	
147:12-20	A	58	8:26-39	A	206	
147:12-20	B	57	9:1-5	A	211	
147:12-20	C	60	10:5-15	A	216	
148	B	53	10:8b-13	C	116	
148	C	56	11:1-2a, 29-32	A	220	
148	C	160	12:1-8	A	225	
148	A	54	12:9-21	A	230	
149	A	233	13:11-14	A	34	
			13:8-14	A	233	
Revelation			14:1-12	A	238	
1:4-8	C	147				

15:4-13	A	39
16:25-27	B	45

Ruth

1:1-18	B	271
3:1-5; 4:13-17	B	275

1 Samuel

1:4-20	B	280
2:1-10	B	281
2:18-20, 26	C	55
3:1-10 (11-20)	B	69
3:1-10 (11-20)	B	170
8:4-11 (12-15), 16-20 (11:14-15)	B	174
15:34—16:13	B	178
16:1-13	A	118
17:(1a, 4-11, 19-23) 32-49	B	182

2 Samuel

1:1, 17-27	B	187
5:1-5, 9-10	B	192
6:1-5, 12b-19	B	196
7:1-14a	B	200
7:1-11, 16	B	43
11:1-15	B	205
11:26—12:13a	B	210
18:5-9, 15, 31-33	B	215
23:1-7	B	284

Song of Solomon

2:8-13	A	193
2:8-13	B	230

1 Thessalonians

1:1-10	A	260
2:1-8	A	264
2:9-13	A	268
3:9-13	C	35

4:13-18	A	273
5:1-11	A	278
5:16-24	B	41

2 Thessalonians

1:1-4, 11-12	C	298
2:1-5, 13-17	C	302
3:6-13	C	306

1 Timothy

1:12-17	C	265
2:1-7	C	270
6:6-19	C	274

2 Timothy

1:1-14	C	279
2:8-15	C	284
3:14—4:5	C	288
4:6-8, 16-18	C	293

Titus

2:11-14	A	51
3:4-7	B	49

Zephaniah

3:14-20	C	41

www.ingramcontent.com/pod-product-compliance
Lightning Source LLC
Chambersburg PA
CBHW070721160426
43192CB00009B/1268